Llewellyn's Whole Life Series

Soul HEALING

Dr. Bruce Goldberg

Author of International Bestseller
Past Lives — Future Lives

1996
Llewellyn Publications
St. Paul, Minnesota, 55164-0383, U.S.A.

FIRST EDITION
First Printing, 1997

Cover Design by Anne Marie Garrison
Cover Photo: Digital Stock Photography
Editing and Interior Design by Connie Hill

Library of Congress Cataloging-in-Publication Data
Goldberg, Bruce, 1948–
Soul healing / Dr. Bruce Goldberg. — 1st ed.
p. cm. -- (Llewellyn's whole life series)
Includes bibliographical references and index.
ISBN 1–56718–317–4 (trade pbk.)
1. Mental healing. 2. Spiritual healing. I. Title. II. Series.
RZ400.G677 1997
615.8'52--dc20 96-35824
CIP

Llewellyn Publications
A Division of Llewellyn Worldwide, Ltd.
St. Paul, Minnesota 55164-0383, U.S.A.

WE CAN ALL BECOME SOUL HEALERS

"*Soul Healing* is a compelling work that will inspire us to create our own miracles of healing."

—Brad Steiger, author of *The Healing Power of Love*
and *Returning from the Light*

" ... a valuable contribution to humanity ... "

—John T. Tokar, M.D.
American Board of Psychiatry and Neurology

"This is a book you can cut your psychic teeth on—full of thought provoking ideas and techniques."

—Marilyn Kroplick, M.D.
Founder, The Center for Attention Deficit Disorder
Author of *A.D.D. and Success*

" ... has opened the doorway to healing for those of us who are sincere in our desire to get well; who are willing to read this book and benefit from what it has to teach."

—Martin Bravin, Ph.D.
Transpersonal psychologist

" ... a book that could become a catalyst for speeding up the changes that have already begun despite resistance from the establishment."

—Bruce W. Christianson, M.D.
Board Certified Psychiatrist

"... deals with the deeper, human soul qualities of people and methods that can free these hidden potentials."

—Lee Bloom, M.D.
Psychiatry and Child Psychiatry

"Rich in psychological insight about our higher self."

—Michael Newton, Ph.D.
Author of *Journey of Souls*

"No fluff, no woo woo. Just the Real Stuff."

—Michael B. Gershman, RN, CHT
Board Certified Hypnotherapy Instructor

ABOUT THE AUTHOR

Dr. Bruce Goldberg holds a B.A. degree in Biology and Chemistry, is a Doctor of Dental Surgery, and has an M.S. degree in Counseling Psychology. He retired from dentistry in 1989, and since then has concentrated on his hypnotherapy practice in Los Angeles. Dr. Goldberg was trained by the American Society of Clinical Hypnosis in the techniques and clinical applications of hypnosis in 1975. This organization trains only licensed dentists, physicians, and psychologists in the use of hypnosis.

Dr. Goldberg has appeared on many television and radio shows. He has been interviewed by Donahue, Oprah, Joan Rivers, The Other Side, Regis and Kathie Lee, Leeza, Tom Snyder, Jerry Springer, Jenny Jones, Montel Williams, CNN, CBS news, and many others.

Through lectures, television and radio appearances, and newspaper articles, including interviews in *TIME, The Los Angeles Times,* and *The Washington Post,* he has been able to educate many people as to the benefits of hypnosis. He was conducted more than 33,000 past life regressions and future life progressions since 1974, and has helped thousands of patients to empower themselves through the use of these techniques. In addition, Dr. Goldberg distributes cassette tapes to teach people self-hypnosis and to guide them into past and future lives. He gives lectures and seminars on hypnosis, regression and progression therapy, and conscious dying as well; he is also a consultant to corporations, attorneys, and the local and network media. His second book, *The Search for Grace,* was made into a television movie by CBS and first aired on May 17, 1994. Dr. Goldberg was the consultant on this film. Dr. Goldberg's column "Hypnotic Highways" appears in *FATE* magazine.

For information on self-hypnosis tapes, speaking engagements, or private sessions, Dr. Goldberg can be contacted directly by writing to the address below. Please include a self-addressed, stamped envelope with your letter.

Bruce Goldberg, D.D.S., M.S.
4300 Natoma Avenue
Woodland Hills, CA 91364
Telephone: (800) KARMA-4-U or (800) 527-6248
Fax: (818) 704-9189

Soul healing demonstrates that our life on Earth is an opportunity to let the energy of love flow through us, to enrich our lives and to heal us.

For when we join with love to the light that is all around us—soul healing must follow.

St. Augustine said that healing miracles do not occur contrary to nature, nor are they supernatural events. These miracles simply transcend what are presently known as natural forces.

OTHER BOOKS BY DR. BRUCE GOLDBERG

Past Lives — Future Lives (Ballantine, 1988)

The Search for Grace: A Documented Case of Murder and Reincarnation (In Print Publishing, 1994)

Forthcoming from Llewellyn Publications

The Search for Grace: The True Story of Murder & Reincarnation, Featured as the CBS Movie of the Week

Peaceful Transition: The Art of Conscious Dying & the Liberation of the Soul

New Age Hypnosis

ACKNOWLEDGEMENTS

First, I would like to express my thanks to Nancy J. Mostad, Acquisitions and Development Manager for Llewellyn Publications. In addition to representing a quality soul who practices what she preaches, Nancy is one of the nicest and most competent souls I have had the pleasure to work with in this incarnation.

Second, I eternally thank Carl Llewellyn Weschcke, President of Llewellyn Publications, for his interest and support in this project.

Third, I am most appreciative for the assistance of my editor, Connie Hill, for her help in bringing this work into its final form.

Next, I would like to thank the Universe and all of its wonders for providing the inspiration that brought this book from my superconscious mind to an earth plane reality. Last, words cannot express the gratitude I extend to the many patients who were kind enough to share their energy with me and make *Soul Healing* possible.

NOTE TO THE READER

This book is the result of the professional experiences accumulated by the author since 1974, working individually with over 11,000 patients. The material included herein is intended to complement, not replace, the advice of your own physician, psychotherapist, and other health professional, whom you should always consult about your circumstances prior to starting or stopping any medication or any other course of treatment, exercise regime, or diet.

Some of the minor details in the case histories have been altered to protect the privacy of my patients. All of the names used, except the celebrities mentioned, have been altered. Everything else in these pages is true.

At times, the masculine pronoun has been used as a convention. It is intended to imply both male and female genders where this is applicable.

CONTENTS

INTRODUCTION

Soul healing deals with energy. Our soul is electromagnetic radiation, equivalent to a television or radio signal. This form of energy is, unfortunately, compromised in quality.

In order to heal ourselves, we must raise the quality of our soul's energy. This is what this book is about. Accessing our higher self (superconscious mind) is the most efficient way I know of raising the quality of our soul's energy, and subsequently the emotional and physical immune system of our body, so that we may fight off diseases.

Since basically all of my patients present themselves with an array of self-defeating sequences (SDSs), it is critical to remove these blocks before any long-lasting progress can be achieved. Good examples of self-defeating sequences are procrastination, tardiness, compulsive spending, alcoholism, overeating, impatience, etc.

"Cleansing" is the process through which the individual introduces their soul (subconscious mind) to its superconscious or higher self. This superconscious mind-level is perfect, and accessing or tapping into this level results in a raising of this energy level of the person's subconscious mind. Soul healing is the natural result of this cleansing. A script of this superconscious mind tap, a technique I developed in 1977, is given in Appendix A.

Why should you read this book? The answer is empowerment. In order to take charge of your life, the karmic "buck" must stop here. You absolutely must be empowered to evolve spiritually, and rise above the need to suffer from disease.

Do we not all want to improve our health and well-being? Taking charge of your life requires empowerment. Soul healing most definitely illustrates the principle of empowerment in relationship to restoring health. Empowerment (i.e. soul healing) is the key to taking control of our lives physically, mentally, emotionally and spiritually.

Only you can take this responsibility. No physician, therapist, well-meaning theologian, or family member can do this for you. Illness is simply our body's natural energy out of harmony. To be healed is to be whole—at one with the universe.

If you truly want to be healed, you already are in contact with your higher self. In 1994 Americans made over 450 million visits to alternative health practitioners. During this same year they made 388 million appointments with mainstream physicians. This search for alternative ways to restore health by soul healing is interwoven within mainstream America.

We must always bear in mind that since the subconscious is where illness of any type originates, it is the subconscious that must remove it. Traditional health care has been guilty of ignoring the patient's consciousness.

For those of you that are skeptical about such paradigms, consider that the newly formed (1992) Office of Alternative Medicine, a component of the National Institute of Health (NIH) near Washington, D.C., has formally recognized hypnotherapy and past life therapy as a classification of alternative medical practices.

The office also acknowledges the following disciplines:

- Acupuncture.
- Biofeedback.
- Ayurveda.
- Homeopathic Medicine.
- Naturopathic Medicine.
- Guided Imagery.
- Sounds, Music Therapy.
- Yoga, Meditation.
- Acupressure.
- Alexander Technique.
- Aromatherapy.
- Biofield Therapeutics.
- Chiropractic Medicine.
- Feldenkrais Method.

- Massage Therapy.
- Osteopathy.
- Reflexology.
- Rolfing.
- Therapeutic Touch.
- Trager Method.
- Shamanism.
- Tibetan Medicine.
- Traditional Oriental Medicine.

In the first part of this book I have pointed out the many limitations of conventional medicine's attempt to treat chronic diseases. The pitfalls of the routine use of drugs to treat only the symptoms is amply illustrated.

In Appendix B, I will give you instructions on how to select a soul healer. Actual questions to ask this prospective practitioner are given. Included are several tips on how to avoid the pitfalls of selecting the wrong soul healer. You will find the "Suggested Reading" list comprehensive and helpful in seeking your own soul healing.

Exploring your own self-awareness, accessing your higher self, and raising the quality of your own soul's energy is the basis of spiritual growth and taking control of your own destiny.

Soul Healing presents the theory and techniques to accomplish both the restoration of health, and the prevention of susceptibility to disease in the first place. Read on and you will learn how to attain these goals.

1

WHAT IS SOUL HEALING?

Webster's Dictionary defines the soul as "an entity which is regarded as being the immortal or spiritual part of the person and, though having no physical or material reality, is credited with the functions of thinking and willing, and hence determining all behavior."

This same reference source describes healing as "to make sound, well, or healthy again." When we combine the two terms, the purpose of this book becomes evident.

My use of the term "soul" is equivalent to what others refer to as spirit or the subconscious mind. In this book I will illustrate how the natural process of healing the soul can be accelerated through the use of simple techniques. The soul is our essence of being. Left to its own devices, it will change very slowly. From a therapist's point of view, that is inefficient and unacceptable. There is absolutely no advantage to procrastination, and delaying the healing of the soul is the worst form of procrastination.

James Hillman, in his essay "Peaks and Valleys," states that the soul is the psyche's actual life, including "the present mess it is in, its discontent, dishonesties, and illusions." You might say that the soul leans toward the past instead of the future, toward attachment to people, places, and events rather than detachment and moving on. These natural, obsessive tendencies can create many problems in one's life.

Without special training, the soul will move at a snail's pace, if at all. Ralph Waldo Emerson once described the soul's advancement as an "ascension of state, like the movement from egg to worm to fly." This may be why most of my patients describe their chief complaint as being "stuck."

How does healing occur? According to East Indian philosophy, *prana* is the universal force that stimulates all activities of the body. If the healer can, in any way, transmit this prana or psychic energy to the patient, healing may occur through a process of stimulating diseased cells and tissues to return to normal function. Remember, it is health that is the norm. Any physical, mental, or spiritual compromise is abnormal, and the universe provides ample ways to return to the normal or healthy condition.

To answer my question, healing occurs when a harmonious relationship is established between the subconscious (soul) and conscious (will power) minds. In medicine, we refer to this state as homeostasis.

There are numerous categories of healing. For simplicity, let us group them into these five types:

1. Psychic or mental healing.
2. Mystical healing.
3. Pranic or magnetic healing.
4. Divine healing.
5. Spiritual healing.

Healing energy is thought to be telepathically transmitted from the subconscious of the patient. This may be accomplished by actually touching the physical body, or by visualization or other mental techniques. My use of hypnosis and the superconscious mind tap will be fully explained in Chapter 4.

The main point in this discussion of soul healing is that, since the subconscious is where illness of any type originates, it is the subconscious that must remove it, thereby returning the soul and its expression through the body to a normal state. Thus, all illnesses fit into the category of psychosomatic medicine. Controlled scientific studies have shown that the psychological state of the patient will exert an effect on the course of a disease, even if that disease is "caused" by a microorganism. In addition, there are numerous hospital cases in which a patient dies, even though the surgery is done correctly. Nobody bothered to ask the patient's subconscious mind if it wanted to continue living.

Traditional health care has been guilty of ignoring the patient's consciousness. Even when healing through consciousness is demonstrated as more effective than traditional approaches, the medical and psychological establishment often refuses to give this alternative method proper credit and respect. One day the establishment will finally accept the theory that all dysfunctions operate on an emotional and consciousness level. Today even the hard science known as quantum physics gives a mathematical value (constant) to consciousness in its equations (see Chapter 23, and Conclusion).

AURAS AND CHAKRAS

Spiritually developed people tend to have a very bright, clear aura that seems to project a little farther than average, especially around the head. This accounts for the halo of light seen around the heads of saints and holy people, depicted by artists in their portrayals of these subjects.

Energies from outside a person, and changes brought about from within through physical, mental, emotional, or spiritual activities, all leave an impression on an individual's energy patterns. The aura is the sum total of these effects, which may be seen as various colors or felt as various intensities.

Penetrating the physical body is a more subtle body, vibrating at a higher frequency. This second body has come to be known as the etheric body.

The etheric body contains an energy blueprint upon which the physical body is shaped and anchored. It contains the structures that allow us to absorb high-frequency energy of various kinds, including the vital force (*prana*). It processes them and passes them into the physical. These etheric structures were seen by Indian seers (*rishis*), who called them *chakras*. Each chakra is represented in the aura by a color. These chakras are the energy centers of the human body. These centers allow energy to flow in and out, and they contain regulating mechanisms to control this flow. The Chinese call them *dantain*.

The seven chakras are identified as follows:

1. The *basal* or *root chakra* is located at the base of the spine. This chakra deals with basic instincts and understanding the physical world. Its color is red or deep pink.
2. The *sacral chakra* is right below the navel. This energy center deals with the lower digestive system, sexuality and

reproduction, basic emotions, and creativity. Orange is associated with this chakra.

3. The *solar plexus chakra* is just below the breast bone. The intellect, stomach, and upper digestive system are its realm. The color attributed to it is yellow.

   Chakras 2 and 3 are vulnerable to negative energies such as anxiety and fear. This appears to explain the link between our mind and emotions. Physical energies also originate from these two chakras.

4. The *heart chakra* deals with emotions such as love, sympathy, and compassion. It is located in the center of the chest and influences the heart, the thymus gland (immune system), chest, lungs, and circulatory system. Green is its characteristic hue.

   The heart chakra stands midway between physical and spiritual life. It is the chakra where both forms of energy are processed. Spiritual energy moving downward may be blocked by the heart. This will deny the lower three chakras the vital energies needed for preparing the human body for spiritual growth (soul healing).

5. The *throat chakra* is involved with creative expression and all forms of communication. Its influence is felt on the organs of the upper chest, throat, and lungs. It is said to be linked to the thyroid gland. Blue is the throat chakra's color.

6. The *brow chakra* deals with intuition and sensory perception. It is also referred to as the "third eye." The color indigo (deep blue) is associated with this chakra.

7. The *crown chakra* is located at the top of the head. It functions as a connection with the higher self and is represented by the color violet.

   There is a chakra above the head which is associated with the color white. Some authorities use this as the color for the crown chakra, and give the brow chakra the color violet.

There is much to be said about positive thinking and soul healing. Disease and illness are the manifestations of energy imbalance or blockages in the etheric system, and physical symptoms can always be traced there. Thoughts attract energies similar in structure to themselves, so thought blocks are quickly built up. When we feel depressed, our thoughts attract similar patterns of energy in the vicinity so that we may quickly find ourselves sinking deeper into negativity. If we exert our will in time to attract a positive-thought block, it will immediately change the situation for the better.

The implications for soul healing are that we can help ourselves and others by trying to keep our thoughts as positive as possible at all times, especially in negative situations or in confrontations with other people.

The two systems of the body—the physical and the etheric—are both essential to life and health. The ancient Indians and Chinese recognized these systems, which still provide the foundations of their current medical practice. The flow of subtle energy between the two systems is the basis of acupuncture, which is designed to remove energy blockages.

KIRLIAN PHOTOGRAPHY

The first scientific evidence for the existence of the aura originated in Russia. The aura was referred to as a bio-energy field in the late nineteenth century. Yakun Yodko-Narkevitch used high-voltage, high-frequency electric charges to measure this phenomenon. He recorded differences in the electromagnetic field between a healthy person and a sick person, between sleeping and wakefulness. He drew attention to the fact that physiological and psychological changes in a person could be monitored using this new technique.

Yodko-Narkevitch's work was lost due to the Russian Revolution, but fortunately his technique was rediscovered by Semyon Kirlian in 1939. Kirlian used no light source, yet when an electrical charge was passed through a living animal and recorded on film, light patterns emerged around these specimens.

Corona-discharge photography (or Kirlian photography, as it is also called) was classified as secret by the Soviet government until 1960, when Kirlian and his wife Valentina published a report. The Kirlians claimed that the corona discharge was the scientific evidence of the existence of a bio-energy field or aura. The term bioplasma was now given to the aura.

The light observed from a specimen was directly proportional to the vital force present. Photographs of healers' hands showed significantly greater light patterns when healing was in progress. A leaf removed from a tree showed decreasing energy patterns as it dried out.

Kirlian photography has shown this bioplasmic field (aura) exists around all living things. Photographs of people with missing fingers or limbs also show the energy matrix as complete, which supports the findings of clairvoyants and healers that there is a complete blueprint of the physical body existing at a higher frequency (the etheric level).

BASIC PRINCIPLES OF SOUL HEALING

- Because healing energies originate at a spiritual level, they can work on any facet of a person's being.
- The patient must be motivated and willing to experience soul healing. Each one of us has free will to accept or reject healing energies.
- The higher self directs the union of the patient and soul healer by way of energy.
- Illness is not seen as a problem to be fought against. It is a condition of imbalance of energies. The purpose of illness is to bring something to our attention.
- Soul healing cooperates with the body's own healing forces rather than overriding them.
- Soul healing is completely natural and every one of us has the ability to draw up this healing energy resource.

This book will focus on hypnosis and the superconscious mind tap. The next three chapters fully explore these concepts and apply them to soul healing. Relaxation is the most significant aspect of the healing process on the physical level. When in pain, the body naturally tightens up. As the muscles contract, the blood flow is constricted, and swelling appears. As more circulation is cut off, there is more pain, swelling, and tightening creating a vicious cycle. Relaxation causes fresh oxygenated blood to be distributed to the wounded tissues so that healing can begin. These are additional soul healing techniques:

Body Work
Shiatsu is a Japanese form of healing during which firm finger pressure is applied to specific points on the body in order to release

healing energy. Western practitioners tend to use a lighter touch than their Asian counterparts.

Feldenkrais work consists of movements, body work, and exercises whose purpose is to retrain the central nervous system to a healthy state. It is remarkably gentle and particularly effective with victims of stroke and trauma.

Trager work uses gentle rocking and bouncing to initiate and maintain relaxation. One of its benefits is that it induces the muscles to respond to the nervous system. Thus, it works well with neuromuscular issues.

Rolfing is a deep-tissue massage, which may elicit pain. Its goal is to restructure the musculoskeletal system by releasing the tensions stored in the tissue. Repressed emotions may surface as a result of this technique.

Therapeutic Touch

Therapeutic touch is a healing modality that is performed by rearranging the energy patterns of the ill person via concentration and meditation by the practitioner. The soul healer keeps his hands approximately six inches above the patient's body, *never touching* it, as he works from the problem area outward in an attempt to cast away the pain. Therapeutic touch is said to reduce pain and muscle tension in the ill individual.

Although there are no formal licenses or state regulations, one can sometimes be certified in therapeutic touch by organizations who hold all-day or weekend seminars in this type of therapy. Cost for training varies, and the practitioners do charge a fee for receiving patients.

Religion

In general, religion is the ability to believe in something or someone—a power greater than ourselves—that can be called upon for answers and strength when life becomes difficult. Those who have abandoned the religious or spiritual side of their lives often may find that they want to return to it for comfort when confronted with immense problems.

In prayer, we seek out the all-embracing relationship by expressing what we feel (anger, doubt, fear, joy, and our needs). We are assured that we are heard and loved. We pray for guidance and to know the will of a supreme being. We listen for answers, for a message, for statements of truth and enlightenment. We read and memorize. Some embrace symbols of their beliefs (pictures, prayer books, a crucifix, rosary beads, tefillin, a tallis, or a mezuzah). We seek out clergy to talk, to gain support, and to offer our services to help others.

Those who are religious believe that our psychological and physical beings are also interwoven with a spiritual being, and that the strength of the individual is directly related to the strength of the weave.

There is evidence that Christian Science healing actually works. Since healing is activated occasionally, and since there is no documented harm, religion has a place in healing. It may even be used as the main treatment in cases with a hopeless prognosis.

Visualization/Guided Imagery

Visualization and guided imagery are not exactly the same, but are often mistaken for each other. With visualization, you might form a mental picture of how you want to be: healthy and free of disease. You can also picture yourself killing off your illness or guiding the hands of your physician toward a cure. Other visualizations might include picturing an alter ego who can be ill in place of your true self, or pictures of your blood cell count rising to normal range. You might visualize a particular treatment working for you.

The idea is to create a self-fulfilling prophecy. Your body is not supposed to be able to distinguish between the vivid mental picture you have conjured up and the actual reality. Thus, the images chosen must be of your own creation, and you must believe they are possible.

Guided imagery is used to induce a state of calm and relaxation. It takes one on a mental journey to a safe, comfortable, peaceful, and soothing place.

Yoga

In yoga breathing exercises (Complete Breath, Corpse Pose, Mountain, Sun Salutation poses), the prana is directed to a part of the body that requires healing. The yogi can anesthetize himself using his thought, help staunch the flow of blood, simulate death, and affect the walls of the heart, the blood pressure, breathing, metabolism, and so on.

The interplay of the yogi's thoughts with his body can create health, peace of mind, and longevity. If a person has an illness, he must not think of it with terror, because his thoughts of fear will aggravate the disease still more. To help restore a patient's physical and mental balance, the yogi uses deep relaxation to erase tension and fear.

Yoga teaches that a healthy person is a harmoniously integrated unit of body, mind, and spirit. Therefore, good health requires a simple, natural diet, exercise in fresh air, a serene mind, and a spirit full of awareness that man's deepest and highest self can be recognized as identical with the spirit of God.

Reflexology

This type of massage utilizes either the foot or the hand to initiate soul healing. Certain areas on the hands and feet correspond to organs and other parts of the body. Massaging the appropriate part of the foot or hand can break up energy blocks in the corresponding part of the body, bringing relief.

Acupuncture

Used mostly to aid pain relief, acupuncture involves the use of presterilized disposable needles of varying lengths, which are passed through the skin at specific points according to charts derived from Eastern medicine. The free end of the needle is then twirled. or can be used to conduct small electrical currents to the preselected point, thereby inducing a type of anesthesia, which in turn causes pain relief or reduction. It is thought that acupuncture may accomplish this by triggering the release of endorphins, which are substances produced by the brain and believed to be the body's natural painkillers.

A person undergoing acupuncture is awake at all times. It is said to be painless, but some people feel discomfort, which may or may not be psychological in nature. Treatments may take place once or twice a week for months or may be limited to a single visit. The length of each session also varies.

Some states require a license to practice acupuncture; others require certification by the National Commission for the Certification of Acupuncturists. Costs vary greatly. If performed by a physician, acupuncture may be covered by some medical insurance policies.

Ayurveda

This Indian discipline originated more than 4,000 years ago. All the Ayurvedic healing techniques operate on the premise that one treats the patient first and the disease second. The Sanskrit term *Ayurveda* literally means "science of life."

Many different circumstances factor into the disease process according to this discipline. The patient's diet, age, immune system, and other elements contribute to the condition diagnosed. The most important condition for healing in Ayurveda is the establishment of deep relaxation. This relaxation will assist the body in returning to a state of balance or homeostasis. Ayurveda groups all human beings into seven different types of constitutions (*Prakriti*), according to the predominance of biological humors (*Doshas*), and similarly groups them into seven psychological constitutions, according to the predominance of mental humors. These factors are always taken into account in diagnosis, prognosis, and treatment of disease. Diseases are caused by imbalance of the humors, which in turn damage various tissues and systems.

Meditation

Meditation is a state of consciousness in which the individual tries to stop his awareness of his surroundings and his internal dialogue so that his mind can focus on a single sound, word, thought, or image. Meditation is a self-induced state of rest and relaxation without sleep, during which you temporarily turn off the outside world. It is also an attempt to quiet a chattering mind.

Through meditation, after time, you may improve your ability to handle stress, lower your blood pressure, normalize your pulse, increase your pain threshold, relax your breathing, and center yourself. You will be capable of reaching a place within yourself that is peaceful, silent, and calm.

To meditate, you close your eyes and sit or lie quietly in a quiet, comfortable atmosphere. You breathe deeply and become aware of your heart beating and your breaths coming calmly and regularly, as you focus on one sound or word.

Meditation must be practiced at home and it takes time to become adept at it. Learning meditation can be accomplished through a center or an instructor. Practitioners are not licensed. There is no regulation of costs, number of sessions, or length of sessions.

SOURCES

Hillman, James. "Peaks and Valleys." In *Puer Papers*, James Hillman, ed. (Irving, Texas: Spring Publications, 1979), p. 66.

2

HEALING – A HISTORICAL OVERVIEW

The exorcism of disease-causing demons by shamans dates back at least 25,000 years, and is still performed today in the Arctic and in Asia, particularly Siberia. Becoming a shaman involves more than just a cruel and self-harmful initiation. Before reaching this point, the candidate must have shown that he is worthy to undergo the tests. It is preferable if his nomination is hereditary, because everyone then expects him to behave as if possessed one day. However, there are various other ways someone can show that he is one of the chosen—one of those whose magical powers make them the most important and revered men in their tribe. It can be by an accident, such as falling from a tree or being touched by lightning; by feeling the call; or by the simple expedient of a bold announcement that he is a shaman, and that he will prove it by bizarre and masochistic behavior.

In addition to the priest-physicians, Egypt had magicians who were adept healers. When they visited the sick, they brought along a papyrus roll filled with incantations, and an ample supply of baked earth to make amulets. The belief was prevalent that demons caused disease. Demons, it was thought, entered the patient's body, broke open the bones, sucked out the marrow, and slowly devoured the flesh. The trick was to drive out these demons, usually by threats and incantations.

These healing rites were often accompanied by massages, by tramping on the patient's body, or by administering potions noxious enough to nauseate the patient, thus subjecting him to a form of "shock therapy."

In the Chinese *Nei Ching*, the 3,000-year-old *Yellow Emperor's Classic of Internal Medicine*, we are told amid discussions of acupuncture needles, herbal remedies, and the physiology of the vital organs that the highest form of doctor uses no medicine, but treats disease solely through the agency of the mind.

Both the Talmud and the Bible contain many references to the laying on of hands in healing. Prayer was introduced at a later date to obtain the same result.

Temples sprang up all over Greece in honor of Aesculapius, the benign healing god. At first, the temples functioned as places of worship, but as time went on they took on the additional function of clinics and hospitals. The fame of such medical centers at Epidaurus, Pergamos, and Cos spread over the ancient world, and their influence reached far into the Christian era.

Once past the initial examination, the patients were taken on a tour of the halls, where impressive images of Aesculapius and other gods were on exhibit. Then one by one the group descended ladders to subterranean baths. Here the patients were scrubbed and cleansed, inside and out. According to reports, some of them underwent a "foodless diet" for about fifteen days. When ready for treatment they were given special white linen vestments, supposed to be especially conductive to dreams, which were the mainstay of Aesculapian therapy.

The priest-physicians tried to induce dreams in which Aesculapius would reveal the cure to the patients. It is believed that hypnosis was utilized here.

These incubation ceremonies were made more mysterious by the use of holy snakes. With the aid of heat and soft flute music, tame reptiles were coaxed to lick the patient's wounds, from ulcerated toes to swollen eyes (dogs were trained to do the same). To enhance the relationship between reptiles and patients, popona, a kind of "snake-biscuit," was sold. The patients bought it, and fed it to the serpents.

Hippocrates was born approximately 460 B.C. on the Greek Island of Cos. At that time, Cos was famous as a health resort, and later on as the site of an Aesculapian temple.

Hippocrates emphasized that medical art consists of three main factors: "the disease, the patient, and the physician." Before

Hippocrates, disease was a divine infliction, the physician was a mere delegate of the gods, and the patient could only recover through faith.

Hippocrates saw disease as a natural process. He saw the patient as an individual whose constitution would react to disease in its own way. This revolutionary concept was neglected for centuries, but it has taken on increased importance in modern times. Hippocrates viewed the doctor as a man of science instead of as a priest. The New Testament recounts Jesus' curing all manners of ills through speech. "Royal touch" was used in healing by the English and French nobility. Edward the Confessor instituted this technique in England as did Francis I in France during the Middle Ages.

HYPNOSIS – A HISTORICAL SUMMARY

The use of hypnosis dates back to religious leaders, witch doctors, medicine men, and shamans. Soothsayers in ancient Egypt used the trance state for their various healings. The healing effect of astral bodies and magnets was promulgated by Paracelsus (1493–1541). He assumed that these magnets were responsible for curing disease.

In Vienna in 1771, Father Hell applied steel plates to the naked bodies of his patients to elicit cures. Mesmer elaborated on this concept and used a means of "passes" to effect his cures. He called this animal magnetism, and this technique became all the rage in Europe during the latter part of the eighteenth century.

Mesmer further expanded his technique to a *baquet,* or large tub filled with iron filings, in order to treat the large following he attracted. Patients grasped the iron rods attached to this contraption to receive the "magnetic" flow. Thirty or more persons were connected to each other by cords and were magnetized as Mesmer touched each person with a glass rod; many developed seizures or crises similar to those observed among some religious sects.

Mesmer theorized that the wand he used transferred the magnetism originating from the astral bodies to the patient. Benjamin Franklin headed a commission in 1784 that disproved Mesmer's theories and showed that it was imagination, not magnetism, that brought on these cures.

Mesmer, unknowingly, established the basis for current-day group psychotherapy, psychoanalysis, and spiritual (soul) healing. His later disciples were Petetin, the discoverer of catalepsy; the Marquis de Puysegur, who first described artificial somnambulism; and de Barbarin, who magnetized without paraphernalia and whose followers called themselves Barbarianists. In Sweden and Germany, the latter group were called Spiritualists. Mesmerism quickly spread all around the world, lasting until about 1840 when it finally disappeared from the world of therapy.

The use of hypnosis for pain control (hypoanalgesia) made its first appearance in 1821 when French physician Recamier used it for surgery. In 1829, Cloquet amputated a breast before the French Academy of Medicine using hypnosis. In the United States, Wheeler used hypnosis while conducting a nasal polypectomy.

The Scottish surgeon James Esdaile reported hundreds of painless operations using hypnosis while in India between 1840 and 1850. In 1849, Crawford Long brought to light the fact that Mesmerism was being used in the United States for surgery. Dr. Long is best known for his work with the general anesthetic ether.

The "father of modern hypnotism" was James Braid from Great Britain. At first a skeptic, Braid began his scientific inquiry into the technique after witnessing a demonstration by La Fontaine (a Swiss Mesmerist) in Manchester in 1843. Braid concluded that the results obtained were not due to magnetic fluids, but that "the phenomena were due to suggestion alone, acting upon a subject whose suggestibility had been artificially increased."

Unfortunately, Braid coined the term "hypnosis" from the Greek word "hypnos," meaning sleep. When he later recognized that hypnosis was not a sleep state, he tried to rename this state as "monoideism," but the term hypnosis had taken hold on the public and the scientific community, and his efforts failed to rectify the situation. Braid's greatest contribution was his discovery that hypnosis could take place without a formal induction. This discovery was ignored for over a century.

How did Mesmer obtain his results? Bernard C. Gines suggested the following formula to explain hypnosis: misdirected attention + belief + expectation = hypnosis.

Considering Mesmer's rituals, his personality, his long robe and wand, it is not difficult to imagine how he achieved what he did. No psychological cures have ever taken place without the presence of some belief on the part of the patient.

The true founder of suggestive therapy was Liebault, whose book *Du Sommeil* was published in 1866. Liebault is known for his statement to his patients, "If you wish to be treated by drugs. you will have to pay my fee; if however, you allow me to treat you by hypnotism, I will do it free of charge!" His integrity, selflessness, devotion to the needy, and success with hypnosis attracted the attention of Hippolyte Bernheim, a renowned French neurologist. At first skeptical, Bernheim later became an ardent proponent of hypnosis. Together, Liebault and Bernheim developed Braid's theories and treated over 12,000 patients.

They both viewed hypnosis as a function of normal behavior and developed the concept of suggestion. Both considered symptom removal to be harmless yet effective. Their views overturned those of Charcot, who maintained that it was a dangerous form of hysteria.

Charcot's theories, based on working repeatedly with only a dozen hysterical patients at the Saltpetriere, an insane asylum, were completely discredited, but since Charcot was a respected practitioner, he gave credibility to the field of hypnosis. Charcot realized that everyone could experience hypnosis and that it was a natural state of mind. He never appreciated the potential that Liebraut and Bernheim achieved in their work.

Hypnosis further evolved as a science in 1886 when Bernheim published *De la Suggestion,* in which he pointed out that suggestion was the basis of hypnosis. It was his credibility that allowed hypnosis to gain stature.

Around 1880, however, Dr. Breuer, a Viennese general practitioner, introduced a most important innovation in hypnotic therapy which extended the application of hypnosis far beyond the mere suggesting away of symptoms. He accidentally discovered that when one of his patients was induced to speak freely under hypnosis, she displayed a profound emotional reaction which was followed by the disappearance of many of her symptoms. When Freud's attention was drawn to this case, he joined Breuer in investigating it more fully and succeeded in confirming Breuer's results. The importance of this discovery lies in the subsequent change in emphasis in hypnotic therapy *from the direct removal of symptoms to the elimination of their apparent causes.*

Later, Freud gave up on hypnosis and concentrated on developing free association and psychoanalysis. His abandoning hypnosis was probably mostly due to the fact that he was not able to induce deep trances in many of his patients. His own ego worked against the field of hypnosis, in that he bad-mouthed the entire discipline of hypnotic suggestion.

This is why devoted followers of Freud even today still adhere to this prejudice. Freud nearly succeeded in dealing a death blow to hypnosis. Fortunately, he failed.

Other therapists showed that hypnosis was effective in psychotherapy. They refused to believe that hypnotic suggestion obscured repressed emotions, as alleged by Freud. An objective review of the facts and clinical experience shows that Freud was incorrect in his conclusions.

The need for rapid treatment of war neuroses during World Wars I and II and the Korean conflict led to a tremendous interest in hypnotherapy. The merger of hypnotic techniques with psychiatry was one of the important advances to come out of these conflicts.

One must wonder why hypnosis has survived, since medicine is filled with fads that come and go. *Prejudice is ignorance educated,* and it is difficult for any individual, in any given era, to see through the "smoke screen" of his own culture, but hypnosis has persisted and continues to gain even stronger scientific interest.

On September 13, 1958, the Council on Mental Health of the American Medical Association formally accepted hypnosis and recommended its inclusion in the curriculum of medical schools and post-graduate residencies. The British Medical Association had previously recognized hypnosis for psychiatric and surgical use.

Today, thousands of dentists, physicians, psychologists, and other health professionals receive training in hypnosis. There are even proprietary schools that will train the lay public in the use of hypnosis. Hypnosis has emerged as a valuable tool in medicine and psychotherapy. Despite the many obstacles it has faced, it is fully recognized and utilized by many credible scientists, myself included.

3

HYPNOSIS – THE ULTIMATE HEALING FORCE

To understand what hypnosis is, one must consider the inner workings of the human mind. Our mind is made up of four different levels of activity.

The first level or stage is called beta. This is the level of complete consciousness. We function in this level for approximately sixteen hours each day. The main purpose of this level is to regulate our life-controlling bodily functions such as heartbeat, breathing, kidney functions, digestion, etc. About seventy-five per cent of the beta level, or conscious mind proper, is spent monitoring these vital bodily functions. Thus, only twenty-five per cent of the conscious mind is left to deal with what we know as our conscious thoughts.

The second level is what we call alpha. Alpha corresponds to the subconscious mind, and this is what we deal with in hypnosis. This level is characterized by ninety-five to 100 per cent concentration efficiency. This is far superior to the twenty-five per cent efficiency of the conscious, or beta, level. Examples of activity on the alpha level are hypnosis, meditation, biofeedback, daydreaming, crossing over into natural sleep, and awakening. Hypnosis is a natural state of mind. It is not sleep. You are fully aware when you are hypnotized.

The next level of mental activity is called *theta*. This is the part of the unconscious mind that functions in light sleep. The term *conscious* means awake; *unconscious* means unawake and unaware.

The last level is called delta. This corresponds to deep sleep. At this level, the unconscious mind is obtaining the greatest amount of rest. Suggestions will not be heard at this level. This level lasts approximately thirty to forty minutes each night.

When we get up in the morning we have just gone from natural hypnosis (alpha) to full consciousness (beta). When we go to sleep at night we go from beta (full consciousness) to alpha (natural hypnosis) to theta (light sleep) to delta (deep sleep) to theta (light sleep) to alpha, and the cycle repeats itself.

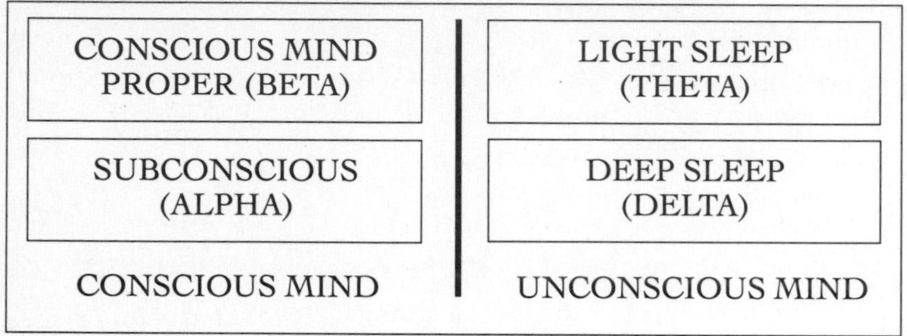

Figure 1 — Consciousness

THE EXPERIENCE OF BEING HYPNOTIZED

If you are hypnotized, you will be in the alpha state. What will you experience? Exactly what is the hypnotic trance like?

Hypnosis is simply the setting aside of the conscious mind proper, and dealing with the subconscious mind directly. At no time will you be asleep.

When we are functioning at full consciousness (beta), both the subconscious and the conscious mind proper are functioning. The physical experience in hypnosis will be identical to that of full consciousness, with three exceptions.

First your concentration will be more focused, nearly 100 per cent as compared with the twenty-five per cent efficiency of the conscious mind proper. Second, every muscle in your body will feel relaxed. (Some people feel a floating sensation, others a warm or tingling feeling. Most people feel a heaviness, especially in the arms and legs.) Third, there is what I call "immobility." This is not technically accurate, because one is always able to move any part of the body at any time. The patient in hypnosis doesn't *want* to move, so he or she doesn't. Many people have compared this effect to having laughing gas (nitrous oxide) in the dentist's office. This is quite accurate, because nitrous oxide will place a patient in a hypnotic trance chemically.

Thus, a hypnotized patient will experience increased concentration, complete relaxation, and lack of movement. Also, our senses are more developed in trance, so that the sense of hearing, touch, smell, etc. will be more accurate in a hypnotic trance state. That's it. There will be no levitation, skyrockets, or any kind of sleep or zombie effect. Examples of natural, day-to-day hypnosis include daydreaming; crossing over into natural sleep at night; watching most television programming; watching windshield wipers on a rainy night; watching light posts or white lines on a highway at night (highway hypnosis); reading a novel and getting so involved in the plot that you lose track of time.

Think about a daydream for a moment. When you daydream you are focusing your mind on a person, place, or event that is usually pleasant. You are not concerned about the weather, what time it is, or whether your clothes are too loose or too tight. If someone were in the same room with you while you were daydreaming, he would probably have to snap his fingers and call your name to get your attention. This is the alpha state and the best example of natural hypnosis. Everyone daydreams, and most people spend between three and four hours daydreaming every day. Thus, most people spend at least three hours every day in natural hypnosis. Hypnosis is therefore a natural and normal state of mind. There is absolutely no danger involved. In fact, without natural hypnosis, the stress in our daily lives would kill us all.

Since our senses are sharper, we are less prone to accidents or other forms of injury when we are in hypnosis. I am not aware of any instances in which hypnosis has ever resulted in either psychological or physical harm to a patient. A person who has a car accident late at night might be the victim of highway hypnosis, but only because he would normally have been asleep, and instead was behind the wheel.

THE LEVELS OF HYPNOSIS

What about the different levels or stages of hypnosis? Today scientists classify more than fifty different levels of hypnosis, but for simplicity I will divide hypnosis into three main levels.

The first is called *light trance*. In this level the patient is relaxed and probably won't feel that he or she is hypnotized. Although regressions and progressions can be accomplished at this level, the information obtained is very sketchy. In addition, when I work with phobias (fears), habits, depression, etc., this level has only limited efficiency in accepting very complex or difficult training techniques. Ninety-five per cent to ninety-five per cent of the public can achieve this level.

The second level is called *medium trance.* This is the level in which I prefer to work. In this level the patient is more completely relaxed and more able to accept very difficult or complex training suggestions. He or she can more easily relive and actually feel an event or scene in regression or progression. At this level the patient may be aware of outside noises but it will not distract him or her. About seventy per cent of the public can achieve this level.

The last level is called *deep* or *somnambulistic trance.* This is the level of hypnosis a stage hypnotist likes to use because one characteristic of it is "hypnoamnesia." In other words, the patient will not remember what he or she did or said in trance unless specifically told to remember upon awakening. Only about five per cent of the public can achieve this level. This level is also characterized by positive hallucinations (seeing an object that is not really there), as well as negative hallucinations (not being able to see an object that is there).

Even in this very deep level, however, the patient cannot be told to do or say anything that is against his or her moral or ethical code. So you see, a hypnotized person is never under anyone's control but his or her own. Unless I am interested in documenting a regression or involved in other types of research, I do not prefer to work with a patient at this level. It is not dangerous, but merely unnecessary.

WHO CAN BE HYPNOTIZED?

As I have already mentioned, ninety-five per cent of the public can be placed in at least a light hypnotic trance. People often ask me to describe the kind of people who make the best hypnotic patients and those who cannot be hypnotized. The best hypnotic patients are intelligent people (contrary to the popular misconception) who have an excellent memory, can focus their concentration, visualize scenes with great detail, can express emotions easily, are not overly critical, and who can go to a lecture or movie and become so deeply involved in the plot that time passes very quickly. Children make excellent patients because of their imagination, respect for authority, and lack of resistance or skepticism. The best hypnotic patients are children between the ages of eight and sixteen, but I will work with children as young as five.

Those people who usually make the worst hypnotic patients are people who have very short attention spans, tend to focus on the past and future rather than the present, are overly critical, use logic instead of emotions, have lower IQs and have great difficulty "letting themselves go." Mental retardation, senility, brain damage, inability to understand the language of the hypnotist, and overly cynical attitudes are also going to inhibit the induction of a hypnotic trance. Considering the number of skeptical media people I work with, belief in the theory of reincarnation or even healing is not necessary for success.

SELF-HYPNOSIS

When I discuss hypnosis, I refer to *self-hypnosis*. All hypnosis is actually self-hypnosis. It is impossible to hypnotize someone against his or her will, unless certain drugs are used, which I never recommend or use. Thus, during a hypnotic session, a patient learns how to hypnotize him or herself, utilizing the services of a hypnotherapist. The term for this is *heterohypnosis*, meaning hypnosis by another (*hetero* means "other").

All of my patients are taught self-hypnosis so that they can condition themselves for deeper trance levels and shorten the time it takes to induce the hypnotic trance. There are many ways to learn self-hypnosis, but I find the use of cassette tapes to be the most efficient. I give tapes to all my patients so that they can be exposed daily to the techniques I give them at their weekly sessions.

OUR OWN NATURAL COMPUTER

Hypnosis takes place in the alpha state, or subconscious mind, which is best described as a computer. Just as a computer is programmed or fed information, the subconscious mind is constantly undergoing a programming process. Everything that we can detect through our five senses, as well as through extrasensory perception (ESP), is permanently stored in the subconscious mind's memory bank. Since the subconscious mind, along with the conscious mind, functions for about sixteen hours each day, scientists estimate that the average human brain is exposed to, and stores, one million separate pieces of information each day.

Each piece of information is stored in what is termed a "memory trace" in the brain. If you multiply one million by 365, and then multiply this total by your age, then you have an idea of how many memory traces you are using. Scientists estimate that the average human mind contains seventy trillion memory traces. Since a trillion is a thousand billion, and a billion is a thousand million, you can see that even a seventy-year-old person has used only a fraction of his memory traces.

There are many common fallacies and needless fears about hypnosis:

- *The fallacy of symptom substitution.* As I have mentioned, by using regression to see the true causes of a negative tendency and by using cleansing techniques to permanently eliminate the problem, symptoms are not substituted. They are permanently removed.

- *The fallacy of mind control.* Earlier in this chapter, I discussed the fact that absolutely nobody can be placed in a hypnotic trance against his or her will. Even a highly skilled hypnotherapist needs the cooperation of the patient in order to induce a trance. The only person capable of controlling a patient's subconscious mind is the patient. All hypnosis is self-hypnosis and is a natural phenomenon.

- *The fallacy of revealing secrets or other information in trance.* Unless the patient wants to reveal it, the information in the patient's subconscious mind will remain hidden. Psychologists use the phrase "the ego cannot be detached" to describe this. For example, in a past life regression if you saw yourself in an embarrassing or even humiliating scene, you would relive this scene in your mind but would not discuss it, even if you were in a very deep trance, unless you wanted to.

- *The fear of not being dehypnotized.* Because hypnosis is a natural process that the mind goes through each and every day, and because we are constantly bringing ourselves into and out of trances, a patient can terminate a hypnotic trance anytime he or she wants to. Patients do not need a hypnotherapist to bring them out of a trance. I usually count from one to five to return the patient to the beta state, but this is not necessary.

The patient will resume beta functioning by him or herself. However, counting forward facilitates this process.

- *The fear of not remembering suggestions afterward.* Unless you are capable of achieving a deep trance, you will always remember the suggestions or scenes afterward. I always give a posthypnotic suggestion (a suggestion that is meant to work long after the trance ends) for patients to remember everything they experienced or reexperienced upon awakening. The term "awakening" is a poor one, since the patient is not asleep, but most people can relate to this description.

  The only time I do not suggest a patient remember what he or she experienced in a trance is when I am working with someone who is emotionally upset and the scene is especially traumatic. If I do not feel that the patient can handle the information, then I will suggest that he or she forget it (hypnoamnesia). In any event, the patient will remember the information or scene eventually as the posthypnotic suggestion wears off (approximately four to ten days). Even patients in a deep trance will remember the scene if you give the appropriate posthypnotic suggestion.

- *The fear of regression.* I know of no case where anyone has ever been harmed by the use of hypnosis in any form. I have done thousands of regressions, superconscious mind taps, and progressions, and can personally testify to the many positive benefits. In all the time that I have used hypnosis, I have never seen or even heard of a negative effect or situation experienced by a patient. In my experience, the worst that can happen is nothing; i.e., no trance is induced.

Hypnosis is simply a way of relaxing and setting aside the conscious mind while at the same time activating the subconscious mind so that suggestions can be made directly to the subconscious, enabling the patient to act on these suggestions with greater ease and efficiency.

Since 1958, the American Medical Association has formally accepted hypnosis as a reputable clinical aid. The British Medical Association accepted hypnosis in 1955. No longer are hypnotherapists thought of as charlatans or stage entertainers. When I first began practicing hypnotherapy, patients would seek my services as a last resort, usually after traditional medicine and psychotherapy had failed. Today, I am more often approached initially, before other traditional forms of therapy are considered. Of course, I refer my patients to physicians to rule out possible physiological causes of their complaints. When the physical causes of illness are eliminated, I begin my therapy. Any therapist you consider should take this clinical approach.

HYPNOSIS – HOLLYWOOD STYLE

I would like to end this chapter with a section on the origin of most people's misconception about hypnosis. The sources appear to be the following three. The first are novels portraying hypnosis as an evil, brainwashing, and dangerous technique. Second, the image portrayed by stage hypnotists that hypnosis gives them "control" over the subject's mind and that this procedure is strictly for entertainment.

Finally, there is the Hollywood film industry portraying hypnosis as dangerous and supernatural. Hypnotists are most often characterized as evil, mind-controlling psychopaths manipulating their "victims" into acts of murder or self-destruction. When feature films do deal with reincarnation, the subjects exploring their previous lives are usually engaged in life-threatening circumstances, and are often harmed as a result.

Of course, nothing could be further from the truth. The films I am about to describe will present a synopsis of Hollywood's version of hypnosis, spanning seventy-five years:

The Cabinet of Dr. Caligari (1919) was a silent film dealing with a hypnotist (Dr. Caligari) and his henchman (Caesare), who was sent out on missions of murder and destruction.

Warner Brothers released *Svengali* in 1931, starring John Barrymore. Barrymore played an evil hypnotist who placed a young girl named Trilby under his spell. While in her trance, Trilby became a talented opera singer, something she could not replicate when the hypnosis ended. This film was remade in 1954.

Boris Karloff starred in *Black Friday* (1940), depicting a brain surgeon and hypnotist. Karloff saved the life of a friend by transplanting part of a criminal's brain into his friend's skull. His friend then acted the part of a murderer and killed a rival gangster, played by Bela Lugosi.

The Frozen Ghost (1945) was a Universal release that starred Lon Chaney, Jr. He played a magician and stage hypnotist who was accused of murder when one of his volunteers died during a performance.

The Woman in Green (1945) by Universal Studios was a Sherlock Holmes movie starring Basil Rathbone as the detective. The villain was an attractive female hypnotist perpetrating a murder for financial gain.

Black Magic (1949) by RKO starred Orson Wells as an evil hypnotist, Count Cagliostro. It took place in Italy during the eighteenth century.

Whirlpool (1950) by 20th Century Fox featured Mel Ferrer as a homicidal hypnotist in Palm Springs, trying to use the kleptomaniac wife of a prominent psychiatrist to take the blame for a murder he committed.

Invasion. USA (1953) was a 20th Century Fox film about the effects of a nuclear war on patrons in a New York bar. The irony was that the bartender simply hypnotized these people into imagining the nuclear war occurred for the purpose of increasing their awareness of the "Red Menace."

Curse of the Demon (1958) by Columbia Pictures starred Dana Andrews as a psychiatrist investigating the murder of a colleague in England. A satanic cult member was placed in trance during his interrogation, but eventually threw himself out of a window and died. Later on, the cult leader used hypnosis on Dana's girlfriend to intimidate him.

Tales of Terror (1959) by American International Pictures showcased stories by Edgar Allen Poe, including "The Facts in the Case of Mr. Valdemer." The story centered on a man in a trance at the exact moment of his death who was unable to move on to his next life. The evil hypnotist cajoled Valdemer's wife into marrying him. Finally, Valdemer rose from his deathbed and strangled the hypnotist.

The Manchurian Candidate (1962) by United Artists was a Cold War story about a Korean War hero who was brainwashed by Red China to be a killer. He was very successful in murdering members of his own platoon in a cold-blooded, machine-like fashion.

On A Clear Day You Can See Forever (1970) by Paramount was an uplifting musical about hypnosis and reincarnation, starring Barbra Streisand. In order to quit smoking, she sought the help of a university professor. While in trance, she recalled various past lives. This is one of my personal favorites because Barbra got a glimpse of her future life, when she and the professor/hypnotist would become lovers.

The Reincarnation of Peter Proud (1975) by Avco Embassy Pictures recreated the life and death of Peter Proud in a past life. Unfortunately, Mr. Proud was murdered again as he investigated this mystery. Hypnosis was used to regress him into his previous lifetime.

Audrey Rose (1977) released by United Artists unfortunately portrayed a twelve-year-old girl dying in trance as she expired in a past life. Anthony Hopkins plays the part of a father who claims Audrey is the reincarnation of his deceased daughter. Of course, we all know that past life regression is completely harmless, which places this film on the very bottom of my must-see list.

The Natural (1984) by TriStar Pictures portrayed Robert Redford as a middle-aged baseball player. A hypnotist was used to help motivate his losing team. Redford stated in this film, "I'm not going to let some sideshow carny hypnotist put me under." The image of hypnosis as silly and frivolous was reinforced in this film.

Dead Again (1992) was a Paramount film portraying a hypnotist (who lived with his disabled mother) as the grown-up murderer of a young woman in her past life, forty years ago. This film illustrated changing sexes in past lives, but portrayed hypnotists as evil and dysfunctional. Robin Williams played a defrocked psychiatrist giving free therapy advice in a meat market freezer. The very thought sends chills down my spine.

My favorite for many obvious reasons is the CBS television movie, "Search for Grace" (1994). Lisa Hartman played the role of Ivy, who was obsessively attracted to a man trying to kill her. Richard Masur played my persona, depicting a competent and ethical hypnotist for a change. Ken Wahl did an excellent job as Johnny, the murderer of Ivy in her past life as a Roaring Twenties flapper. My capacity as technical advisor to this film is reflected in the accuracy of the hypnosis sequences, some of which were taken from the actual data I retrieved when I regressed the real Ivy. I highly recommend both the movie and the book of the same name.

4

THE PROCESS

One of the most misconstrued words in the English language is "hypnosis." The word is taken from the Greek "hypnos" and literally means sleep. Hypnosis, however, occurs on the natural daydream level that we all experience from three to four hours daily, in addition to three hours (REM) when we dream at night.

It is an alpha brain-wave level, as measured by electroencephalograph (EEG). Without the restorative effects of the alpha level, we would die of a stroke or heart attack due to the body's inability to deal with stress.

Hypnosis is a natural state, and everyone logs approximately 2,500 hours of it every year of his life. Since everyone goes through self-hypnosis daily, everyone, theoretically, can be hypnotized. In fact, only five per cent of the population is refractive, meaning they block any attempt of a therapist to guide them into self-hypnosis. The patient has so much control over this state that he or she may block it or terminate the trance at any time.

Most therapists assume that hypnosis must deal with visual imagery and behavior modification, and must be administered at a fairly deep level to be effective. With all due respect to my colleagues, this simply is not true. First of all, the depth of a trance is irrelevant. Any "cleansing," regression, and progression technique can be done at light, medium, or deep trance levels. Also, visual imagery is not necessary or even desirable when "cleansing" is performed. Finally, this technique is not behavior modification. What I generally achieve with my patients is an energy cleansing or a raising of the vibrational rate of their alpha brain wave (subconscious mind).

This alpha level produces electromagnetic radiation, which is equivalent to a television or radio signal. Unfortunately, the undeveloped soul (or spirit, or subconscious mind—the terms are interchangeable) operates in our current body at a relatively low frequency of vibrational rate. Chapters 3, 5, 24, and 25 in *Past Lives—Future Lives* explain this concept in greater detail. Since the purpose of karma, and thus the process of reincarnation, is to purify the soul, it must raise this frequency somehow.

As we go through each life we face challenges, sometimes referred to as karmic tests. If we pass the test, our frequency is raised. However, if we fail a challenge, our frequency vibrational rate remains unchanged. You cannot lower the frequency of your subconscious.

CLEANSING

Cleansing is the process through which the hypnotherapist introduces the patient's subconscious mind to its superconscious or higher self. This superconscious mind level is perfect, and thus accessing or tapping into this level results in a raising, of the energy level of the patient's subconscious mind. Therapy is accomplished through tapping into this superconscious mind.

As I stated in *Past Lives—Future Lives* (167–168):

> Since basically all of my patients present themselves with an array of self-defeating sequences (SDS), it is critical to remove these blocks before any long-lasting progress can be achieved. Good examples of self-defeating sequences are procrastination, lateness, compulsive spending, alcoholism, overeating, impatience, etc. One tends to create difficulties in one's life (and lives) which prevent one from achieving desired goals, whether personal or professional. The self-image (how we perceive ourselves, not how others perceive us) is lowered.

The first step in hypnotherapy is to improve this self-image. If you build a house on quicksand, it won't be around to benefit from appreciation. I have already discussed the use of cassette tapes to help establish a sound and strong psychological foundation from which patients can more fully understand their karmic purpose and make strides toward fulfilling their karma.

Most of a patient's therapy will take effect during the dream level at night. Recent medical research establishes that we enter REM (rapid eye movement), a characteristic of the dream state, for three hours each night. Since our defense mechanisms (willpower or analytical mind) cannot function once we enter the sleep cycle, this is a most efficient cleansing opportunity.

During this dream state, the emotional cleansing necessary for our survival occurs, but deeper energy cleansing is not part of this survival function. It will not occur unless we are trained for it. If we are properly trained, we will use approximately one hour of the REM cycle to cleanse our alpha level. Since each minute in hypnosis is equivalent to three to four earth minutes, three to four hours of therapeutic energy cleansing is actually experienced by the patient. It is no wonder that this therapy is so short, successful, and popular. The patient is trained in relatively few sessions to be totally independent of the therapist and to attain any goal that is humanly possible. The patient uses superconscious mind cassette tapes to assist in this goal.

There are three levels of manifestation of an issue. First, there is the physical level. Using depression as an example, the associated lack of energy and malaise are examples of the physical level. Next is the emotional level. In this example, unexplained crying would be a symptom of this level. The last and most important level is the energy level. This level is the actual frequency vibrational rate of the patient's alpha level or subconscious mind. In other words, this is the level of spiritual growth or karmic status of the individual. The energy level controls the emotional level, which in turn influences the physical level. Thus, the only level I am concerned with when I conduct a hypnotherapy session is the energy level. Once we raise the patient's frequency vibrational rate to a new threshold—a major breakthrough—this new level or rate is established and irreversible. The patient may plateau for a while, but this new rate cannot be lowered. Thus, the emotional and physical symptoms as well as the causes are resolved by treating the ultimate cause, which is the patient's energy level or frequency vibrational rate.

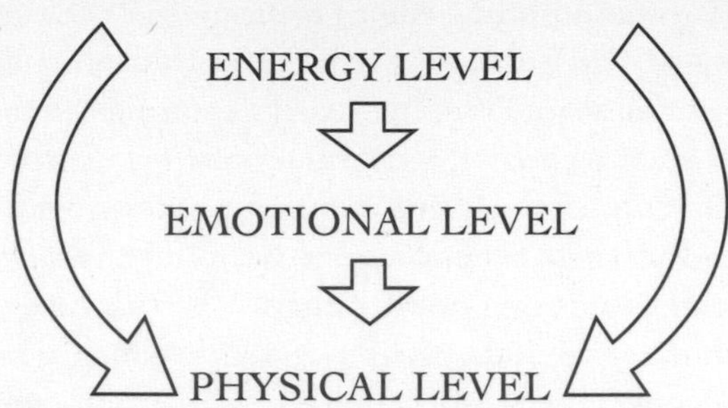

Figure 2 — Cleansing

You will note that the arrows always flow down from the energy level to the physical but not in reverse; also observe that the energy level can change the physical level directly without having to use the emotional level as an intermediary. An example of this latter phenomenon would be the removal of psychosomatic pain or a headache.

How does past life regression, age progression, or future life progression fit into this approach? The answer is simple. These techniques are used as stepping stones to reach the superconscious mind and to satisfy the patient's curiosity. These techniques taken together account for approximately five percent of the therapy. Ninety-five percent of any therapeutic result will come from cleansing at the superconscious level. This cleansing will also greatly reduce the time and number of sessions required to train patients to resolve their conflicts and maximize their potential. Thus, it is not necessary to explore past or future lives for this therapy to work.

Since this is not cognitive or analytical therapy, I am not particularly interested in the intellectual "cause" of the issue. In this type of therapy, process is everything. The whys are not important. All that is necessary is that the patient must be motivated to attain a goal, that goal must be possible to attain, and the patient must trust the therapist he works with. As long as these three conditions are met, any goal is achievable.

Throughout the therapeutic process, a patient will experience good days and bad days. The bad days are actually more therapeutic, because during these days the energy needed by the conscious mind in order to interfere with the therapy is drained, so the defense mechanism is disengaged.

The purpose of our defense mechanisms (rationalization, intellectualization, displacement, etc.) is to keep our behavior the same. To this end, they will do anything to disrupt change. Fortunately, the defense mechanisms' energy supply is limited and every time they exert themselves, they are literally burning themselves out.

Good days do not result in a direct drain to the defense mechanisms, but do indirectly sap their energy. By raising one's energy level (frequency vibrational rate), as a result of these good days, the defense mechanisms must expend even more energy in their attempt to reverse this therapeutic progress. Since our subconscious mind has an unlimited energy supply (by accessing the superconscious mind), it will always win in the end.

APPLICATIONS OF THE SUPERCONSCIOUS MIND TAP

- Scanning past lives, the future of one's current life, and future lifetimes.
- Contacting departed loved ones, masters and guides, and one's own higher self.
- Obtaining spiritual guidance and growth by raising the frequency vibrational rate of the subconscious mind (soul).
- Removing attached entities and poltergeists (ghosts).
- Contacting the souls of children before they are born. A mother or father can actually communicate with the soul of a developing fetus while it is still in the womb.

A transcript of my superconscious mind tap cassette is presented in Appendix A (Healing Yourself through Hypnosis).

There is a growing need in all fields of psychotherapy today for more effective methods of treatment. Successful therapy should facilitate the patient's gaining increased mastery over himself so he can learn to cope with and overcome his problems. The majority of psychotherapy methods are either too limited in their applications, too lengthy, or too costly. The recovery rate, judged by empirical observations, can be meaningful only if it exceeds the sixty-five per cent spontaneous cure rate (the placebo effect).

Hypnotherapy is classified as Code 07.01.05, and parapsychology as Code 270 on the American Psychological Association's APA field system. The American Association for the Advancement of Science in Washington, D.C. formally accepted parapsychology into its family of sciences in 1969. Most people are unfamiliar with the enormous credibility of this "unconventional" field. Also, since past-life regression/progression hypnotherapy is based on the principles of quantum physics (see Chapter 23), that makes this field the only one accepted by the APA that is based on a hard science.

5

THE ROLE OF KARMA

Karma is simply cause and effect. If you throw a rock through a window, making a hole in the window, you have a cause (throwing the rock), and an effect (a hole in the window). Every effect that exists has some cause. If you are unhappy about your life, your financial situation, your relationships, your health, etc., then you must realize that a cause exists. These causes can be traced back to past lives. Your subconscious mind retains all of these causes because it has a perfect memory bank. The subconscious mind also survives death, so that a new life means merely exchanging one body for another. You have the same subconscious, only now it has learned some lessons and grown spiritually.

All of the things you have or have not done in this and all of your past lives will generate certain effects in this life as well as in future lifetimes. The laws of karma are perfectly just. The soul always has free will. Karma can bring you happiness or sadness, depending on the effects you have earned and the paths you have chosen to take. It is not the purpose of karma to reward or punish. Its purpose is to educate the subconscious, and to purify it. Once the subconscious is purified, it no longer needs karma, or the "karmic cycle," as we refer to it. The karmic cycle is the chain of lives we live in order to work out all of the negativity we have earned in previous lifetimes.

The balance sheet or final result of the karmic cycle is zero. When all of the positive causes we've amassed cancel out all of the negative causes, and we have learned all of the lessons that we are supposed to learn, then we have completed our karmic cycle. The balance sheet is zero and the subconscious is purified. We then no longer need to come back again to learn.

If, however, we react to certain tests in our lives negatively (with hatred, revenge, jealousy, pettiness, or some other negative emotion), then we have not learned our lesson but have failed the test and will have to retake this test in either this or a future lifetime.

KARMA – AN EASTERN TRADITION WITH A WESTERN APPLICATION

The belief in the preexistence of an individual soul (or subconscious) has been called by many names. The terms *metempsychosis, transmigration, reincarnation, rebirth,* and *reembodiment* have been used to describe this mechanism. Karma is a Sanskrit word that literally means "action." (Sanskrit is an ancient Indo-European written language, dating from about 1500 B.C.) Karma is the force that leads to reincarnation. *Destiny* is another synonym for karma. In any one life we plant the seeds of the personality that will grow during that and subsequent incarnations (lifetimes). Thus, reincarnation is the mechanism by which karma works. The two must be considered together.

The basic law of karma has come to mean action and reaction, or cause and effect. This is equivalent to the Christian philosophy: "As ye do unto others, so shall it be done unto you." Any action that is considered harmful or evil to the well-being of another is recompensed exactly in proportion to the harm done.

One of the basic principles of karma is that every soul (entity) has free will. There is always freedom of choice. Each soul is drawn to parents who can provide the biological heredity and physical environment needed to learn karmic lessons. Psychic genetics is more important than biological genetics in determining the character of our lives. In addition, all lessons and deeds are recorded in the entity's Akashic records, which are used to determine each new lifetime. These records are the sum total of our past, present, and future lives and are accessible through our superconscious mind.

A law of retribution extends over the entire karmic cycle. This law allows an entity to enjoy, in one lifetime, what it has earned in previous incarnations.

Often people will say that they are incapable of doing something because of their karma. In this case karma is being used as a crutch. Karma neither rewards nor punishes. This universal law of cause and effect gives meaning to all actions. Nothing happens by chance. It is only through ignorance and misuse that karma results in destruction, pain, sorrow, and suffering.

The concept of *transmigration* is included in Eastern karmic thought. Transmigration is the passage of the human soul from the mineral kingdom through lower animals and finally to man. Many Eastern philosophers reject this concept, as do the majority of Western karmic followers. Even those who do accept transmigration feel that it is impossible to revert back to the lower animal form once human form is achieved. I personally do not accept transmigration, and none of the 33,000 regression and progressions that I have personally conducted have revealed a non-human existence.

Every culture since ancient times has accepted the idea of karma in some form or other.

The Principle of Forgiveness

What is interesting to note about working out our karma is the principle of forgiveness. When I have the patient speak from the superconscious (the highest level of the subconscious) mind level I am informed of how this principle works. Assume that you lived during the time of the Vikings, about 1,200 years ago. Raiding villages, burning buildings, raping the women, and murdering the villagers would have been commonplace. This would incur much negative karma. If during one of these raids a certain group of villagers would have their lives spared because of your kindness, then you would earn positive karma. It wouldn't be just one positive episode against many negative ones. The fact that you showed this kindness would erase many negative episodes during that particular incarnation. If you spent the rest of that life helping other people, all of the past murders, thefts, and other crimes could be removed from your karmic cycle.

Free Will

Since the soul always has free will, it is our decision to be born at a certain time and place. It is our decision to choose our parents, friends, lovers, and enemies. We cannot blame other people or a bad childhood or marriage for our present problems. We are directly responsible for our lives because we have chosen the environment.

The basic framework of your new life will be preplanned by you, but you cannot plan every situation. Not only does your soul have free will, but so do all the souls that you will come into contact with in this new life. The main point is that you choose the tests.

Lords of Karma

Theosophists believe karma is regulated by the Lipika, or Lords of Karma, beings so powerful and objective that they work as a spiritual natural law.

For a nonbeliever, the assumption of a Lipika is identical with the classical mythological personifications of natural powers and natural laws.

Group Karma

We do not reincarnate individually. Rather, as I have been suggesting, our own separate karmic cycles are intertwined with many others. For example, your parents may have been your children in a former life. Your wife may have been your brother or son, etc. This is not to say that karma involves any form of incest or other such moral judgment. It simply implies that our lessons are intermingled with the lessons of their entities. These lessons have an effect between entities and among others around them,

Group karma applies to everything we do. People who are killed in airplane crashes, wars, or other catastrophes actually chose that time and place to die. Case histories later in the book will develop this concept further.

The Theosophic view of karma has three levels:

1. As natural law, without providence or release.
2. As reward or punishment.
3. As guidance, compensation, evolution, and healing.

It is level number three that we are dealing with in this book. There are many instances where health issues are carried over from previous lives. Drowning in a past life leads to a fear of water, or falling off a cliff centuries ago with a resulting fear of heights are but two examples of this principle.

SUMMARIZING REINCARNATION AND KARMA

Karma means "action" or "reaction." Another way to define it is simply as cause and effect. Christians say, "Do unto others as it should be done unto you." The Christian philosophy views this cause and effect as occurring during a single lifetime.

Followers of karma and reincarnation carry it over from lifetime to lifetime. The law of karma states that any single entity is born into a particular lifetime under the exact set of circumstances and with the exact set of capabilities to best utilize his or her karmic cycle. These qualities were the result of previous incarnations.

The law of retribution encompasses the entire karmic cycle. Thus the soul may benefit or suffer in one lifetime from the events of its previous lifetimes.

The law of karma has many advantages for its students. It offers an understanding of the frustrations and obstacles that are experienced by people who do not seem to deserve their environment. Second, it offers a more scientific explanation for the teachings of Christ and all other religious leaders. Third, it acts as a deterrent to selfish, thoughtless, and harmful actions. Fourth, it facilitates the belief in an orderly universe, one in which law and order and a sense of moral purpose dominate.

One of the very attractive qualities about reincarnation and karma is the opportunity to meet challenges in new lives and to have a great deal of control over one's destiny. You might consider it a concept of evolution based on the laws of cause and effect. "As you sow, so shall you reap."

6

CONVENTIONAL MEDICINE vs. SOUL HEALING

As we have discussed earlier, the term "healing" means to make whole. To heal is to restore balance and integrity to our being. The body has a wonderful, innate capacity to heal itself. Modern medicine has a nonholistic approach to healing. Generally, it initiates treatment from the outside, using artificial methods such as surgery, radiation, and drugs. In truth, healing occurs from within. Healing is a natural property of life, and life itself is a continual process of healing.

This is not to suggest that modern medicine should be totally ignored or discarded, but we need to understand the limitations of conventional treatments and expand our awareness of alternative approaches to health and healing—especially in relation to chronic conditions which conventional medicine has traditionally failed to treat effectively.

For example, conventional medicine is unable to properly deal with allergies, cancer, viral infections, and psychosomatic illnesses. Even when conventional treatment appears to work, it is often in spite of the traditional therapy. The results more likely represent the activation of the body's own intrinsic healing mechanisms. In other words, it is most probably the body's own inner restorative powers which effected the healing, rather than the outside stimulus from traditional medicine.

Interestingly, the word "doctor," comes from the Latin word for "teacher": *docure.* The primary concern of a doctor should be to teach the prevention of illness. The direct treatment of the disease itself should be secondary. Preventing illness in the first place is far easier, wiser, and less costly than treating the disease once it occurs. Most of the common drugs prescribed today by conventional medicine begin with the prefix "anti," which, of course, means against For example, anti-depressants, anti-histamines, anti-inflammatories, anti-arrhythemics, anti-pyretics, and anti-hypertensives are commonly used today. Medicine is dominated by this suppressive, combative and counteractive approach.

Conventional medicine is usually effective, sometimes with the help of these drugs, for the management of acute conditions on a short-term basis. Where it is less effective or not effective at all relates to long-term use for chronic conditions. Two major types of problems arise in this connection. First, the patient is exposed to many side effects with these drugs (toxicity). Second, the disease process may actually be strengthened over time by these suppressive drugs. Suppressive measures can actually drive the disease process inward and affect the body's vital organs. For example, patients who take Prednisone for many months to control rheumatoid arthritis, lupus, asthma, or allergic disorders, commonly experience depression, ulcers, weight gain, acne, and weakened bones. In fact, patients experience a recurrence of symptoms when they stop using these drugs. The result is unfortunate. The disease remains and a dependency on the medication is established.

Hippocrates stated, "First do no harm" (*primam non nocere*) and "Honor the healing power of nature" (*vis medicatrix naturae*). In its treatment of chronic diseases, conventional medicine has failed miserably on both accounts.

Conversely, soul healing, with its holistic approach, has a positive perspective. It assumes the body can and will heal itself. Remember the key points from Chapter 4. The soul's energy affects the emotions which, in turn, stimulates the body's innate healing processes. Thus, there is no separation of mind and body. Further, the beliefs of the health practitioner strongly influence the patient's natural healing forces. By communicating this dedication and love nonverbally as well as verbally, soul healing will be effectively facilitated.

The body as a whole and all of its parts are connected. The body's organs and systems are dependent on each other. In addition, our energy and emotional states are linked to our physical self. The body, in fact, has a natural desire to be healthy. This natural condition requires the least amount of energy expenditure. In medicine we call this *homeostasis*. When the body is out of balance it truly wants to return to this natural state of balance and health. If this was not so, the human species would have become extinct long ago. We have not persisted for 35,000 years by accident!

Traditional medicine is dominated by a pessimistic attitude. It stresses the treatment of disease rather than the maintenance of health and the prevention of illness. The biomedical model is the basis of conventional medicine. The emphasis is placed on form rather than function. However, the body's natural healing system is based on function rather than on form or structure alone. The biomedical model ignores the importance of the mind and our psychological state. Instead, the model focuses on organic (physical) causes of disease. We have no National Institute of Health and Healing. We do, however, have the National Cancer Institute, the National Institute of Neurological Disorders, the National Institute of Allergy and Infectious Diseases, etc. The preoccupation is with the disease rather than the healing process.

The amount of medical research done on healing is minute and far too narrow in scope. Most of it concerns "spontaneous remission" of cancer tumors. This is unacceptable. The term remission is misleading; it is not synonymous with healing. Remission implies a temporary abatement of a disease process, which can still resurface at times. The whole field of healing can and should be rigorously researched. The main problem is the prejudice exhibited by the medical establishment, which regards this topic with little or no respect.

In his book *Spontaneous Healing*, Dr. Andrew Weil offers the following observations about our natural healing process:

- Healing directs the normal functioning along with neutralizing the effects of injury to the body.
- Healing is spontaneous.
- Healing is continuous and is available twenty-four hours a day.
- Healing is a part of our constitution functioning through our DNA, which manufactures the enzymes needed to repair the body.
- The body's healing system can recognize disease and injury and can remove damaged tissue and replace it with normal, healthy structures.

During the last fifteen years, researchers from various backgrounds have been gradually drawn to the new discipline of psychoneuroimmunology (PNI). Social psychologists, experimental psychologists, psychiatrists, immunologists, neuroendocrinologists, neuroanatomists, biologists, oncologists, and epidemiologists, among other specialists, have all made contributions to PNI research. Unfortunately, the medical establishment has shown much reluctance and suspicion toward this discipline. Lawrence LeShan, a cancer researcher, encountered so much difficulty when he sought funding for his research linking cancer to personality traits that his work had to be supported by a private laboratory.

The Behavioral Medicine Branch, a division of the National Cancer Institute, provides yet another example of hostility toward PNI research. In the early 1980s, researchers noted that women with breast cancer who were aggressive in assuming control of their choice of treatment and physician had better survival rates. These researchers wanted to test this hypothesis and develop methods for other women to deal with their cancer more assertively and more productively.

In 1982, the new head of the Behavioral Medicine division disbanded that branch. He said, "Psychoneuroimmunological research is not a large part of the Institute and won't be for the present. The issue of how emotions affect cancer is very difficult for us to deal with here."

Dr. Truman Schnabel, of the University of Pennsylvania School of Medicine, authored an article, "Is Medicine Still an Art?" which appeared in the prestigious *New England Journal of Medicine*. In it, he compared the way his father, an internist, practiced medicine with the way it is currently administered.

Although medicine in the 1920s and 1930s was primitive compared to today's practices, a much closer relationship existed with the patient. Referring to his father, Schnabel said, "To him, medicine's art lay in a skillful manipulation of the relationship between doctor and patient which, when combined with the logical use of medicine's science, led to the best kind of patient care."

Referring to our current mania for specialists, Schnabel adds, "The sick person seems to have changed. No longer a single entity, the body demanded an expert in each specific organ system." What the technology of medicine gained by this approach, the art of healing has lost. Not surprisingly, says Schnabel, this raises a basic question: Is anyone focused on the whole being?

An excellent example of soul healing can be found in a study of miracle cures: specifically, sudden and dramatic reversals of disease experienced by people who made pilgrimages to Lourdes near the French Pyrenees. Legend has it that the Virgin Mary appeared there in 1858 to a French peasant girl, Bernadette Soubirous. Water from a spring discovered at the time of the holy apparition is believed to effect miraculous cures. Every year an estimated three million people (a half million of whom are sick people seeking a cure) travel to the shrine to drink and bathe in its icy waters. Since 1858, the Catholic Church claims to have authenticated more than sixty instances of miracle cures that have occurred here. The ritual of making the pilgrimage, attending the ceremonies, and praying at the shrine all played a part in this process of non-medical healing.

Dr. Andrew Weil presents another example of healing at Lourdes in his book *Spontaneous Healing* (pp. 84–85). Vittorio Micheli, inducted into the Italian Army in 1961, complained of pains in his left hip. A comprehensive series of medical tests revealed that Micheli had cancer (sarcoma)of the left pelvis.

This condition worsened, and by August of that year x-rays showed "almost complete destruction of the left pelvis." Micheli was placed in a hip-to-toe cast and treated with chemotherapy. After two months of this treatment, with no improvement, the chemotherapy was discontinued.

In May of 1963 Micheli went to Lourdes. By now he had had severe and continuous pain, loss of appetite, and could no longer stand. Immediately after plunging himself in the Lourdes water, his appetite improved and he no longer experienced pain.

Micheli started walking within a month. X-rays then showed a regression of the sarcoma, which completely disappeared by 1974. He began working in a factory where he was required to stand for eight to ten hours a day. Bureau records show that Micheli's left hip and leg are "the same as normal."

David Sobel, an expert in the use of placebos, has strongly advocated the use of these harmless aids. The classic criticism leveled against the use of placebos is that it is a form of deception by the physician and is thus unethical. One possible solution is for the doctor to state that this medication (the placebo) has no known chemical activity but may still work, as do hypnosis, relaxation therapy, body work, yoga, etc. Sobel firmly believes that placebos are effective and can be ethically administered to summon the placebo response. Ultimately, "the placebo makes a statement that we have within us a certain self-regulatory mechanism, a self-healing mechanism, which can be mobilized given proper situational and environmental cues."

Dr. Herbert Benson feels the placebo response is the relaxation response. He has recommended combining religious cues by the patient to induce this response (prayer, for example). Since the placebo is inert and has no chemical medicinal properties, I believe it is the expectations created by the substance which induces the healing.

Placebos are used in the clinical tests of all drugs being researched. In fact, in order to obtain FDA approval, the drug tested must show that it is more effective than the placebo. Approximately one-third of the people using them "get better" with the use of placebos alone.

As mentioned earlier, few members of the medical establishment regard the field of mind/body medicine seriously. What is even worse is that the most prestigious researchers show nothing but contempt for their colleagues who do research work in this field. Regardless of the recent surge of books, television shows, magazine articles, lectures, and workshops featuring doctors and researchers advocating these concepts, the research actually done is often of poor quality. In the next chapter, we will deal with this research.

Mind/body medicine (especially soul healing) is not routinely taught in medical schools. The most a medical student will be offered is an occasional elective on the topic. Conventional medicine erroneously assumes the mind is the effect rather than the cause. Even psychiatry students spend most of their four-year residency programs on psychopharmacology, emphasizing the dogma that psychopathology is a problem solely related to brain circuitry and biochemistry. One of my patients gave me a pin several years ago that reads, "My karma ran over my dogma."

Healing responses have occurred immediately following a traumatic situation. Numerous examples include escaping from physical danger, ending a dysfunctional relationship, terminating a stressful job, etc. Even the act of falling in love has been correlated with the healing of chronic fatigue, chronic back and neck pain, rheumatoid arthritis, and many more syndromes. Falling "head over heels" for someone and committing "body and soul" does have its advantages in soul healing.

Even anger helps initiate a healing process. Seismophobia is a fear of earthquakes, a syndrome that is often exhibited by those who live in Los Angeles (where my office is located). A simple technique that is rather effective in healing this simple phobia is to displace anger against the earthquake as it is happening. Appropriate and focused expressions of anger can, in many instances, activate the healing process.

In my experience with patients, a total acceptance of the circumstances surrounding one's illness and life in general is usually a prerequisite to soul healing. In fact, acceptance is Stage 5 in Elizabeth Kübler-Ross' thanatology process. This submission to a higher power is, in reality, an acceptance of one's own higher self or superconscious mind.

The only reason we get sick is that the capacity of the healing system to restore balance is exceeded by the forces of imbalance. For the sake of simplicity, I am describing only the physical level and purposely neglecting the karmic and spiritual aspects.

Remember, healing is a process of becoming whole. This inner sense of peace and balance can still be attained while some aspects of a disease are in the body. These subclinical circumstances do not manifest themselves, and therefore, are not a problem. The ability of our body to compensate is truly amazing. Blind people can hear better than seeing people. A patient with a missing limb can still function by adaptation.

Spiritual causes of our problems can be karmic (the result of actions or inactions in previous lives), possession by spirits, a psychic attack, or the influence of deceased ancestors on our soul. Conventional medicine rejects this hypothesis and focuses only on physical (organic) causes of illness.

Conventional medicine is effective when dealing with acute trauma. Thus, if you are injured in a car accident, please get yourself to a hospital first. Once you are out of physical danger, you can then safely consult a soul healer.

Acute conditions such as appendicitis, heart attacks, diabetic comas, bowel obstructions, etc. are, for the most part, largely treatable in the realm of modern medicine. In chronic disease, conventional (allopathic) medicine fails to offer effective treatment.

To summarize, conventional medicine can greatly help with cases of trauma, acute bacterial, fungal, and parasitic infections, surgical emergencies, hormonal deficiencies, infectious disease (by immunization), the replacement of damaged hips and knees, and so forth. Allopathic medicine cannot cure cancer, combat viral infections, cure allergies, manage psychosomatic illnesses, or cure most chronic degenerative diseases.

My rule of thumb is this: do not rely on soul healing for a condition which conventional medicine can handle well, and do not consult a physician for a condition which conventional medicine cannot treat. However, if your physician is also a soul healer, you have the best of both worlds.

Therapeutic touch needs to be discussed here. Dolores Krieger, a professor of nursing at New York University, is a pioneer of this method. She was influenced by the work of the soul healer, Oskar Estebany. Since the 1970s, she has been educating her students in this art. More than fifty universities offer a course in therapeutic touch, mostly in their nursing programs.

The ritual of therapeutic touch is quite simple. The healer first centers himself or herself. The healer then eases into an altered state of consciousness where he or she concentrates or focuses energies on the healing process. Next, the healer passes his or her hands slowly over the person to be healed, hovering four to six inches above the body of the patient, trying to activate the intrinsic energy radiating from the patient's body.

Krieger has utilized therapeutic touch for the treatment of illnesses such as musculoskeletal problems, fevers, inflammation, and many psychosomatic diseases.

Dr. Janet Quinn, of the University of South Carolina, received the first federal grant to study therapeutic touch. In a study she conducted, she had two groups of "healers." One group centered themselves and concentrated on their patients. The control group did not center themselves and simply counted back from 100 as they moved their hands over the patients. These sessions were videotaped; no one who watched them could tell the healers from the control group. The patients who received true soul healing showed a significant drop in anxiety, which was absent from those of the control group.

One point I would like to emphasize is this: do your own research regarding alternative treatments. Initiate your own search for other forms of therapy regarding your illness. Read books, talk to friends, seek out authors, visit libraries, watch talk shows, and, if necessary, travel to meet with soul healers who pass your credibility tests. Conventional doctors may consider you an annoying patient for doing this, but it is your life. As Leo Durocher used to say, "Nice guys finish last." Out-maneuver your own ego and let the body heal itself. Trust that your body knows how to do this.

Shortcomings of Conventional Medicine

I would like to conclude this chapter with my main criticisms of conventional medicine:

- The biomedical model completely works against the concept of soul healing. Physicians dismiss this field as "unscientific" and unworthy of investigation.
- Insurance companies have far too much influence on the medical community. These companies will not pay for soul healing approaches because they claim there isn't enough research data to support their use. However, since the medical establishment is biased against such research to begin with, we are stuck with a Catch-22 situation.
- Doctors are more afraid of lawsuits than they are interested in true healing. They are unwilling to "deviate from the standard of conventional care" and use soul healing techniques. They fear being vulnerable to litigation.
- Medicine is stuck in its disease-oriented and strictly symptom treatment modalities. Until there is a basic change in medical education, the problems will only worsen.

Dr. Weil makes many of the following recommendations to medical educators. He believes these would begin the process of updating conventional medicine into the soul healing twenty-first century:

- Incorporate alternative medicine disciplines such as nutrition, herbalism, acupuncture, guided imagery, and hypnosis into the curriculum.
- Offer courses in spirituality and transpersonal psychology.
- Emphasize mind/body interactions, including psychoneuroimmunology and placebo responses.
- Instruct students on communication skills in relationship to taking medical histories and the presentation of treatment plans which will enhance the body's healing system.
- Offer courses on quantum physics, the holographic memory theory, and others to account for the nonphysical causation of physical events.
- Emphasize the healing power of nature and the body's innate healing system.

7

SCIENTIFIC RESEARCH SUPPORTING SOUL HEALING

Dr. Herbert Benson, a cardiologist and professor at Harvard Medical School, has done much work with the relaxation response by studying the effects of Transcendental Meditation (TM). Dr. Benson initially felt the very idea of people lowering their blood pressure, for example, through the use of TM was absurd.

The work of a California physiologist named Keith Wallace changed Dr. Benson's mind. Wallace published a paper in *Science* magazine titled, "Physiological Effects of Transcendental Meditation." He found that meditators had lower blood pressure. Their oxygen consumption stopped, and their brain waves (alpha) resembled those of people experiencing hypnosis and biofeedback.

Later, Wallace worked with Dr. Benson at Harvard Medical School's Thorndike Laboratory. They discovered that subjects practicing yoga and Zen were able to duplicate the results of the TM practitioners. Benson also noted that when people prayed or meditated, especially deeply religious people, they settled into an identical soothing state of mind.

After additional research, Benson and his fellow scientists found that all these methods had four basic features in common.

1. Each was performed in a quiet place: a cool, shaded room, a temple, church, or chapel.

2. Each focused on an object of concentration: a symbol or single sound, such as the famous Om.
3. Each practitioner assumed a comfortable position.
4. Most importantly, to perform the exercise successfully, individuals assumed a passive attitude, a willingness to let thoughts pass through the mind without dwelling on them. They were not to worry whether they were performing the exercise correctly or well. The resulting exercise could summon forth Benson's relaxation response: a calming state of body and spirit.

Benson based some of his conclusions on the work done on cats by Swiss Nobel Laureate Dr. Walter Hess. Hess deduced that the hypothalamus in the brain was the center through which the relaxation response operated. The hypothalamus has significant control over the body's immune system. When Hess stimulated one section of the hypothalamus with small pulses of electricity, he obtained a trophotropic response, the feline cat equivalent of the relaxation response. The animal was placid and displayed some of the same body patterns—lowered blood pressure and relaxed muscles—of those of the TM and relaxation response groups.

In the 1960s, psychologist Lawrence LeShan discovered that there was a "cancer personality." He suggested that people with certain kinds of personality traits had a higher than average incidence of cancer, an incidence that conventional medicine could not explain.

Those characterized as having low self-esteem, found to be longer suffering, repressed their hostile emotions, and, before their diagnosis, had experienced a personal loss such as divorce or a death of a loved one. These were the people who most often evidenced a "cancer personality." LeShan, a respected researcher, had voluminous evidence to support his theories.

Nicholas Hall, a neuroendocrinologist in the Department of Biochemistry at George Washington University, had conducted research with visual imagery and cancer patients. As part of his experiment, one of his subjects, a retired school administrator, kept a detailed diary of his feelings about his daily imagery sessions. Hall monitored the subject's level of the hormone thymosin in his blood. Thymosin is an important component of our immune system. The levels of this hormone were checked against the man's attitudes and needs, as recorded in his diary. On days when he felt his imagery exercises were going well, the man's thymosin levels were high. On those days when his diary revealed that he did not participate fully in the imaging, his thymosin levels were lower. During this study, the man's wife died. In his diary, he said he had lost interest in the experiment. A blood sample was drawn at this time. Laboratory tests showed his thymosin levels to be noticeably depressed. The man stopped doing the imagery work, and two months later he was dead. "The emotional setbacks, coupled with cancer, were too much," Hall concluded. "In my opinion, he essentially gave up hope," he added.

From the evidence accumulated thus far, it appears that imagery exercises have some effect, but that the specific image does not. There are no inherently healthful images. They are healthful only to the degree that those who use them experience some feeling of well-being or security—the same kind of feeling that accompanies hope of recovery. Many people have always believed that the mind does affect the body; now that belief can be confirmed.

Psychologist Robert Ader coined the term psychoneuroimmunology (PNI) to describe how the mind, the immune system, and the nervous system all respond to disease. Among the goals of psychoneuroimmunology is to understand and explore the concept of hope. Part of PNI's quest is to call forth the "biology" of hope through an appreciation of the healing powers of the human spirit, plus a deeper understanding of the intimate neuronal and hormonal bonds between the mind and body. In the twenty-first century the art of soul healing and the science of medicine will be transformed by that far-reaching quest.

Psychiatrist Fred Hencker, a professor of psychiatry at the University of Arkansas, developed an approach to increase hope in patients scheduled for kidney transplants and heart surgery. Patients and their families meet with the surgeon and their staff, who calmly explain the various procedures. The hospital staff further encourages the patients to do as much as possible for themselves after surgery. The results of this study are encouraging. Hencker has found a greater success rate in surgery and a less compromised patient, both psychologically and medically.

BIOFEEDBACK

The effects of biofeedback on the immune system were demonstrated by Barbara Peavey at North Texas University. Participants learned to raise the temperature of their hands and psychological tests showed that they were less stressed. More impressively, blood tests revealed that phagocytes (immune system cells) were more potent after the biofeedback sessions.

Janice Kiecolt-Glaser at Ohio State University has shown that teaching progressive relaxation to geriatric patients resulted in an increase in the potency of the natural killer cells of the immune system. This was confirmed by blood tests following these exercises.

David McClelland, a psychologist at Harvard University, referring to self-healing, has stated:

> It may turn out to be something fairly existential or religious, a kind of personal disengagement combined with a kind of faith in something beyond the self, something beyond, or bigger than the self that you can trust.

The appearance of pills seems to affect one's healing ability. The average person ingests 76,000 pills during a lifetime. Dr. David Sobel of Kaiser Hospital in California points out that injections are interpreted by patients as more powerful than pills. As far as pills are concerned, capsules are considered more potent than tablets. Yellow or orange capsules are traditionally thought of as mind manipulators. Lavender pills connote hallucinogens. A sedative is expected to be gray or dark red. White pills signify pain killers and black pills suggest hallucinogenic substances. As Dr. Sobel points out, most diseases are self-limiting; that is, they run their course and end. As Mark Twain once said: "God cures and the doctor sends the bill."

A nineteenth century French doctor noted: "You should treat as many patients as possible with the new drugs while they still have the power to heal." The message is that doctors follow fads in medicine with the same waxing and waning of enthusiasm for a new medicine or a new therapy as everyone else.

Belief is potent medicine. Doctors Herbert Benson of Harvard Medical School and David P. McCallie, Jr., of Harvard's Thorndike Laboratory compared various treatments for angina pectoris (heart pain). They found that an unusually high number of patients (approximately eight out of ten) reported relief from heart pain when treated by certain doctors. Benson and McCallie classified these highly successful doctors "enthusiasts," because in each case the individual had introduced the therapy into medical practice. Of course, these doctors believed in their own work and were able to transmit their faith and confidence to their patients. The effect transcended general positive feelings of well-being; measurable improvements resulted. For example, the enthusiasts' patients tolerated more strenuous exercise, reduced their nitroglycerin intake, and had improved electrocardiographic results. These improvements occurred despite the fact that, in some instances, the treatment was later shown to be ineffective.

Additional factors in self-healing relate to the environment surrounding the treatment. Being treated in a hospital or in a doctor's private office is healing in itself. More importantly, the caring attitude of the practitioner can liken him to the ancient Shaman and his techniques. A positive, loving attitude greatly facilitates healing.

Dr. Morgan Martin described his conversations with a Native American healer named Russell in an article in the *Journal of the American Medical Association.* Russell pointed out that both the healer and the patient share a belief about the nature of disease. The healer focuses on the reactions of the family and friends to the disease, not on the disease itself. The shaman involves the patient's family in the healing ceremony. In the end, the healer dispenses "a remedy and a ritual." Russell emphasized that it is the patient's faith in the healer which determines the ultimate success (or failure) of the healing.

In the Pacific Northwest, programs were started to incorporate the best of shamanic techniques with modern medicine. The healers often had better success than the clinic doctors. The National Institute of Mental Health has initiated similar programs in New Mexico where apprentice Navajo medicine men learn the traditional ways of healing. This includes ceremonies, dances, rituals, and prayers.

The work of Harvard psychologist George Vaillant in his book, *Adaptation to Life,* shows that individuals who typically handle the trials and pressures of life in an immature way also tend to become ill four times more often. Clearly, the immune system is responding to mental states. His work and those of others illustrate that disease occurs if the immune system:

- Is overactive in response to an antigen from outside the body—ragweed pollen, for example, where allergy is the medical result.

- Is overactive in responding to an antigen that is the body itself—if the immune system attacks its own body's healthy tissues, such as the cartilage in joints, the result is an autoimmune disease such as rheumatoid arthritis.
- Underreacts, ignores, or is unable to destroy an outside antigen—a bacterium, for example, which could result in an infection.
- Underreacts to or simply ignores an abnormal antigen that appears to be a normal part of the inside of the body—the result may be cancer, in which abnormal body cells are allowed to proliferate unchecked.

Soloman and Moos (1965) became convinced that distinct personality traits characterize those individuals most prone to autoimmune diseases. Generally, such people are described as "quiet, introverted, reliable, conscientious, restricted in their expression of emotion (particularly anger), conforming, self-sacrificing, tending to allow themselves to be imposed upon, sensitive to criticism, distant, over-active and busy, stubborn, rigid, and controlling."

As a possible explanation for these results, University of Texas psychologist Jean Achterberg-Lawlis suggests that alexithyrnia, the inability to verbalize emotions, could account for the unemotional manner of some arthritic patients. According to the theory, this emotional flatness is not the result of any personality disorder, but rather a poor neuronal link between the two halves of the brain. The right emotional side of the brain cannot find expression through the verbal left side of the brain because of poor communication of emotional information between the two sides of the brain. In order to compensate for the inability to express emotions verbally, a person does so physically, through bodily illness.

In 1994 the American Psychiatric Associations *DMS-IV* (*Diagnostic and Statistical Manual of Mental Disorders*) presented a V code labeled "Religious or Spiritual Problem" (Lukoff, Lu and Turner, 1992). This category recognizes religious and spiritual issues that are not attributed to a mental disorder.

In a study by Eisenberg, Kessler, Foster, Norlock, Calkins and Delbanco (1993) reported in the *New England Journal of Medicine*, one of three respondents (thirty-four per cent) reported using at least one unconventional therapy in the past year. In addition, "Roughly one in four Americans who see their medical doctors for a serious health problem may be using unconventional therapy in addition to conventional medicine for that problem" (p. 251). Several of the unconventional therapies were psychospiritual in nature (e.g., spiritual healing, prayer, homeopathy, energy healing, and imagery).

Other publications have addressed the religious and spiritual issues in psychotherapy; for example, the book *Sacred Landscapes* (Randour, 1993) contains case studies and essays on these subjects.

The media also targeted religious and spiritual aspects of healing on television shows, magazine articles, and newspaper articles. Bill Moyer's five-part television series on "Healing and the Mind" brought these issues into millions of living rooms. *The New York Times* published a report on changes in "How Therapists See Religion as an Aid, not Illusion" (Goldman, 1991).

Psychiatrists and psychologists are relatively uninvolved in religion, and fifty to sixty per cent describe themselves as atheists or agnostics, in contrast to one per cent to five per cent of the population (Lukoff, et al., 1992).

In the Allman, de la Roche, Elkins, and Weathers (1992) study, fifty per cent of the psychologists reported personally having a mystical experience, which is significantly higher than the thirty to forty per cent incidence of mystical experiences in the general population (Lukoff and Lu, 1988).

Another survey (Bergin and Jensen, 1990) of psychiatrists, psychologists, social workers, and marriage and family counselors found that sixty-eight per cent of those questioned "Seek a spiritual understanding of the universe and one's place in it." The authors concluded, "There may be a reservoir of spiritual interests among therapists that is often unexpressed due to the secular framework of professional education and practice" (p. 3). They named this phenomenon "spiritual humanism" and emphasized this could bridge the cultural gap between medical clinicians and the more spiritually inclined public.

The Spiritual Orientation Inventory (SOI) specifically attempted to be sensitive to the spirituality of those unaffiliated with any traditional religion. In this study, D. W. Smith (1991) compared the scores of 172 polio survivors with eighty individuals sho had not had the disease. Her prediction that the polio survivors would have higher scores was confirmed. Another study (Lee and Bainum, 1991) compared thirteen hospice workers with twenty-three hospital nurses. Nurses who dealt more directly with death scored higher on the SOI.

Unlike physicians, nurses have traditionally adopted a more holistic perspective toward patients, an integration of body, mind, and spirit. Their awareness of the spiritual dimension of their patients was strikingly evident in the accepted nursing diagnostic classification system (Carpenito, 1983). This included categories for spiritual concerns, spiritual distress, and spiritual despair.

The word *kundalini* is from the Hindu and is translated as "she who is coiled," symbolizing psycho-biospiritual energy. According to traditional Indian philosophy, this coiled-up energy lies at the base of the spine and is dormant. The image of a coiled-up snake is sometimes used to depict this.

Indian philosophy symbolizes the Cosmic Energy, or Creative Intelligence, of the universe as bipolar. Shiva, one of the Hindu trinity, is the Godhead, or pure consciousness. He is the transcendent or Absolute, the father aspect. Shakti is the Mother of the Universe, the dynamic creative energy or primal energy of the universe, located at the base of the spine. Shiva resides in the head, between the eyebrows or sixth center of consciousness, sometimes called in Hindu the *anja*. Between the two Energy symbols, the head and the base of the spine, are a series of powerful energy points or wheels called Chakras (five in Buddhism, seven in Hinduism). A central channel, called the *sushumna,* connects them along a vertical axis. As the kundali rises, it ascends the sushumna, opening the dhakras and producing myriad superconscious experiences. Those who practice the awakening of the *hundalini* (kundalini yoga) believe they will eventually attain higher spiritual states of consciousness, leading ultimately to samadhi or enlightenment. Many believe that before enlightenment, one may experience various consciousness-expanding states. These may include increased intuition, clairvoyance, and an expansion of compassion, among other psychic or spiritual experiences.

The practice of meditation, touch, or simply being in the same room as the teacher may awaken a person's kundalini. Adherents believe this process rapidly advances personal growth and spiritual evolution. While studying this phenomena, Sannella (1987) observed,

> ... a process of psychophysiological transmutation most usefully viewed as "awakening of the kundalini" is indeed a reality ... This process is a part of evolutionary mechanism and that as such it must not be viewed as a pathological development rather the kundalini process is in aspect of human psycho-spirtiual unfolding that is intrinsically desirable. The pathway of

> the kundalini can be blocked anywhere along its upward trajectory. We can look upon these blockages as stress points. Thus, in its ascent, the kundalini causes the central nervous system to throw off stress. This is usually associated with experience of pain.
>
> When the kundalini encounters these blocks, it works away at them until they are dissolved. It appears to act of its own volition, spreading through the entire psychophysiological system to effect its transformation. In Eastern terminology such spontaneous movements are called kriyas and are "physical purificatory movements initiated by the awakened kundalini. Kriyas purify the body and nervous system and help the person tolerate greater levels of energy (Muktananda, 1979, p. 52).

Kenneth Ring (1984) was the first Western consciousness researcher to speculate in detail about the role of kundalini in near-death experiences. He presented anecdotal evidence of similarities between kundalini awakenings and the common aftereffects of NDEs.

VISUAL IMAGERY

Visual imagery, as an aspect of soul healing, dates back as far as the Aesculapian temples of ancient Greece, where treatment involved the dreams of the patient (Horowitz, 1978). Its use in formal psychotherapy can be traced to Freud, during the time he first developed his theories of psychoanalysis. By means of relaxation and hypnosis, enhanced when patients lie down with their eyes closed, Freud created a favorable atmosphere for eliciting vivid images and fantasies, which he then analyzed. Freud eventually abandoned hypnosis, and his psychoanalytic treatment became more verbal than visual. Perhaps this change was influenced by the fact that Freud himself was not a visual thinker. He claimed that his memories were represented in ideas rather than pictures. Ironically, studies today indicate that most psychologists tend to be verbalizers rather than visualizers. This raises the provocative question of what course psychotherapy might have taken had Freud been a visualizer (Sommer, 1978).

Pope (1977) suggests that the constraints of the scientific method encouraged the study of the structured, "rational" aspects of thought rather than the stream of consciousness which includes fantasy and imagery. Soul healers decry the fact that for the last seventy-five years the literature of psychotherapy reveals sparse research in this area, and they contend that bias in favor of verbal thought has stunted the growth of current research. This indicates that subjective experiences are linked more closely with images and imaginings than with rational processes, and important changes are taking place. Reflecting this new awareness, Anees Sheikh (1978, p. 197) observes: "it appears that after having been severed from visions, warped by words, and stifled by semantics for a long time, Western man is ready to restore his wholeness by returning to the nonverbal springs of his existence."

In the last two decades, the challenging field of creative visualization and imagery has prompted research in areas as diverse as the performance of athletes and the treatment of cancer. These studies have attracted the attention of therapists with many different orientations. Psychoanalysis, hypnotherapy, behavior modification, biofeedback, body movement therapies, symbolic meditation, cognitive theories, covert aversive conditioning, personal construct therapy, and European mental imagery are among the therapies which currently utilize imagery. Goldberg (1984) and Meichenbaum (1978) suggest there are at least twenty alternative therapies that explore the value of imagery.

What are the specific benefits that motivate therapists to use visual imagery? Sheikh enumerates several:

1. Many traumatic and vivid events seem to be revealed in imagery.
2. Imagery can reveal proverbial memories which lead to basic conflicts.
3. Images are less likely to be filtered through critical processes.
4. Because images are spatial and simultaneous, they tend to be more accurate than sequential and linear representations.
5. Emotions respond more to visual than verbal thought.

Guided Affective Imagery (GAI), widely practiced in Europe, is the focus of an international society with chapters in Germany, Switzerland, Austria and Sweden. GAI employs a system of graduated methods and models for the therapeutic use of daydreams, which is probably the most highly systematized of all image therapies.

Ten standard motifs of GAI are used as guidelines and interpreted in relation to a patient's individual background. Motifs, which have specific purposes and goals, are ranked: (A) Elementary (meadow, brook, mountain, house, edge of the woods), (B) Intermediate (encounter with relatives, sexual attitudes, aggressive orientation, ego ideal), (C) Advanced (cave, swamp, volcano, folio). In the advanced level, free visual associations are used much like the free-word associations used in classic psychoanalysis. This associative process often sparks spontaneous occurrences of age regression, where childhood trauma can be experienced and eventually healed (Leuner, 1978). In addition, images and emotions from past and future lifetimes have been reported (Goldberg, 1984, 1988).

In his book, *In the Mind's Eyes,* Arnold Lazarus (1977) offers image therapy as a way of working through all types of problems. Using case histories, he cites many examples of the success of imagery therapy to overcome anxiety, depression, phobias, psychosomatic disorders, suicidal tendencies, obsessive-compulsive behavior, and other personality problems or disorders. One exercise which Lazarus calls "goal rehearsal" is defined as "practicing in the mind the specific goals one wishes to attain" (p. 49). For example, he details how goal rehearsal can help enhance athletic performance.

There is ample evidence to support the value of using Imagery as an adjunct to various therapies. One of the most valuable, perhaps, is that imagery seems to lessen dependence on the therapist and helps the patient gain mastery over his or her own inner processes. This leads to a sense of *empowerment* (which we will discuss in Chapter 24).

Thus, visual imagery is an important part of various therapeutic treatments, and one form of soul healing.

SOURCES

Allman, L. S., O. De La Roche, D. N. Elkins, and R. S. Weathers. "Psychotherapists' Attitudes towards Clients Reporting Mystical Experiences." *Psychotherapy,* 1992; 29(4), 654–69.

Bergin, A. and J. Jensen. "Religiosity of Psychotherapists: A National Survey." *Psychotherapy,* 1990: 27, 3–7.

Carpenito, L. *Nursing Diagnosis: Application to Clinical Practice.* New York: J. B. Lippincott, 1983.

Eisenberg, D., R. Kessler, C. Foster, F. Norlock, D. Calkins, and T. Delbanco. "Unconventional medicine in the United States." *The New England Journal of Medicine,* 1993; 328, 246–52.

Goldberg, Bruce, D.D.S., M.S. *Past Lives — Future Lives.* New York: Ballantine. 1988.

______. "Treating Dental Phobias through Past Life Therapy; a Case Report." *Journal of the Maryland State Dental Association,* 1984; 27(3), 137–139.

______. "The Treatment of Cancer through Hypnosis." *Psychology—A Journal of Human Behavior,* 1985; 3 (4), 36–39.

Goldman, D. "Therapists see Religion as an Aid, Not Illusion." *New York Times,* Sept. 10, 1991; p. c1, 8.

Horowitz, M. J. "Controls of Visual Imagery and Therapist Intervention." In J. Singer and K. Pope (Eds.). *The Power of Human Imagination*. New York; Plenum, 1978.

Lazarus, A. *In the Mind's Eye.* New York: Rawson Associates Publishers, Inc. 1977.

Lee, J. R. and B. Bainum. "Spiritual Orientation in Hospital Workers, Crisis Help Workers, and College Students." Unpublished study, 1991, Northern Pacific Union College.

Leuner, H. "Basic Principles and Therapeutic Efficacy of Guided Affective Imagery" (GAI). In J. Singer and K. Pope (Eds.) *The Power of Human Imagination*. New York: Plenum, 1978.

Lukoff, D. and F. Lu. "Transpersonal Psychology Research Review Topic: Mystical Experience." *Journal of Transpersonal Psychology,* 1988; 20, 161–84.

Lukoff, D., F. Lu, and R. Turner. "Toward a More Culturally Sensitive DSM–IV: Psychoreligious and Psychospiritual Problems." *Journal of Nervous and Mental Disease,* 1992; 180(11), 673–82.

Meichenbaum, R. "Why Does Using Imagery in Psychotherapy Lead to Change?" In J. Singer and K. Pope (Eds.). *The Power of Human Imagination*. New York, Plenum, 1978.

Muktanada. *Kundalini: "The secret of life."* Ganesphuri, India: Gurudev Siddha Peeth, 1979.

Pope, K. S. "The Flow of Consciousness." Unpublished doctoral dissertation. Yale University, In J. Singer and K. Pope (Eds.). *The Power of Human Imagination*. New York; Plenum, 1977.

Randour, M. L. (Ed.) *Exploring Sacred Landscapes: Religious and Spiritual Dimensions in Psychotherapy*. New York: Columbia University Press, 1993.

Ring, Kenneth. *Heading Towards Omega*. New York: William Morrow, 1984.

Sannella, L. *Kundalini—Psychosis or Transcendence?* Self-published, 1976.

Sannella, L. *Kundalini Experience: Psychosis or Transcendence?* Lower Lake, Ca: Integral Publishing, 1987.

Sheikh, A. "Eidetic Psychotherapy." In J. Singer and K. Pope (Eds.). *The Power of Human Imagination*. New York: Plenum, 1978.

Smith, D. W. "A Study of Power and Spirituality in Polio Survivors Using the Nursing Model of Martha E. Rogers." Doctoral Dissertation; New York University, 1991.

Solomon, G. and R. Moos. "The Relationship of Personality to the Presence of Pheumatic Factor in Asymptomatic Relatives with Rheumatoid Arthritis." *Psychosomatic Medicine,* 1965; 27; 350–360.

Sommer, R. *The Mind's Eye: Imagery in Everyday Life.* New York: Delacorte, 1978.

8

CANCER AND AIDS

Many types of stress impact on human beings in the ordinary course of life. Serious illnesses, especially those which are life-threatening, cause additional stress on one's body and emotional/mental states. Cancer is an especially stressful illness which can create a variety of biological and psychological stresses. Confronting the possibility of pain, mutilation, amputation, inability to function, alienation from family and friends (pain creates its own "abnormal" world), and eventual death, is an overwhelming challenge to any human being and impacts on one's self-esteem.

Human beings are mind/body/spirit complexes. Scientific research has confirmed this. An ongoing communication exists between the mind and the body. This dialogue between the body and the mind has been demonstrated to facilitate the body's immune system, as it reacts to stress and responds to disease.

The work of Dr. George Solomon, a professor at the University of California Medical Schools (Los Angeles and San Francisco) was described in 1964 in his article titled "Emotions, Immunity and Disease: A Speculative Theoretical Integration." The thrust of Dr. Solomon's thesis was that stress compromised the immune system. Twenty years after Dr. Solomon's work, others like him have proven the truth of this theory. There are more than thirty hypotheses for which much hard scientific evidence has been established.

Sandra Levy (University of Pittsburgh) has done similar research. In a 1984 article, she points to "associations" to be strong. Her research has focused on breast cancer in women. Not surprisingly, Levy found longer survival rates in patients who had a fighting spirit. This conclusion is supported by the work of dozens of other researchers during a thirty-year span. Levy states, "lower survival rates from cancer are associated with depression or helplessness and higher rates are associated with a sense of coping."

Levy's research also uncovered a new vulnerability in cancer survival rates. The main factor which predicted survival rate was the length of time between initial diagnosis and recurrence. The next most important factor was a sense of joy, and not a fighting spirit as Levy expected. Joy, in fact, proved to be a more powerful predictor of survival than the number or location of metastatic sites. Another factor included the support of one's mate and rapport with one's physician. Other medical investigators have linked the healing of cancer to how our DNA communicates with our mind. If we listen to the "wisdom of the body," and heed its message, we will achieve a truer healing, a soul healing. Psychoneuroimmunology (PNI) is the term which describes the combined disciplines of psychology, neurophysiology, endocrinology, and immunology.

Dr. Lydia Temoshok, who worked with Dr. Solomon at the University of California, defined an "immunosuppression-prone" personality pattern in AIDS patients, which is similar to the "Type C" coping style that Dr. Temoshok observed with cancer patients. "Compliance, conformity, self-sacrifice, denial of hostility or anger, and non-expression of emotion were qualities associated with an unfavorable prognosis in cancer patients. They also related to cancer susceptibility as well." Thus, Temoshok speculated that a similarly repressed personality type may also be vulnerable to AIDS.

Type C was the exact opposite of the Type A individual (angry, tense, hard-driving), a high-risk candidate for a heart attack. Type C was also different from the more relaxed, confident Type B personality. The Type C person always has to feel happy and in control. The dominant characteristic of the Type C, according to Temoshok, is the *nonexpression* of emotion.

Among the most common stresses and psychological traits associated with cancer are the following:

- Experiencing loss of an important relationship or a significant person, thing, or position in life.

- Being a rigid, conforming person with an overly critical attitude toward oneself.
- Having a disturbed or emotionally sterile relationship with one's parents.
- Lacking satisfactory emotional outlets—a habit of bottling up or suppressing anger and other strong emotions.
- Having a poor ability to deal with stressful life change, a sense of hopelessness of helplessness in the face of stress.
- Being depressed, not necessarily so severely as to require professional help, but sufficient to register far above average on a psychological test.

All cancers begin as single cells somewhere in the body. Every component of the bones, muscles, blood, glands, the linings of tubes and ducts, etc., consists of microscopic cells. Most cells periodically reproduce themselves by splitting in half. This creates two daughter cells identical with the original. The new cells replace damaged or dead cells. A cancer begins when the original cell loses its capacity to reproduce its normal characteristics because the DNA, a vital component in the process of replication, is either damaged or unable to function properly. Abnormal cells thus result and reproduce, creating more and larger numbers of aberrant cells. In the process called metastasis, individual unhealthy cells break off from the original mass and travel to other areas of the body via the bloodstream or lymph system, affecting the organs and tissues, and creating new tumors.

The traditional concept of cure (i.e., permanent removal of a disease) is often not even an appropriate medical goal for malignancies which are deemed "treatable." Traditional thinking focuses on illness and on the negatives of disease. Orthodox attitudes may work well for acute illnesses, especially those that are infectious in nature. A person with an infected wound takes an antibiotic, swelling and pain recede, and the person is "cured." In conventional thinking, the absence of illness denotes cure, but, in treatment for cancer, removal of apparent signs of disease does not equal cure. The aim of holistic therapy, conversely, is the achievement of wellness.

Cancer often recurs after a tumor is excised because malignant cells still remain at the site of the original lesion, or are hidden undetected elsewhere in the body. It is more accurate to characterize a successfully treated patient as having "no evidence of disease" or as being "in remission," rather than being "cured." In absence of valid clinical evidence of a genuine cure, many scientists use statistical definitions based on longevity of survival after diagnosis. "Five-year survival," for example, indicates a cure, and is the most familiar criteria used. Medical doctors interpret five-year survival to mean that a person has not experienced a recurrence for five years after initial treatment and presumably harbors no malignant cells or undetected tumors. After five years, the assumption is that the risk of cancer is virtually eliminated, and one's life expectancy equals others with similar demographic characteristics. However, this interpretation of five-year survival is faulty for many forms of cancer, although five-year survival is always a hopeful sign. The truth is that generally people with a history of cancer are more likely to develop malignancies in the future than people with no such history. Breast cancer is a frequently cited example of the limits of five-year survival as a definition of cure, but breast cancer recurrences have been known to occur in persons who showed no signs of cancer ten to fifteen years after initial treatment. Prostate cancer reveals another limitation of this often-cited criterion. A high proportion of men with this disease, which often develops very slowly, live for five years or longer, even in the absence of treatment. Is this another example of soul healing?

CONVENTIONAL TREATMENT MODALITIES FOR CANCER

Surgery

Surgery is the most basic, oldest, and still most often used method in the treatment of cancer. This most blatantly invasive of therapies, surgery still imparts an aura of heroism to both doctor and patient.

Radiation

Radiation consists of high energy waves or particles produced by electromagnetic devices (e.g., high-voltage vacuum tubes) or radioactive elements and their compounds.

Chemotherapy

Toxic drugs used to "kill" cancer cells are administered via infusion or injection or, less frequently, oral medication. Chemotherapy is the primary treatment for several forms of cancer, particularly those in which surgery is inappropriate or deemed to be ineffective. These include cancers that do not form "solid" tumors (for instance, leukemia) and cancers widely disseminated throughout the body (for instance, lymphoma). Chemotherapy is the only feasible conventional treatment for cancers that are widely disseminated throughout the body.

SOUL HEALING

There is a vast difference between the mere absence of illness and feeling "okay," and a positive sense of wellness, the goal of soul healing. Soul healing has proven valuable in my practice and is confirmed in scientific literature. Whenever an oncologist refers a cancer patient to me for hypnotherapy, he or she invariably mentions the names of Carl Simonton, a radiation oncologist, and Stephanie Matthews-Simonton, a psychotherapist. Noting the apparent relationship between the immune system and cancer, the Simontons developed a visualization relaxation technique which they used in conjunction with traditional medical treatment for cancer patients. The approach is two-fold: first the cancer patient relaxes, then he or she visualizes the immune system's white blood cells attacking and destroying the "weak" or "confused" cancer cells in the body like "strong powerful" sharks attacking meat. For example, patients are also encouraged to develop other images in harmony with the same theme (Simonton, Matthews-Simonton and Creighton, 1978).

The Simontons (1978) clinically tested this procedure with 159 selected patients diagnosed with medically incurable cancer and given one year to live. The results were remarkable. Sixty-three of the original 159 patients were alive two years after their diagnosis, one year beyond their original prognosis. Even more inspiring, of those sixty-three patients alive two years later who had practiced the visualization/relaxation process procedure, 22.2 per cent showed no evidence of cancer, 19.1 per cent demonstrated tumor regression, while 27.1 per cent of these patients were "stabilized." The Simontons attributed these findings to the fact that visualization/relaxation procedures resulted in an enhancement of the immune system.

T-lymphocytes, which are responsible for the cell-mediated immune response, migrate to the thymus. These cells constitute part of the immune surveillance mechanism which protects the body from cells that have molecular structures that are different from its normal cellular pattern (cancer cells). According to this proposition, a cancer cell would be detected as a different or "non-self" cell and destroyed by these T-lymphocytes.

If operating properly, the immune system (specifically T-lymphocytes) will detect and destroy a cancer (neoplasm) before it becomes a clinically significant tumor. When this surveillance system is not operating properly, however, due to a number of psychological and physical conditions, cancer cells escape detection as being "non-self" and are free to establish themselves at the expense of the host. Given this theory of immunological defense against cancer cells, it is important to determine how psychological factors such as stress affect immune functioning.

Stress appears to inhibit the immune system through the production of elevated levels of adrenal corticoid hormones in the plasma. These hormones result in a decrease in the number of lymphocytes, or a condition termed leukocytopenia. Research with animals has revealed that the immune system of unstressed mice was able to "partially or totally" contain the growth of experimentally implanted lymphosarcoma cancer cells (Riley, 1981). Animals experimentally stressed experienced tumor growth. The type of stress used resulted in an increase of corticosterone (an adrenal corticoid). Thus, this enhancement of tumor growth was attributed to the damaging effects of these hormones on cell-mediated immune defense.

The relationship between stress, the production of adrenal corticoid hormones, the suppression of the immune system, and the progression of cancer suggests that methods of reducing stress and corticoid production could play an important role in the treatment of cancer. It is interesting to note that a hypnotic trance results in significant decreases in plasma 17-hydroxy-corticosteroid concentrations and cortisol levels (Sachar, Fishman and Mason, 1965; Sachar, Cobb, and Shor, 1966). Thus, hypnosis may be one method to mitigate the suppressive effects of adrenal corticoid hormones on the immune system, and thus effecting a form of soul healing.

As one gets older, there is an increase in the production of cancer cells, possibly because of the waning immune system. In a study by Howard Hall at Pennsylvania State University, twenty healthy individuals, ages twenty-two to eighty-five, were hypnotized. A 25 cc sample of blood was taken from each subject in order to have a prehypnosis baseline recording of lymphocyte function. The subjects were hypnotized with a relaxation induction. During hypnosis they were asked to imagine their white blood cells as "strong powerful" sharks with teeth which attacked and destroyed the "weak confused" germ cells in their body which caused colds and influenza. One hour after the end of hypnosis, another 25cc post-hypnosis blood sample was taken. After the hypnosis sessions, subjects received written and verbal instructions in self-hypnosis. They were instructed to practice this two times each day until the second session, one week later.

One week later subjects returned for their second session. Hypnosis and visualization were repeated, and a third post-hypnotic blood sample was drawn. The purpose of this second session was to determine the effects of practice on hypnosis and immune function. After completing both hypnosis sessions, each subject was individually assessed on hypnotizability with the Stanford Hypnotic Susceptibility Scale, Form C. Two major findings emerged from this study. First, when subjects were divided into two age groups with a median split at age fifty, the younger group had an overall higher level of immune functioning. An examination of the lymphocyte count revealed a significant increase from baseline to one hour post-hypnosis for only the highly hypnotizable subjects. A week later, the increase in lymphocyte count for this group was not maintained at the one-hour level, but decreased somewhat. The low-hypnotizable subjects, on the other hand, did not show any significant changes across the three blood-measurement periods. This study clearly indicated that hypnosis and visualization may indeed result in an increase in immune function for individuals who are highly hypnotizable.

Kiecolt-Glaser, et al. (1985) did a similar study utilizing relaxation training and guided imagery. After one month of three-times-weekly sessions, only the relaxation imagery group showed increases in T-lymphocytes.

Some research suggests that hypnosis with only suggestions of relaxation does not result in any significant changes in either the number of white blood cells or lymphocytes from waking state (Goldwyn, 1930). Thus, the relaxation aspect of hypnosis was probably not solely responsible for the observed increases in immune functioning. A relaxation/humoral explanation accounts for decreases in adrenal corticoid hormones with hypnosis that could not explain both inhibition and enhancement of immune responses. These data suggest a neural rather than a humoral mechanism. Neural processes have been offered to explain how hypnosis can result in alterations in immune responses (Mason, 1961; Rogers, Dubey, and Reich, 1979).

George was referred to me about fifteen years ago by a local oncologist. He had lung cancer and was still an active smoker. He brought his chest x-rays with him to show me what his lungs looked like radiographically.

The tumor I observed was the size of a fist. Eliminating George's smoking habit was not difficult. Next, superconscious mind taps were initiated to facilitate his natural healing processes. Finally, I gave him a superconscious mind tape cassette to accelerate his "cleansing." Six months after I completed my training with him, George called with an urgent need to see me. When he came to my office, I was presented with two pieces of outstanding news. First, George was still a non-smoker with absolutely no desire to smoke. Secondly, his fist-sized tumor was now the size of a pea. He brought his most recent chest x-ray to prove his point.

George was so excited and happy he cried. This was not his typical behavior. He had the classic Type C personality exhibited by many cancer patients. George's visit was followed by a call from his oncologist. The doctor wanted to know what kind of "magic" I performed. I responded, "Soul healing." George was sixty-three when I saw him. He was not expected to live out the year. Now his prognosis is excellent. Spontaneous cancer cures have been extensively researched in both the United States and Japan. Most of these patients experience a dramatic shift in awareness just prior to their cure. The patient, convinced that he or she will be healed, is aware that a force responsible for healing lies within his or her ability, but beyond one's self. This jump to a new level of consciousness prevents the cancer from existing. This quantum leap will be explored more fully in Chapter 19. Additional examples of spontaneous cures of cancer are given in Chapter 15.

AIDS

The virus that causes AIDS was discovered separately in mid-1984 by three different scientific teams (led by Drs. Gallo, Montagnier, and Levy, respectively). It was given various names through the years, but the one finally settled upon in 1986 is HIV, which stands for human immunodeficiency virus. HIV is somewhat unique among human viruses because of the type of genetic material it possesses and the way in which it destroys the immune system.

AIDS appeared on the medical horizon rather abruptly in a short report in the June 5, 1981, issue of a then somewhat obscure pamphlet published by the Centers for Disease Control and Prevention (CDC), titled "The Morbidity and Mortality Weekly Report."

In this particular issue of MMWR, doctors in California described a cluster of cases of a rare pneumonia called Pneumocystis carinii (PCP) among homosexual men. About a month later, another report discussed the appearance (again, among young homosexual men) of a cancer called Kaposi's Sarcoma (KS), which usually afflicts older men. Soon the CDC began tracking all cases of PCP and KS. The hunt was on to try to solve the enigma of this syndrome of rare and opportunistic infections and malignancies. In 1982 the CDC officially adopted the name: Acquired Immunodeficiency Syndrome, or AIDS.

AIDS sufferers may manifest fever, weakness, diarrhea, and a general debilitation. They may also suffer from memory loss, attention deficits, psychological problems, difficulties with maintaining balance, and, more extremely, seizures and paralysis. Others may develop rashes, mouth lesions; and in female patients, vaginitis, pelvic infections, or abnormal Pap smears.

In 1986, Dr. Gerald Friedland of Montefior Medical Center (Bronx, New York) shocked the country with the news that AIDS was not strictly a disease of gay, promiscuous men. He had uncovered multiple cases of AIDS among heterosexuals, both male and female, who were also intravenous drug users. As if the world community was not frightened and dismayed enough to learn that AIDS could infect those with rather atypical lifestyles, the news really hit home as report after report identified new at-risk groups (hemophiliacs and blood transfusion recipients, among others) until we reached the reality which confronts us today. Virtually every person is at risk. Teenagers, college students, yuppies, or retirees, males, females, blacks, whites or Asians; neither your age, the color of your skin, nor your ethnicity determines your risk. Instead, it is your lifestyle and your behavior. By the mid-1980s AIDS had been definitely determined to be a sexually transmitted disease—a blood and body fluid-borne virus. However, it is still hypothesized by some researchers that other factors, or "cofactors," may determine why some people carry HIV without developing AIDS, and others quickly succumb to the full AIDS syndrome. Some of the cofactors known to suppress the immune system include: use of recreational drugs, reported infections with diseases such as herpes simplex, cytomegalovirus, and Epstein-Barr virus, and the direct entry of sperm into the bloodstream through small tears made in the rectal lining during anal intercourse. Of course, other environmental conditions (heavy drinking, stress, poor nutrition) also play a role.

Our bone marrow is the birthplace of the immune system. Within the bone marrow, immature blood cells develop into various components of the immune system. Some are called leukocytes, or white blood cells. There are leukocytes (phagocytes) whose primary responsibility is to surround or engulf a foreign invader and chemically digest it in a process called phagocytosis. Others contain special chemicals that attack and destroy molecules (usually proteins) that the body recognizes as foreign. These foreign molecules are known as antigens. Antigens trigger the production by the immune system of substances called antibodies, designed to oppose them.

Of all the different leukocyte types, probably the most important ones (which held the key to the proper functioning of the immune system) are the lymphocytes. The lymphocytes are to the immune system what the brain is to the rest of the body. Constituting about a third of all immune system cells, lymphocytes turn on, turn off, and regulate the functioning of all of the remaining sixty per cent of leukocytes involved in immunity.

Lymphocytes are divided into three main types: B-cells, T-cells, and null cells (which are neither B nor T). Each B-cell produces an antibody to only one specific antigen. Once the antibody comes in contact with the antigen, they fit together like a key and a lock. The antibody effectively neutralizes the harmful effects of that antigen by together forming into an inactive complex which may then be destroyed by other elements of the immune system (collectively called complement). This is done in a series of steps known as the "complement cascade."

This process works very well against simple bacteria. However, when the body is confronted with a more complex enemy, such as a virus (HIV is a retrovirus, which means it contains RNA instead of DNA), B-cells require assistance from a particular subgroup of T-cells called T-helper cells. In essence, they help the antibody-antigen reaction. T-helper cells also play a role in activating other T-cells, such as those involved in fighting cancers.

HIV reproduces abundantly from the outset, killing numerous CD4 cells in the process. However, the immune system initially keeps pace with this destruction, churning out CD4 cells to replace those destroyed. Eventually, the immune system cannot create enough replacement cells, and thus AIDS symptoms develop.

In recent articles, *Science* magazine (266:1642–1649, 267:157–160, 313–316 and 945–946) examined in detail the theory promulgated by Dr. Peter Duesberg who claims that drugs, not HIV, causes AIDS.

Duesberg, a University of California–Berkeley virologist, was the first to isolate a gene associated with cancer. Duesberg, a well-respected scientist, won notoriety by voicing the outspoken opinion that AIDS may not be caused by the human immunodeficiency virus (HIV). He felt that AIDS was caused by the chronic use of recreational drugs and AZT, the only pharmaceutical agent presently approved for AIDS treatment. Duesberg has taken the field with his ideas, debating their merit in the prestigious pages of *The Lancet, The New England Journal of Medicine,* and the *Journal of AIDS,* among other referenced scholarly publications.

A fundamental characteristic of all disease-producing viruses is their tendency to kill more cells than the body can possibly regenerate. This is not the case with patients suffering from AIDS. Even in those who've had long-term infections, the virus has proven very difficult to find. In fact, it can only be detected indirectly, through the presence of antibodies. HIV is estimated to infect only one in every 500 to 1,000 cells. No other virus with so fractionally small an invasion rate has ever been known to kill the host.

Infectious diseases have predictable latencies. In terms of incubation kinetics, HIV ought to be able to infect every cell in the human body within two short weeks after initial infection, but contemporary estimates put the actual measured minimum figure at one year, while the hypothesized average latency is ten years! It is also possible to suffer from AIDS without having any HIV viruses in one's system. There are more than 4,000 cases reported in the literature of AIDS—defined in terms of low T-cell counts and the presence of a suite of opportunistic diseases associated with the illness—in patients that are certifiably HIV-free. The HIV model runs aground against the hard data provided by the best scientific research presently available.

The AIDS epidemic directly parallels the resurgence of drug use in the 1980s, particularly nitrates and amphetamines. These drugs are implicated in many homosexual AIDS patients as well.

HIV can indeed be transmitted sexually, yet the statistical odds of transmission are surprisingly small: it would take 1,000 sexual encounters with HIV-positive partners to acquire the disease (from the point of view of statistical averages, of course). Since nitrates and amphetamines, among other drugs, are often employed as aphrodisiacs, it would be plausible to infer that people who have the most sex will also use the most drugs, increasing the risk of becoming infected with HIV, but it simply does not follow that HIV is what caused their death.

AZT works like most chemotherapies. Scientists have recognized from the outset that AZT is a toxic drug. It has been misrepresented as a compound that targets the HIV virus, when in point of fact it indiscriminately kills every cell in its path.

The approval of AZT by the FDA was based in large part on a single study that compared the mortality rates of a population of individuals over a highly truncated timespan (less than four months). As Bruce Nussbaum pointed out in his illuminating volume, Good Intentions (North Atlantic Press, 1990), the pressure to fast-track the approval of AZT was orchestrated by factions anxious to promote their prestige and to earn big money. When these early clinical results were first published, it was hastily decided that further placebo-controlled testing was "unethical," thus terminating all objective research on the matter.

If HIV was responsible for killing of IV drug users, an increase in morbidity and reduction of lifespan should be in evidence in this particular HIV-positive sub-population. Yet, a recent study conducted in Europe concluded that HIV-positive and HIV-negative addicts had identical life expectancies: thirty years. Among infants with AIDS, eighty percent had been born to mothers who used IV drugs while with child.

Each year, $7.5 billion is spent on AIDS research and treatment, most of which is being funneled into HIV research. To understand why research is being unproductively rerouted into various dead-ends, simply follow the money. Most researchers realize that focusing on HIV, whether or not such research is actually a blind alley devoid of any possibility of an AIDS cure, is the only financially tenable thing to do. Alternate viewpoints are, in essence, defunded. This, despite the irrefutable fact that ten years of research has turned up no pattern of AIDS among any population that has avoided both AZT and recreational drug use.

Five to ten percent of HIV infected people can live for ten years, or even twenty years, without showing any symptoms of AIDS. Temoshok and Solomon are currently studying long-term AIDS survivors. On the basis of studies by themselves and others, they have noted a number of common personality traits among these survivors. These traits include a sense of personal responsibility for one's health, a sense of meaning and purpose in life, a sense of humor, and an ability to express one's needs and emotions. Successful patients are motivated to participate in their own healing. In essence, they have mastered the mind-body connection (soul healing). Conventional medicine cannot even begin to duplicate such healing.

Mary's case is a most impressive one of soul healing in response to AIDS. She came to my Los Angeles office from the East Coast in 1993. Her CD4 count was 50 and overall she was not in good shape.

Following superconscious mind taps, I guided Mary through a series of simple age progressions (this technique is described in detail in Chapter 4). She chose an ideal frequency during which, surprisingly, she was placed on an experimental drug which proved ineffective. Following this failure, and being free of medication, her immune system responded quite well.

Mary was later given Nevirapine, a drug which did not work. She was taken off this medication and several months later her CD4 count rose to 150. Today, Mary is alive and doing quite well. She is responsible for her soul healing through her subconscious-superconscious mind connection. The fact that her ideal frequency (as perceived by her during her age progression) came true is only one aspect of her soul healing.

SOURCES

Goldwyn, J. "The Effect of Hypnosis on Basal Metabolism." *Archives of Internal Medicine,* 1930, 45, 109–114.

Kiecolt-Glaser, J. K., Glaser, R., Williger, D., Stout, J., Messick, G., Sheppard, S., Ricker, D., Romisher, S. C., Briner, W., Bonnell, G., and Donnerberg, R. "Psychosocial Enhancement of Immunocompetence in a Geriatric Population." *Health Psychology,* 1985 4, 25–41.

Levy, S. M. "Emotions and the Progression of Cancer: A Review," *Advances: Journal of the Institute for the Advancement of Health* 1 (1), Winter 1984: 10–15.

Levy, S. M., J. Lee, C. Bagley, and M. Lippman, "Survival Hazards Analysis in Recurrent Breast Cancer Patients: Seven Year Follow-up," *Psychosomatic Medicine* L (5), September/October 1988.

Mason, A. A. *Hypnotism for Medical and Dental Practitioners.* London: Secker and Warburg, 1961.

Riley, V. "Psychoneuroendocrine Influences on Immunocompetence and Neoplasia." *Science,* 1981, 212, 1100–1109.

Rogers, M.P., D. Dubly, and P. Reich. "The Influence of the Psyche and the Brain on Immunity and Disease Susceptibility: A Critical Review." *Psychosomatic Medicine,* 1979, 41, 147–164.

Sachar, E. J., J. C. Cobb, and R. E. Shor. "Plasma Cortisol Changes During Hypnotic Trance." *Archives of General Psychiatry,* 1966, 14, 482–490.

Sachar, E. J., J. R. Fishman, and J. W. Mason. "Influence of the Hypnotic Trance on Plasma 17-hydroxycorticosteroid Concentration." *Psychosomatic Medicine,* 1963, 27, 330–341.

Simonton, O. C., S. Matthews-Simonton, and J. L. Creighton. *Getting Well Again.* Los Angeles: Tarcher-St. Martins, 1978.

Soloman G. F., and L. Temoshok. "Psychoneuroimmunologic Perspective on AIDS Research: Questions, Preliminary Findings, and Suggestions," *Applied Social Psychology* (V. H. Winston and Sons, Inc.), 286–307. 1987.

Solomon G. F., L. Temoshok, A. O'Leary, and J. Zich. "An Intensive Psychoimmunologic Study of Long-Surviving Persons with AIDS." *Annuals of the New York Academy of Sciences*, 496, 1987: 647–55.

9

SLOWING DOWN THE AGING PROCESS

Since 1974, I have been engaged in doing soul healing. Over the years, one thing has become abundantly clear. When patients do alpha techniques for several years, they seem to appear and act younger than their chronological age. Whether it be because of hypnosis, meditation, yoga, guided imagery, etc., they simply "do not look their age." When patients meet me in person they are astounded at my appearance. Most say I look ten to fifteen years younger than my chronological age. I have been utilizing self-hypnosis informally since my college years and formally since 1974.

In 1975, I worked with a thirty-two-year-old female chiropractor from the east coast. Early in 1995 she visited my Los Angeles office with her best friend, whom she had referred to me. My former patient looked perhaps five years older than my last mental image of her. Precisely how does soul healing slow down the aging process? The answer can be found in scientific research which we will explore in this chapter.

In ancient Greece and Rome the average life span was twenty-two years. By 1900, it increased to forty-seven years. In the U.S. today, humans, on the average, live well into their seventies. At the turn of the century, one in sixteen Americans were sixty or older. Today, it is one in six. This figure will shrink to one in four by the time baby-boomers near retirement. Inactivity and bad habits seem to account for our "normal aging." Scientists estimate that our body is capable of reaching 140 years before crossing into spirit. One of the longest-living human beings with complete credentials was Fanny Thomas, who attributed her longevity to eating applesauce three times a day and never marrying. "I never had a man to bother me," she declared. Fanny died in 1980 in California at the age of 113 years, 215 days.

The benefits gained from simply overcoming diseases are limited. Curing all forms of cancer, for instance, would only boost the average life span in the United States by two years. If we eliminated all human disease from the planet, plus all wars and accidents, the average life span would be increased only into the low nineties.

According to the January 1973 issue of *National Geographic,* the Andean village of Vilcabama in Ecuador, the Hunza of Kashmir in Pakistan, and Abkhazia in the Georgian region of Russia, contain the largest percentage of humans over the age of 100. These people "live much longer and remain more vigorous in old age than in most modern societies" (p. 93).

Researchers have observed a select group of people who do not age normally as most of us do. These people are referred to as "supernormals." They are relatively free of physical and mental problems, have solid relationships, high activity levels, and their personalities are outgoing and shrewd, well-adjusted and happy. About one person in seven over the age of sixty-five fall into this group. Obviously, these "supernormals" are probably practicing their own form of soul healing.

Our immune system is the most important factor in determining the rate at which we age. Cancer, arthritis, heart disease, and infectious diseases such as pneumonia occur only after the immune system declines in potency with age. As we age, our immune system becomes less efficient in removing defective or dead normal cells from our body. Also, auto-immune diseases (arthritis, for example) appear, in which our body is actually attacked by our own immune system. The thymus is the master gland of the immune system. It turns immature white blood cells from the bone marrow into mature T-cells. The thymus makes hormones that circulate throughout the body and help T- and B-cells interact effectively.

People have about the same number of white blood cells at age eighty as they did at age twenty. However, the white blood cells no longer mature as they should; they stop sending and receiving commands as effectively. Sometimes they have trouble getting to where they are needed. This results in a significant decline in the efficiency of the entire immune system, except for the phagocytes, which do not seem to lose any of their abilities with advancing age.

Hypnosis shares many commonalities with other altered states of consciousness, such as transcendental meditation (TM), yoga, etc., and is identical to them neurophysiologically (Fromm, 1977; Goldberg, 1988). Individuals over fifty-five who practice TM have a younger physiological age than a control population on a standardized index, which estimates biological age using blood pressure, auditory threshold, and near-point vision (Wallace, et al., 1982). Biological age shows how well a person's body is functioning, compared to the norms of the whole population, giving a truer measure of how the aging process is progressing than does chronological age. Some of Wallace's female subjects were twenty years younger than their chronological age. The longer the subjects meditated, the younger they appeared to be. The dividing line was between those who had meditated fewer than five years and those who had meditated five years or more. The first group averaged five years younger than their chronological age on the biological index, while the second averaged twelve years younger. A backup study conducted in England later calculated that each year of regular meditation takes off roughly one year of aging.

A recent study of 2,000 TM practitioners who subscribed to a major health insurance carrier found reduced medical utilization rates for sixteen of seventeen major medical treatment categories. TM practitioners may have lower morbidity (Alexander, et al., 1989).

Pavlov (et al., 1986) showed that age-related decline was related to a decrease in serum DHEA-S levels produced by the adrenal gland. Some mechanism in the TM group apparently prevents the usual age-related reduction in those biochemical processes. The higher DHEA-S levels seen in the TM group may reflect protection against chronic overstimulation of the adrenal in response to stress. The age-related decline in DHEA-S, retarded in the TM group, may be due to decreased adrenal-cell responsiveness to ACTH, some other factor, or is intrinsic to the adrenal cell. It is still unclear whether higher DHEA-S levels significantly contribute to longevity and improved health in older individuals, or whether elevated DHEA-S levels simply reflect the lack of cumulative physical deterioration due to age, chronic stress, and illness.

Since the hormone DHEA-S appears to be the key as to how hypnosis and other soul healing techniques retard the aging process, let's discuss this naturally produced chemical in greater detail.

The older you are, the less DHEA you have. At the age of eighty, you produce only ten to twenty per cent of the DHEA produced in the second decade of life (Orentreich, 1984). Studies have shown a direct relationship between blood levels of DHEA and the inhibition of many diseases.

If you have high levels of DHEA you are far less likely to:

- Develop atherosclerosis (and suffer from cardiovascular disease).
- Develop malignant tumors (and generate cancer).
- Lose insulin sensitivity (and acquire diabetes).
- Suffer a decline in mental function (and lapse into dementia, Alzheimer's or Parkinson's disease or stroke-related).

Because the above-named diseases are the principal benchmarks of aging, DHEA may be the best biomarker of aging and longevity.

DHEA protects against bacterial and viral infections. Although most major adrenocortical hormones cause immune suppression, DHEA has prevented death from infection with two different types of viruses and a fatal streptococcus infection. It is believed that DHEA stimulates T-cells, B-cells, and machrophages by interfering with glucocorticoid immunosuppression (Loria, 1990).

Several studies have shown the ability of DHEA to reduce replication of the AIDS (HIV-I) virus (Henderson, 1992). The thymus gland regulates T-cells, the immune system's principal "detectives" and "killers." Immune function "normally" declines with advancing age, and thymic involution. Shrinkage and incapacitation of the thymus gland is associated with increased susceptibility to bacterial infections, viral infections, cancers, and other types of diseases. DHEA protects thymic function by slowing shrinkage of the thymus gland. In one controlled study, the immunosuppressive impact of dexamethasone, a synthetic flucocorticoid, was successfully antagonized by DHEA. Compared with controls, pretreatment with DHEA also resulted in significantly lessened dexamethasone-induced thymic atrophy (Blauer, 1991). In another study, the thymus showed improved regulatory control over the function capabilities of mature recalculating T-cells when repotentiated by DHEA (Widemeier, 1991).

A recent study in diabetes-prone rats indicates that one of DHEA's weight-reducing mechanisms may operate through the increase of serotonin levels in the hypothalamus region of the brain, thereby increasing the release of cholecytoknin (CCK), the satiation hormone. CCK reduced the desire for foods by creating a feeling of fullness. Rats fed DHEA showed an increase in serotonin levels in the hypothalamus, which was associated with increased CCK activity, reduced food intake and lower body fat (Wright, 1992). DHEA has prevented the occurrence of many different types of spontaneous and chemically induced tumors, including chemically induced adenocarcinoma of the colon (Schulz, 1991), lung cancer (Pashko, 1984), skin cancer (Pashko, 1985), and spontaneous viral-induced breast cancer (Schwartz, 1981).

Acute heart attacks are associated with low levels of DHEA and high density lipoprotein (HDL) (Ruiz Salmeron, 1992). DHEA was able to prevent certain induced hypertension in rats. In a study spanning nearly two decades, male DHEA-S levels were found to be lower in patients who died of coronary heart disease than in controls (LaCroix, 1992). DHEA may relieve amnesia that contributes to dementia or is caused by it (Nasman, 1991). DHEA may help to slow "normal" aging. (Daynes, 1993). Studies have shown that DHEA can increase lifespans by fifty per cent in laboratory animals (Regelson, 1986).

From the scientific literature presented and research conducted, it is abundantly clear that soul healing works through the immune system and adrenal gland (the producer of DHEA-S) to slow down the aging process, thus allowing us to live longer and better.

SOURCES

Alexander, C. N., H. M. Chandler, E. J. Langer, R. I. Newman, and J. L. Davies. "Transcendental Mediation, Mindfulness and Longevity: An Experimental Study with the Elderly." *Journal of Personal and Social Psychology*, 1989; 57: 950–964.

Blauer, K. L., M. Poth, W. M. Rogers, and E. W. Bernton. "Dehydroepiandrosterolle Antagonizes the Suppressive Effects of Dexamethoasone on Lymphocyte Proliferation." *Endocrinology*, 1991; 129 (6): 3174–3179.

Daynes, R. A, B. A. Araneo, W B. Ershler, and C. Maloney. Li G-Z, Ryu S-Y. "Altered Regulation of IL-6 Production with Normal Aging: Possible Linkage to the Age Associated Decline in DehydroePiandrosterone and Its Sulfated Derivative." *Journal of Immunol*, 1993; 150(12): 5219–5230.

Fromm. E. "Altered States of Consciousness and Hypnosis: A Discussion." *International Journal Clinical Exp. Hypnosis*, 1977; 25: 325–334.

Goldberg, B. *Past Lives — Future Lives*. New York; Ballantine, 1988.

Henderson E., J. Y. Yang, and A. Schwartz. "Dehydroepiandrosterone (DHEA) and Synthetic DHEA Analogs are Modest Inhibitors of HIV-1 IIJB Replication." *AIDS ResHum Restroviruses*, 1992; 8 (5): 625–631.

LaCroix A. Z., K. Yano, and D. M. Reed. "Dehydroepiandrosterone Sulfate, Incidence of Myocardial Infarction and Extent of Ahterosclerosis in Men." *Circulation*, 1992; 86(5): 1529–1535.

Loria, R. M., W. Regelson, and D. A. Padgett, "Immune Response Facilitation and Resistance to Virus and Bacterial Infections with Dehydroepiandrosterone (DHEA)." In *The Biologic Role of Dehydroepiandrosterone*. (Kalimi, M., Regelson, W., eds) Walter de Gruyter, New York 1990: 107–130.

Nasman, B., T. Olsson, T. Backstrom, S. Eriksson, K. Grankvist, M. Viitanen, G. Bucht. "Serum Dehydroepiandrosterone Sulfate in Alzheimer's Disease and in Multi-infarct Dementia." *Biological Psychiatry*, 1991; 30(7): 684–690.

Orentreich N, J. L. Brind, R. L. Rizer, et al. "Age Changes and Sex Differences in Serum Dehydroepiandrosterone Sulfate Concentrations Throughout Childhood." *Journal of Clinical Endcrinology*, 1984; 59: 551–555.

Pashko L. L , G. C. Hard, R. J. Rovito, J. R. Williams, E. L. Soberl, A. G. Schwartz, "Inhibition of 7, 12-dimethylbenz(a)anthracene-induced Skin Papillomas and Carcinomas by Dehydroepiandrosterone and 3-beta-methylandrost-5-en-17-one in Mice." *Cancer Res.*, 1985;45(1): 164–66.

Pashko L. L., R. J. Rovito, J. R. Williams, E. L. Sobel, A. G. Schwartz. "Dehydroepiandrosterone (DHEA) and 3 beta-methylandrost-5-en-17-one: Inhibitors of 7, 12 Dimethylbenz[a]anthracene (DMBA)-initiated and 12-0-tetradecanoyl-phorbol-13-acetate (TPA)-promoted Skin Papilloma Formation in Mice." *Carcinogenesis*, 1984; 5(4): 463–466.

Pavlov, E. P., S. M. Harman, G. P. Chrousos, D. L. Loriaux, and M. R. Blackman. "Responses of Plasma Adrenocorticotropin, Cortisol, and Dehydroepiandrosterone to Ovine Corticotropin-releasing Hormone in Healthy Aging Men." *Journal of Clinical Endocrinological Metabolism*, 1986; 62: 767.

Regelson, W. Speech given to the Life Extension Conference, May 1986 (Tape #7 available from the Life Extension Foundation).

Ruiz Salmeron, R. J., J. L. del Arbol, J. Torrededia Raya, J. Munoz, A. Luque, Rico Lopez, J. Irles Ruiz, M. E. Requenta, J. Bolanos. "Dehydroepiandrosterone Sulfate and Lipids in Acute Myocardial Infarct." *Rev Clin Esp*, 1992; 190(8): 398–402.

Schulz, S, and J. W. Nyce. "Inhibition of Protein Isoprenylation and p21ras Membrane Association by Dehydroepiandrosterone in Human Colonic Adenocarcinhoma Cells in Vitro." *Cancer Res.*, 1991; 51(24): 6563–6567.

Schwartz, A. G., G. C. Hard, L. L. Pashko, M. Abou-Gharbia, D. Swern. "Dehydroepiandrosterone: an Anti-obesity and Anticarcinogenic Agent." *Nutr Cancer*, 1981; 3(1): 46–53.

Wallace, R. K., M. C. Dillbec, E. Jacobe, and B. Harrington. "Effects of the TM and TM-Sidhi Program on the Aging Process." *International Journal of Neuroscience*, 1982; 16: 53–58.

Wiedmeier, S. E., B. A. Aranco, K. Huang, and R. A. Daynes. "Thymic Modulation of IL-2 and IL-4 Synthesis by Peripheral T-cells." *Cell Immunol*, 1991; 135(2) 501–518.

Wright, B. E., J. R. Poiter, E. S. Browne, F. Svee. "Antiglucocorticid Action of Dehydroepiandrosterone in Young Obese Zucker Rats." *International Journal on Obesity*, 1992; 16(8): 579–583.

10

INSOMNIA

Imagine this picture of a typical run-in with insomnia. You have been lying in your usual sleeping position for the past hour or so. Your body is tense, a solid knot of muscle. Your mind is spinning at high speed with random, mostly self-defeating thoughts—a myriad of past, present, and future problems. In the midst of all this turmoil and unrest, your eyelids keep flipping open. The pillow seems too high, too low, too hard, too soft. At some time during the night the sheets turn to sandpaper. Someone has sucked all the air out of the room. You start noticing noises you never heard before.

At this point you flop over into a new, fake relaxed position and lie there suffering until you drift off to sleep hours later. Or you may choose the quick alternative, a sleeping pill that gives you instant sleep and a mind-fogging hangover the next morning. Throughout the next day you are a zombie. You feel as though you never slept, and the worst of it is you fear that the next night is going to be a rerun of the night before. You may even lie there convinced that, once again, sleep will elude you. This is how many people "cope" with insomnia and end up losing their sleep and their peace of mind.

Two out of every ten women have trouble sleeping, as compared with only one out of every ten men. Also, people over age sixty are more prone to insomnia. When insomnia strikes, it will assume one of three different forms. The first: sleep-onset insomnia (type 1) is basically the inability to fall asleep. Sleep experts say you qualify for this category if it takes you over thirty minutes to doze off at night. The second is sleep-maintenance insomnia (type 2), meaning that you can get to sleep, but you cannot stay asleep. With this type of insomnia, you may wake up periodically during the night. Your wakeups may come hours apart or as frequently as every twenty seconds, depending on their cause. The third and most devastating type is early-morning awakening insomnia (type 3). With this kind you may find yourself alert and miserable at about four or five o'clock in the morning. Most often you cannot get back to sleep, and you may succumb to the "dark night of the soul"—hopelessness and depression—condition which sometimes accompanies this type of insomnia.

In 1953, University of Chicago researchers Eugene Aserinsky and Nathanial Kleitman discovered that during one of the stages of sleep, which change roughly every ninety minutes, rapid eye movements can be recorded. Most dreaming occurs during this rapideeye movement, or REM sleep. During REM sleep, our large muscles are completely paralyzed. We cannot walk or talk. Conversely, most of our brain cells are vigorously active. Among them are the cells in our motor centers, a phenomenon that may explain sensations of movement, such as the ability to fly in dreams. Nerve cells that govern motivation and memory, however, turn off during REM; consequently most dreams are involuntary and amnesic.

Sleep should begin within twenty minutes of retiring. There are two types of sleep, REM and non-REM. Non-REM, which comes first, has four stages or levels. Each is a step deeper into an unconscious state. Your sleep starts with stage 1 of non-REM, initially signaled by a brief twitch in your legs or body, the sign of one last spark of restlessness from the brain. Your stay in stage 1 is very brief, no more than six or seven minutes, and then you are down to stage 2, which many feel is the true beginning of sleep. At this point your body is more relaxed, your temperature is beginning to drop slightly, and pulse and breathing start to slow. Your brain waves are looser, more relaxed, similar to the alpha state, and your mind retreats more into itself. You may have brief flashes of minidreams, disconnected thoughts, and bits of mental flotsam (things to do tomorrow, fragments of a TV show, flashes of the day's events, etc.) Stages 1 and 2 are very shallow levels of sleep. You can easily awaken at this time, and if you do, you will remember it the next day. This is not true of the deeper levels of sleep, stages 3 and 4, that follow. Sometimes lumped together and called "delta sleep," after the name of a distinctive brain wave, stages 3 and 4 are the deepest and, some believe, the most refreshing, restorative parts of your night's sleep. These stages start about a half-hour after sleep has begun, and last from a few minutes to as much as an hour. Stage 4 is as far from consciousness as you'll get in an ordinary day. Your body has slowed way down. Pulse, blood pressure, and temperature have all dropped. Your brain is extremely relaxed and, while you may have a rare dream or two at this time, it will be brief and colorless, usually not worth remembering. It is tremendously difficult to wake you at this time, and if someone manages it, you probably will not remember anything you said or did.

Delta sleep is the time for bizarre behavior, when sleeptalkers sit up and engage in long conversations with themselves, or get out of bed and begin to wander around. This is also the time of night when children have trouble with bedwetting or with a strange problem called night terrors. Some children have attacks of hysteria and fear, and will awake screaming with horror. Very often they will not even remember what caused the panic, and by morning none of them even remember waking up. As disturbing as it may be to those that are awakened by these things, night terrors do not seem to significantly affect children in any negative way. No one knows why these things happen, but children eventually outgrow the problem. Adults may also have this syndrome. Once your delta sleep ends, your brain starts to tighten up its wave tempo and head back up toward the more shallow levels of sleep. You have now been "out" for about ninety minutes and are getting ready to shift into the other kind of sleep, REM sleep. This is as different from being awake as it is from non-REM sleep. It is a state of body and mind so different that some refer to it as a third state of existence.

As REM sleep begins, your body is totally limp. If someone dragged you out of bed and tried to stand you up, you would collapse like a wet towel. Your body is not moving at all, except for the side-to-side eye twitching discovered by Kleitman and Aserinsky. If you are a man, you may have an automatic erection; if you are a woman, your vaginal tissue will begin to swell with blood. At the same time, your brain is electric with activity. In fact, it is difficult to tell the difference between a recording of a fully awake, alert brain, and one in REM sleep. All kinds of fantastic scenes and images soar through your mind. During this time, you will have most of your dreams and nightmares, as well as out-of-body experiences. When this REM period is over, so is the first whole sleep cycle of the evening. Then brain and body shuttle over to non-REM sleep and start a new non-REM/REM cycle. In an average night's sleep, a normal, healthy adult, age twenty-five to forty-five, has between four and six of these cycles in a steady, predictable sequence. The total time spent in REM is about three hours, based on a total sleep time of about eight hours. This REM cycle is utilized by the patients to effect "energy cleansing." While I train patients to access their superconscious mind during a session in my office, they also receive a superconscious mind training tape. A patient with insomnia receives a separate insomnia tape with instructions to play it just prior to retiring. The REM "cleaning" initiated accounts for ninety-eight per cent of my patients' soul healing. In REM, there are no defense mechanisms to block the raising of this energy, and the patient enjoys the deepest level of trance humanly possible.

Often I train a patient to do "lucid dreaming." A "lucid dreamer" is able to recognize, during a dream, the fact that she or he is dreaming, and can then control the plot. The obvious clinical benefit is to train a patient to escape from a difficult situation and to continue dreaming about more tranquil subjects.

Harvard psychologist and physician Dr. Morton Prince called this "double consciousness." Dr. Stephen LaBerge, a researcher at the Stanford Sleep Laboratory, refers to lucid dreaming as being "fully there, awake in the middle of the dream world." Most of us seldom realize we are dreaming; we accept all that is happening to us as reality. Countless examples exist of scientists who made great breakthroughs during dreams and awoke with the solution to their problems.

In 1974, at the meeting of the Association for the Psychophysiological Study of Sleep (APSS), psychologist Patricia Garfield offered evidence that by "self-conditioning"—intense interest in dreams and advance planning—we can determine the contents of our dream and induce long, lucid dreams. She insists we can all have lucid dreams and do anything we want in them.

Is it really possible to free yourself of your own bad dreams-nightmares? Yes, says Rosalind Cartwright, director of the Sleep Disorder Service and Research Center at Rush Presbyterian St. Luke's Medical Center in Chicago. Several years ago, Dr.

Cartwright taught patients who had recurrent bad dreams to press a buzzer when they began the dream. Awakened, they could recount their dream. The patient and her psychotherapist then planned how best to change the dream. When the patient slept again in the lab, she would signal the start of the nightmare, the technician would buzz back as a reminder to change the dream, and the patient would successfully do so. One woman, who had dreamed repeatedly of being sucked under by huge waves, realized during therapy that she should be able to swim as well in dreams as in reality, and taught herself to dive under the dream waves. She never again had that dream.

When he arrived at Stanford to work on his doctoral degree, LaBerge was inspired to revive his own lucid dreaming for scientific purposes. He developed a method he calls MILD—mnemonic induction of lucid dreams. Waking from a dream, he first memorized it, then spent ten or fifteen minutes reading or doing some activity that required full wakefulness. As he tried to go back to sleep, he would tell himself: "Next time I'm dreaming, I want to recognize I'm dreaming." Through MILD, LaBerge found he could stimulate lucid dreams as often as he chose.

Toni's case of insomnia illustrates many concepts and advantages of soul healing. This thirty-year-old, rather bright and attractive accountant was a lucid dreamer. She had experienced nightmares at least twice a week for the past five years. She would awaken screaming, usually around 4:00 A.M.

Toni recalled the details of these nightmares upon awakening. The themes were unvaried. She was being chased and about to be killed. In most of these dreams her grandmother (who died in 1990) was also in danger.

The DMS IV of the American Psychiatric Association would label this as nightmare disorder. More importantly, coinciding with the onset of the dreams, Toni suffered from occasional panic attacks during the day.

In addition to not being able to return to sleep (type III insomnia), Toni's life was being turned upside down. Her husband unfortunately was not very supportive, and this situation did not help their recent marriage.

The first thing I did was give Toni an insomnia self-hypnosis cassette to help train her to ease her mind prior to retiring at night. Next we began her soul healing with white light protection and a superconscious mind tap. It is not necessary to regress patients back to a previous life (assuming Toni's nightmares in this example were due to past life death scenes) to remove the cause of their disruptive dreams.

As part of Toni's cleansing, I trained her to send love and white light to her grandmother's soul to assist her to enter the white light, ascend to the soul plane, and be at peace while deciding her next lifetime.

The presence of her grandmother's disturbed spirit (her grandmother died of cancer and had been in great pain during the last year of her life) was unquestionably a factor in Toni's nightmares. This was not, however, the only reason for her sleep disturbance.

Toni's nightmares disappeared after only a few sessions. One extra benefit she received was the knowledge that she helped her late grandmother to attain a peaceful state. This facilitated the removal of any bereavement issues Toni had, in addition to helping her resolve her insomnia. Eventually, Toni became a soul healer as well as a successfully treated patient.

For those of you interested in past life death scenes which can return to haunt a patient, the case of Dan is classic. Dan, a very aggressive salesman, is married to a rather timid woman, Marie. When Dan came to my office for therapy, his only stated problem was insomnia. He had had the same nightmare for nearly twenty years. It consisted of his being chased in the woods by wild animals and eventually being torn apart limb by limb by these beasts. Dan would wake up screaming in the middle of the night. This disturbing pattern persisted for twenty years.

The past life Dan lived occurred in the tenth century in Europe. He was a young boy living in the south of France, along the coast. One day Viking raiders plundered his village and kidnapped him along with dozens of other youths. The boys were taken back to Scandinavia by ship and trained to be warriors. At the time Dan was about eighteen, he and his fellow captives decided to plan their escape. One night they overcame their guards and headed for the woods. Their plan was discovered and several wolves were turned loose on Dan and his comrades. Dan described the gruesome death scene. He screamed in trance in my therapy room, even though, of course, he was in no present danger.

Due more to the superconscious mind tap (cleansing) than the regression, Dan's nightmares finally ended. Marie was totally amazed. She had always known about and witnessed Dan's nightmares. For the first time in her life with Dan, they could have a peaceful night's rest.

11

PAST LIFE REGRESSION

The soul, which is immaterial and invisible in its nature, exists in no material place without having a body suited to the nature of that place; accordingly, it at one time puts off one body, which was necessary before, but which is no longer adequate in its changed state, and it exchanges it for a second body (Origen, A.D. 185–254).

As I globally assess the various techniques utilized in soul healing, the one that seems to stand out is past life regression. However, the details or data obtained from a previous life are not sufficient in themselves to heal the soul. As I stated in *Past Lives — Future Lives* (p. 58):

> The most important benefit of regression and progression therapy is not the retelling of scenes from past or future lives. It is a change in perspectives on life, an enlightenment as to who you are and what you are supposed to be doing here. The realization of constant evolution to something bigger, better, and more fulfilling is very beautiful to witness. I witness this every week of my life.

A review of Chapter 4 will further illuminate this point. *Regression* is simply going back in time. If you think about what you had for lunch yesterday, you are regressing with your *conscious* mind. Hypnotic regression is going back in time utilizing the *subconscious* mind, endowed with its perfect memory bank. I will use the term *simple age regression* to refer to going back in time to events that transpired in our present life. The term *past life regression* will refer to going back in time to events and experiences from a prior lifetime.

Many people are curious about what they will experience in a past life regression. There are many possibilities. First, you may see a scene and become simultaneously aware of information related to this scene, as if you were watching a movie or television show. I refer to this as being an audio and visual experience, and it generally provides excellent data. Unfortunately, it is not the most common experience with my patients.

The second and most common type of experience consists of seeing cloudy or swiftly passing impressions that tend to disappear just as you are about to grasp their meaning and significance. Another reported reaction is to become palpably and intimately aware of an environment, an awareness proceeding from an apparently deep-seated knowledge, without actually seeing or hearing anything at all. Feeling as if someone were whispering in your ear is another possibility. Reading words that pass before your inner eyes is a very rare type of experience, al-though this may be how some people learn what the date is, or in what country they are living during the regression.

Although there are clinicians who regress large groups of people into past lives all at once, I am a firm believer in conducting regression therapy on an individual basis. I have done both individual and group past life regressions, and I have achieved better results, yielding more detailed information, while working one-on-one. When I work with patients individually, I can be much more effective in helping them to overcome a problem, or to find out more about themselves and their karmic cycle. A number of so-called coincidences can be traced back to prior lives, and these scenes can be most helpful to patients in explaining why certain things have happened to them.

Shielding or protective techniques are always applied to a patient undergoing a past life regression. In all of the thousands of regressions that I have done, I have never presided over a traumatic episode, or any other type of negative experience. I shield my patients with what I call "spiritual protection." This technique consists of having the patient imagine a pure white light entering the top of the head and filling the entire body, surrounding each and every muscle, bone, and organ. The technique is powerful, despite being disarmingly simple. The white light protects the patient from any harm or negativity that he or she may potentially encounter during therapy.

Before describing various patients of mine who have re-experienced their own past lives and resolved sundry issues clouding the present, I would like to deal with the issue of "past life readers." There are many people claiming to read past lives. Some are quite accurate (they are referred to as "sensitives"), but most are as phony as a three-dollar bill.

Even if you seek out a "sensitive," potential hazards remain. If there is a therapeutic goal in mind, the reading will prove ineffective in addressing underlying causes. As I stated earlier, the raw data from past lives are simply not curative in themselves. Second, you have no way of knowing whether or not the material transcribed for you actually reflects one of your own past lives, or that of a loved one you focused on during the reading. Since the psychic is picking up alpha waves (your subconscious mind), contamination is quite possible.

Last, far from empowering the individual, the practice of "past life reading" renders one codependent. The more accurate the reading, the greater the likelihood you will be "hooked" and that you will return for many more readings. There is enough codependency in the world already. Please don't let yourself fall into this trap.

Always use your common sense when undergoing past life regression hypnotherapy. Please don't attach any significance to what a psychic or "past life reader" tells you about your past lives. Anyone can say that you were Queen Nefertiti. The reality is that, having conducting over 33,000 past life regressions since 1974, I have never regressed anyone to the life of an historical figure. I would recognize the authenticity of such a "claim to fame" only if it issued directly from the patient during a session conducted by a credible hypnotherapist.

Before presenting several examples of past life regressions, I would like to discuss a most unusual case involving simple age regression.

SIMPLE AGE REGRESSION

Nicole had a most unusual situation. She simply could not remember anything about her life prior to the age of twenty-two. She was from the Midwest and had moved several times during the past fifteen years. There were no members of her family she could contact for help.

Neurologists and psychologists tell us that the average person can remember events as far back as age three. In all my years of practice, I had never encountered such an extreme instance of memory truncation as Nicole was manifesting.

Nicole was not interested in going back to previous lives, nor in progressing into the future. She merely wanted to obtain information on who she was in her current lifetime. She was fifty-one years old when I treated her in 1993.

I conducted a simple age regression during her initial session, in which she first reported her experiences in college, and then high school. This was a minor breakthrough: she remembered things about her life as far back as the age of fifteen. At the end of our session, I gave her an age-regression conditioning tape to condition her subconscious mind for further explorations.

It was her next session that opened up the floodgates of early childhood memories. She recalled events from her fourth birthday up through the age of twelve. She exhibited naturally many emotions, most commonly tears of joy. This session was her last, and she was deeply appreciative of the experiences. About six months later, she called to inform me that as a result of the information unearthed during her sessions, she was able to contact some lost family members. They confirmed much of the data Nicole reported in trance.

POST-TRAUMATIC STRESS DISORDER

Patients who have been exposed to a traumatic event involving intense fear, helplessness, or horror sometimes suffer aftereffects. These can include recurrent dreams of the event, acting or feeling as if the event were recurring (flashback episodes), intense psychological distress from exposure to cues that symbolize or resemble an aspect of the event, repression of actual memories of the event, and feelings of detachment. We refer to this syndrome as post-traumatic stress disorder.

Carmella is a Mexican woman in her mid-thirties. She had been living in Los Angeles for about ten years when she called my office. After reading my first book (*Past Lives — Future Lives*), she decided that I could help her, and sought me out.

Post-traumatic stress disorder (PTSD) can have many causes. In Carmella's case, there were metaphysical overtones that significantly complicated her situation. When she was eighteen and living with her parents in Mexico, Carmella was engaged to a man twelve years older than she. She was in love, but this did not sit well with her Mother, Anna.

Anna was a cold woman who did everything in her power to make Carmella's life miserable. Anna did not want her daughter to get married. To achieve this goal, Anna invited a "shaman" into her home to see Carmella.

I use the term "shaman" only because Carmella knew no other term to describe him. She never even knew his name. The "shaman" interviewed Carmella and recommended that she come to his apartment for a week or more of intensive "treatment." I had to use simple age regression to obtain the details of Carmella's experience with the "shaman," since she had repressed most of these traumatic memories.

Anna brought the shy and impressionable Carmella over to the "shaman." Carmella then described a rather traumatic series of incidents during her "treatment." She was not allowed to leave this apartment for nearly ten weeks. During this time, the "shaman" verbally and physically abused her. He raped her repeatedly and brainwashed her, using drugs and sensory deprivation techniques (keeping her awake for days at a time). He also used "black magic," or negative projection techniques, on her. The "shaman's" wife was both his assistant and an active participant in this "treatment."

Finally, Carmella was allowed to return home for one day. During this visit, she saw a psychic, who advised Anna not to bring Carmella back to the "shaman." Anna agreed, thus terminating Carmella's confinement. Carmella later learned that the "shaman" had wanted her all along for his personal sexual pleasure, and nothing more.

The psychic who saved Carmella then arranged a marriage between Carmella and one of her (the psychic's) male clients. By this time, Carmella's fiancee gave up on her and became involved with another woman. Carmella's arranged marriage resulted in her relocation to Los Angeles, where she bore a son. Shortly after she had this child, her husband beat her horribly.

Eventually, she left her husband and met another man who was to soon become her second husband. In 1987, Carmella started having flashbacks of her confinement with the "shaman," This abated temporarily, but began to flare up once again in 1995, at which point she came to my Los Angeles office.

Carmella presented herself with PTSD, depression, high blood pressure, headaches, anger toward her mother and the "shaman," and nightmares of demonic spirits attacking her.

Her recovery from some of these symptoms as a result of shielding techniques and superconscious mind taps was quite rapid. Eventually, her blood pressure dropped to 120/80, her depression lifted, and the flashbacks disappeared, as did her headaches and nightmares. Lastly, she no longer exhibited anger toward her mother or the "shaman." It is impossible to describe how amazed Carmella's husband was at her phenomenal progress.

PAST LIFE REGRESSION

The rest of the cases presented in this chapter involve regression back into previous lifetimes. I have arranged these examples into categories reflecting the various pathologies reported by the patients.

Obsessive-Compulsive Disorder

Obsessive people have an innate drive to control both themselves and their environment. This can be a good thing—within reason. The research scientist, for example, needs such a drive, together with the capacity for meticulous and painstaking detail that often accompanies it. However, when over-emphasized, this type of personality becomes tyrannically governed by organization and ritual. Individuals under its sway are often fanatically tidy and quite "neurotic."

Obsessive people often carry out a ritual several times during the day, as though they were driven to it by an inner compulsion. This repeated activity is really a defense mechanism interposed to prevent some forbidden thought or desire from impinging upon the conscious mind. It comes into operation as a result of subconscious guilt. The patient is actually aware that such repetitive activity or behavior serves no useful purpose, at least so far as conscious apprehension is concerned. However, the urges prove completely uncontrollable, compelling the individual to repeat the ritual again and again, *ad infinitum*.

Often, obsessional behavior manifests itself in relationships. Some of the cases presented illustrate this principle, fortunately with positive results.

Nymphomania

A twenty-seven-year-old flight attendant came to me to help her with a serious nymphomania problem. She could never turn down a man's advances. It was as if she had an uncontrollable need (compulsion) to sexually satisfy every man she met. In a past life in Persia (present-day Iran) during the tenth century B.C., she had been a temple maiden, representing the goddess of fertility. It was her sacred and sworn duty to sexually please the noblemen who sought her. She very much enjoyed her work until one fateful day when a noblemen approached her for sexual favors. She recognized him as the man who had beaten and killed one of her friends (also a temple maiden). She refused his advances and was later beheaded for her actions.

Compulsive Spending

Farah came to my office to deal with an obsession with her daughter, Ronnie. Farah had quite a low opinion of hypnosis, so it was quite unusual that she even contacted my office at all. She had no formal exposure to this therapeutic technique, and like most people probably based her opinion on it from stage hypnosis shows and old horror movies.

A few weeks prior to contacting me, Farah had an unusual experience with automatic writing. She was writing a letter to a relative across the country when suddenly her right hand began writing things on its own. The communication established was with her late father's spirit. He advised her to seek hypnosis as a way of solving her problem with Ronnie.

Ronnie was a compulsive shopper whose severe financial problems only grew worse with time. Farah always bailed her out, becoming obsessed with attending to Ronnie's constant needs. In an Egyptian past life, Farah was a healer and Ronnie her daughter.

The karmic pattern was first established during this earlier lifetime. Ronnie got into trouble with regularity, and Farah had to intervene each time to save her. Eventually, both women were banished, ultimately dying of exposure in the desert.

This regression was conducted on May 17, 1994, the day "Search for Grace," my CBS movie, aired. Farah described her experience as a "revelation," finally accepting the fact that her karmic debt to Ronnie was paid.

An interesting sidenote is that Ronnie overcame her compulsive spending habit on her own. The relationship between Farah and Ronnie had at long last become a healthy one. The automatic writing experience Farah originally had represents the first scientific proof we have of the existence of the subconscious mind. This research dates back to the nineteenth century.

This case took an even more unusual turn in the spring of 1995. Shortly after Farah had returned from a trip to Brazil (a country known for its energy vortexes), she developed sores on both of her hands and feet. These "wounds" appeared in the form of a *stigmata* (symbolic of Jesus' wounds) during the Easter month of April.

After three months of conventional medical treatment, consisting of topical creams applied to the sores, Farah gave up on the traditional approach. She began playing my superconscious mind self-hypnosis tape, and soon her sores began to heal.

Most patients can be taught to do automatic writing while in very deep hypnosis. By placing a pencil in the patient's hand during the trance, the suggestion may be given that the hand and arm feel as if they are completely detached and no longer under the patient's control. It is then suggested that the hand will begin to write, moving along automatically so that the patient will not be aware of what is being written. The product of such writing is usually quite different from the patient's normal handwriting. It may even be quite indecipherable. Some patients can acquire the technique in very light trances. A few may even be able to write automatically upon suggestion in the waking state. The disadvantage is that such patients may be quite unable to give the real meaning of their communications, which would only become apparent in the deep hypnotic state.

Obsession with Having a Baby

Sara was obsessed with the desire to have a child. Specifically, she wanted a daughter. This twenty-five year-old receptionist was married to a loving husband, but their efforts to conceive a child proved fruitless.

During a past life in Sweden in the early 1700s, Sara was married to a farmer (her current-life husband). He was very demanding and abusive toward her. He would frequently take off and leave Sara all alone with endless chores to complete.

She eventually got pregnant, but lost the baby girl, and her husband soon abandoned her. Sara was depressed and a few years later died of pneumonia. Her resentment toward her current-life husband because of his actions nearly 300 years earlier was the cause of her fertility problem. The fact that she lost a baby daughter explains why she so desired one now. One year later, Sara gave birth to a baby girl. She and her family are now doing quite well.

Obsession with Boots

A forty-year-old male engineer had a fascination for certain kinds of boots, so much so that it became a fetish. In the 1870s in New Mexico, this patient was a woman named Deluvina Maxwell who befriended William Bonney ("Billy the Kid"). Bonney was hired by the Maxwells to settle a feud between the ranchers. Deluvina became very close (i.e., virtually a surrogate mother) to Bonney, and became very depressed when Sheriff Garrett killed him.

The key to the engineer's fixation was that Deluvina took off Billy's boots prior to the burial, keeping them as a standing memorial of the fallen gunman. The boot fetish disappeared after the engineer relived this pivotal life.

Obsession with Scotland

A thirty-two-year-old junior high school science teacher came to me to deal with an obsession with Scotland.

She recalled living in Scotland as Emily Douglas, the wife of the wealthy Hugh Douglas. Under hypnosis, she emotionally described the battle of Culloden, in which the English defeated the Scots and stripped them of the plaids that signified their respective clans. Her husband, Hugh, had managed to survive the battle by hiding under his fallen horse. Emily and Hugh were eventually forced to hide their valuables and take a boat to Canada to escape the British. Emily Douglas did not want to live anywhere but Scotland, so she gave her food to the children and starved. Subsequent research showed that Hugh had in fact fought in the battle of Culloden in 1746.

Frigidity

A forty-one-year-old female came to my office, intent on overcoming a problem with frigidity (sexual dysfunction).

In a past life in Southeast Asia, she was married to a merchant who traveled often. One day, while he was away, she was raped by an escaped prisoner. When her husband returned, she told him of the incident, whereupon he rejected her sexually. She was given a separate bedroom to sleep in, and their relationship deteriorated into a marriage of convenience. She eventually died of malaria. The husband in her past life is her current husband. She was getting even with him in this life by rejecting him sexually.

Weight Reduction

Elaine was obese. She was five feet three inches tall and weighed 175 pounds when she came to my office in 1993. As a dental hygienist, she was well trained in nutrition and knew better than to engage in immoderate eating.

Another problem affecting Elaine concerned her relationships with men. She simply didn't trust men, having invited quite a few "Mr. Wrongs" into her life.

The western United States during the early 1800s was the setting for her past life. She lived in a small cabin in the woods with her husband. They were married only a few months when a group of escaped convicts murdered her husband and raped her.

These desperados used her cabin as a hideout for several years, keeping Elaine a prisoner while continually abusing her. One day, they decided to leave, complaining that she was getting old and that they wanted someone younger. Elaine died of starvation shortly after their departure. She merely wasted away, having lost the will to live.

The karmic carryover of starvation manifested itself as a desire to overcompensate in this present life with excess food consumption. After applying cleansing techniques, and a two-year follow-up, Elaine now weighs 125 pounds and is engaged to a man she loves, and who appears to love her.

A fifty-three-year-old widowed female realtor came to see me in order to have me help her lose weight. In a past life in Switzerland in the 1700s, she was a very attractive female. However, she had three sisters who were very obese, and they tried to force my patient to overeat. When she refused, one of her sisters tried to kill her. Her father saved her, but over the next five years her life remained in constant danger. She finally gave in and became obese. In her present life, she now weighs over 300 pounds and has lost her job. In addition, the man she loves has abandoned her for another woman. Her sisters in the previous life are her sisters in this life. The man she loved but lost was her husband (now deceased) in this life.

Weight Loss and Infertility

This twenty-nine-year-old registered nurse was five-feet-five inches tall and weighed 245 pounds. She also couldn't conceive a child, a circumstance which is fairly common among obese women. To make matters worse, her husband's sperm count was too low to assure fertilization.

In a past life as a Swiss farmer, she was a female (Karen) and her father died when she was young. When her brother (her brother in this life) went off to war, all of the work on the farm fell on her shoulders. Her brother returned as a cripple, and Karen had to minister to his needs in addition to working the farm. Eating became her only comfort.

In another life as a *male* Eskimo, the nurse was the husband of a woman who almost perished while giving birth to the couple's son. Overpowering feelings of guilt completely obliterated any sexual interest in his wife. He subsequently had an affair with another Eskimo's wife. Upon being discovered, he and his new girlfriend were banished from the tribe.

The now-compounded guilt was transferred into this life, and became strongly associated with procreation and childbirth. In her earlier life as a male Eskimo, the nurse's son married the chief's daughter, precipitating full acceptance back into the tribe. However, the guilt remained "unexpiated," to be carried once again into future lives.

Today, eleven years later, this nurse has a son and a daughter, and weighs a much healthier 130 pounds.

Smoking

A forty-three-year-old male building contractor came to me for help in quitting smoking. Since smoking is a response to stress, we traced back the origins of his stress and his underlying desire for self-punishment.

David, in an eighteenth-century life as a shepherd, was frustrated in his attempt to go after a group of thieves. These thieves raided David's flock of sheep, killed some of the shepherds, and burned down a number of the tribe's tents. As a nomad, David experienced stress and frustration. A council of elders ruled David's tribe. They made all of the decisions concerning the tribe's actions.

These elders felt that pursuing the murderers would leave the flocks, women, and children defenseless. The elders were soon proven correct. A second attack by another gang of rustlers was fortunately repelled by David's tribe. Had they left the camp unguarded in order to capture the first band of marauders, a complete disaster would have resulted.

During the Middle Ages, this patient was also a priest in India, whose name was Bevar. Bevar was a scholarly, dedicated priest who had a true concern for people. Unfortunately, the head priest didn't share Bevar's attitude. This head priest, Navu, was very greedy. He would increase the tax burden on the already impoverished townspeople, many of whom were starving. Bevar sought to return some of the Church's money to the people. Navu objected, frustrating Bevar's every attempt to be truly charitable. As a result, Bevar became angry but couldn't express his emotions. Navu eventually died, and Bevar collected funds for the poor.

Stress was involved in both these past lives. In both lives, the patient encountered serious obstructions. Navu would not let Bevar do what he wanted. Like David the shepherd, he was frustrated: the tension was rising. Note also that Bevar had to submit to the orders of an authority figure, a situation to which David could very well relate.

One additional past life was uncovered, one that helped this patient to permanently eliminate his tobacco addiction. In the nineteenth century, he described a number of scenes depicting himself in the process of murdering various people. He was a member of a band of orphans, all of whom were in their early twenties. In this particular life, he was a Jewish youth disguised in Arab garb. He and his band would drift from town to town murdering Arabs. Apparently, certain Arabs had killed his parents, as well as the parents of the other orphaned youths in the gang. These youths had escaped certain death, and were hellbent on finding the men responsible for murdering their parents.

When they became frustrated by the fruitlessness of their vengeful search, these youths would indiscriminately open fire on any Arab they saw. The attacks had been going on for over two years. Finally, the youths were able to avenge their parents' deaths by killing those responsible, but this did not end the band's thirst for Arab blood. Their killing raids continued.

Finally, the gang was butchered in an ambush, and the Jewish youth with them. He was on a real vengeance trip in that life, venting his frustrations with abandon. He sought out violence and revenge, but they brought only death in their wake. Today, my patient is about the least vengeful person I have ever met.

I compared many of his present experiences with those of his three past lives. In all three of his lives, he was frustrated. As David, he had violent thoughts but never acted on them. As the Jewish band leader, he acted on these urges. He is presently a builder. He waits for money and projects to come in. Sometimes he is all set to go to work, but cannot proceed until approvals are issued. He might have to deal with weather delays, labor problems, construction delays, and bureaucratic red tape. Most of the pressures that drove him to smoke were business pressures. He no longer smokes.

Insomnia

A thirty-three-year-old art teacher came to me to help her overcome her fear of having her throat cut. It seems that when she would go to bed at night, she couldn't sleep unless she pulled the covers right up to her chin, covering her throat. This regimen was far from failsafe, for she still occasionally had nightmares and developed insomnia.

In a past life as Martinelli, a *male* monk working on an Italian farm in the sixteenth century, he was a very happy man. One day while he was farming, soldiers attacked the monastery. All of the monks were killed. When Martinelli went inside the building to see what was happening, a soldier grabbed him and cut his throat. After this regression, the woman's nightmares and insomnia disappeared.

In another life in China, circa A.D. 1000, she was a poor boy who was blind and crippled. He made pottery to support himself. One day in the market place, there was an attack by a band of thieves. He (she) was strangled to death by one of the thieves, throwing additional light on the art teacher's symptomology.

In a different case, a twenty-seven-year-old female benefits administrator came to me, asking me to help her overcome the nightmares she was experiencing. It seems that she would wake up screaming *every night*, a pattern that had persisted now for five years. After undergoing the following past life regressions, the nightmares and screaming disappeared completely.

First, in a frontier life, she was a male stable worker who felt empty and lifeless. His wife, child, and he went out for a ride one day, but their wagon ran into trouble on a high cliff. As a result of this incident, his wife and child fell to their deaths while my patient screamed while trying, unsuccessfully, to save them.

In a primitive life on a tropical island, she (as a male) was the people's leader. He opposed violence, so that when another tribe threatened his people, he counseled his subjects to peaceably depart and avoid conflict. His people rejected this advice, voting rather to stand and fight, whereupon they were soundly defeated, banished, and dispersed. Renegades from his former tribe forced him to lead a nocturnal attack against the aggressors. He (she) was caught and tortured to death by the enemy, culminating a night of ritualistic victory celebrations.

A thirty-eight-year-old housewife suffered from a severe case of insomnia. In 1880, she was a nun in Africa. Her role was to aid the village physician. The drums and musical instruments the natives played kept her up at night. One day the doctor assisted in the delivery of the tribal chief's granddaughter. The baby was stillborn, and the nun and doctor were tortured and killed.

In another life, this same housewife was a male farmer in Kentucky during the early 1880s. The indigenous Indians made a cacaphonous noise almost every night, trying thereby to force the farmer out of the area. He (she) had insomnia, and before long the Indians had burned their cabin to the ground.

Depression

Debbie came to see me over ten years ago to be treated for depression. This mood disorder began shortly after she started dating Mark. Debbie was taking a night course when she developed a tremendous attraction to Mark.

Mark, an older man, felt their relationship seemed to fit into an established pattern from the beginning. "We stayed in it comfortably and it seemed like we had been in it for years," Debbie said.

As certain events transpired, Debbie seemed to turn inward. "A couple of Saturdays ago, nothing was going right," Debbie said. "It turned out Mark had fallen and hurt his leg. I kept telling my mother, 'Something feels wrong today.' It's really awful, It's strange, but Mark and I, we seem to have that kind of tie."

Debbie stated, "Our personalities felt so compatible. We felt that we had been through this before, yet we never discussed it. Once he kidded me, 'Maybe we did love before. Maybe there is no other explanation.' I've never felt this way with anyone else."

In her past life, she was a psychic named Aya, living in Athens in 50 B.C. A Roman politician named Marcus convinced her to live with him in Rome. Because she broke her vow of celibacy, she lost much of her psychic ability. She was thus prevented from reaching her full potential.

I surmised that by reliving her Grecian life—a lot of her life was spent in Rome with Marcus—she was able to understand why she was attracted to her boyfriend in this life (Mark). He is the reincarnation of Marcus.

By recognizing that Mark was the Roman politician of her past life, Debbie was able to discern that, their good relationship notwithstanding, it had still resulted in the earlier loss of her psychic abilities, and had imposed severe limits on her ability to live up to her potential. In this life, had Mark maintained another relationship with her, Debbie might have been tremendously limited in her personal and professional growth.

After her hypnotherapy, Debbie overcame her depressions. She realized that she wasn't supposed to be with her old love because it would have limited her. She is now quite an independent person, and very career-oriented. Her goal is not to be the "typical American housewife."

After I regressed Debbie past her death as Aya, I asked her what she had learned. She replied, "I no longer need to be with Marcus. The dark cloud lifted. I can now go on."

Debbie reflected, "Maybe Mark is presenting a lesson I have yet to learn. Maybe this particular life is presenting the same situation again and I have to choose again, because I am tending to go the same way." She later terminated her relationship with Mark.

"I have had certain psychic things happen to me that are totally unexplained, dreams that come to me, feelings that I've been somewhere before," Debbie said.

Even so, she felt that reliving her past life not only "liberated" her, it also explained the origin of her psychic abilities.

In an altogether different vein, Yvonne's depression was a low grade condition, but it had persisted for many years. She was also a compulsive eater. Her depression usually set in when she was alone in her apartment. Her husband worked longer hours than she.

During World War II, she had been a twenty-year-old seamstress in Germany. In that past life, she went on a trip to visit relatives. Upon her return, she discovered that all of her family had been killed by the Nazis. She starved herself to death to join them. Yvonne just couldn't bear the thought of being alone in that lifetime. This selfsame pattern manifested itself in her current lifetime.

Elsa was a middle-aged, divorced woman who experienced severe depression in cycles lasting approximately one month. During a past life as a young male farmer who was studying geology, his father died, forcing him to abandon his schooling and a planned career change in order to support his widowed mother. My patient's obligation to keep this farm going persisted long after his mother died. He felt he had wasted his life. In her current lifetime, Elsa also feels she has missed her purpose in life.

Homosexuality

Most therapists believe homosexual behavior is genetically imprinted onto the child and is therefore incurable. The case of Aaron suggests otherwise.

For fourteen years, Aaron had been married to a woman he thought he loved. They had no children and were fairly happy. However, Aaron had strong desires to sleep with men. Such impulses preoccupied him most of his life, but he repressed these urges until recently. During the past five years, he has had several homosexual affairs while on business trips.

These patterns did not manifest themselves when he was home. His relationship with his wife was mostly unaffected, and his bisexuality only surfaced when he traveled. Aaron's goal was to obliterate these urges and return to a heterosexual lifestyle.

During several primitive past lives, Aaron had been a sexual perpetrator. He was always a male, and either raped women or forced them to perform acts that disgusted and traumatized them. Aaron is a kind and gentle man in his current life, and these actions carried over to the present as a tremendous burden of subconscious guilt.

To compound his situation, the most positive life he described took place in Peru, approximately 500 years ago. He was the male leader of his tribe and maintained a homosexual relationship with one of the tribe's men for many years. As this Peruvian experience was the only past life with any positive connotations for Aaron (he had proven to be a good leader), the appeal of homosexuality in the present becomes quite clear.

Subsequent superconscious mind taps finalized this case and Aaron lost his bisexual tendencies. This case is over ten years old. I spoke with Aaron recently, who reports that he is no longer drawn toward bisexuality. His relationship with his wife has never been better.

Adult Attention Deficit Disorder (AADD)

Although most commonly noted in children (as hyperactivity), this disorder is frequently observed in adults. Children usually receive Ritalin to deal with this condition. Adults, however, usually end up on antidepressants, which provide only partial symptomatic relief but nothing approaching a substantive cure.

AADD is characterized by short attention spans, inability to listen, lack of follow-up on tasks, difficulty with organization, forgetfulness, restlessness, procrastination, excessive talking, a tendency to become easily frustrated, bored, impatient, impulsive, and a strong dislike for being told what to do.

Marie worked with computers and had a very demanding and high-level position with a major corporation. She quit her job due to the various symptoms of AADD, and for the past four years experienced migraine headaches, depression, panic attacks, insomnia, procrastination, and a very poor self-image.

Her past treatment consisted of various drugs. She had taken antidepressants, narcotics (for the migraines), and tranquilizers, just to name a few. None of this appeared to work, and after four years of conventional medicine her symptoms were worse than ever.

I only guided her into one past life as part of her therapy. She described being male and fighting in the Mexican-American War (1846–1848) for the United States. Her name had been Bart. He was compelled to leave his family to go to war.

Bart was very uncomfortable as a soldier. He was constantly fearful of his life and couldn't concentrate on his duties. One evening he fell asleep at his post. He and dozens of his fellow soldiers were killed. Bart was shot in the head.

The insomnia and migraines might be explained by the circumstances of Bart's death, but, as Chapter 4 illustrates, the main issue is lowered soul's energy.

Marie experienced several superconscious mind taps to raise her soul's energy and overcome these issues. In just a few months of soul healing (ninety-eight percent of this is accomplished while she is dreaming), Marie achieved more relief than four years of conventional medical treatments had provided.

Today, Marie is free from migraines (none have arisen in over two years), insomnia, and AADD. Marie is completely amazed at what happened. Soul healing does seem to have a powerful effect.

Alcoholism

It has been estimated that over 100 million Americans consume alcohol. The majority of these individuals can do so without developing a drinking problem; however, for one out of ten people who drink, alcohol can become a serious problem. Contrary to the widely accepted stereotype of the alcoholic, ninety-five per cent of alcoholics are either employed or capable of working. In half of all the murders in the United States, either the killer or the victim or both have been drinking. A fourth of all suicides are found to have significant amounts of alcohol in their bloodstreams. The economic cost associated with the misuse of alcohol is estimated at more than $25 billion each year.

Kerry came to me with a severe drinking problem. She was on her third marriage and her drinking was the worst it had ever been. Kerry's life was hardly typical. The last man she dated prior to marrying Ed (her current husband) had become good friends with Ed.

This circumstance significantly affected Kerry's drinking. Ed was not supportive when she suggested that he scuttle his friendship with her old paramour. Apparently, Kerry and Ed's marriage was shaky even on its best days.

Kerry had tried many forms of therapy over the years to deal with her drinking. She was placed on Antabuse, joined Alcoholics Anonymous (AA), participated in group therapy, etc. Nothing seemed to work. After reading *Past Lives — Future Lives,* she decided to give past life regression a try.

During a medieval past life, Kerry had been the owner of a castle. She was female and her husband had been killed in a war several years earlier. Kerry was lonely, and began to drink. Later her army again went to war and was defeated. She was imprisoned and fed terrible food, but was given wine instead of water to drink (the water was apparently unpotable). Her drinking simply worsened in captivity. She died shortly thereafter of food poisoning. Happily, Kerry responded well to superconscious mind taps and no longer harbors an insatiable desire for alcohol.

Doreen's case of excessive drinking involved an "attached entity." She had had a problem with alcohol since she was in college. This was causing problems with her current husband, who didn't drink at all. As this was Doreen's second marriage in three years, she was determined to make it work.

In a past life in Portugal, Doreen had been married to a man who was obsessively jealous. Doreen was young and beautiful in this eighteenth-century lifetime, and was faithful to her wealthy husband, Jose.

One night, Jose killed Doreen in a fit of unjustified jealous rage. His spirit found her in her current life and literally attached itself to her. He has been bothering her all her life, exacerbating her drinking problem in both of her marriages.

Jose was still jealous of Doreen's mates. Through superconscious mind taps, I was able to identify Jose and remove him from her presence. He was instructed to go into the white light. As he left Doreen, he took her desire for alcohol with him.

Claustrophobia

Bertha had a fear of being in closed areas, a condition commonly known as claustrophobia. In ancient Egypt, she was a male slave working on a construction site for a pyramid. She was part of a team that excavated one of many secret entrances to the pyramid. After the work was completed, he and the other slaves were killed to protect the secret of this passageway. When he was stabbed and buried outside the pyramid, he was not quite dead. He panicked as the dirt was thrown on his paralyzed body; he was being buried alive.

In another life in New England during the 1700s, Bertha was a sixteen-year-old girl from a wealthy family. One day, while going into the wine cellar to retrieve some wine for her father, the stairway collapsed and Bertha was buried beneath the rubble. She slowly died a painful death before she could be found.

Agoraphobia
A forty-seven-year-old housewife suffered from agoraphobia for most of her adult life. She was afraid to leave her house and locked herself in her bedroom for most of the day. This pattern persisted for twelve years.

In a monk's life in the tenth century, he (she) was forced into the clergy by his domineering father. He was persecuted by the Church for his opinions and eventually sent on one of the Crusades (Holy Wars). There he witnessed numerous killings and later went insane.

As a wealthy male landowner during the twelfth century in Southern France, my patient rebelled against an evil church official who sat in judgment over his people. This official eventually tortured his daughter, who thereafter became a "vegetable." He cared for his incapacitated daughter for the rest of her life. When she finally died, he took action. He killed the church official one night and was soon executed for this murder.

A subsequent library check revealed that there indeed was an inquisition during the twelfth and thirteenth centuries in Northern Italy and Southern France.

Fear of Snakes
A twenty-nine-year-old female insurance saleswoman came to me to help her overcome a terrible fear of snakes. The sight of a mere garter snake sliding across her lawn could immobilize her for half an hour. Since her husband was an avid camper, she had to overcome this phobia.

In a past life in Malaysia, approximately 2,500 years ago, she had been a healer for her tribe. Snakes played a significant part in her various rituals. These snakes were trained to kill the human sacrifices, which were sometimes required for the ceremonies she conducted. One day the snakes turned on her instead, and she died a terrifying, painful death.

As an American Indian female about 3,000 years ago, she was a psychic named Mirami. She tapped into a past life in Atlantis from 30,000 B.C. and helped her people find a red crystal, which was prophesied as a source of healing and a very valuable sign. Having acquired it, her people didn't know what to do with it. They decided to go to war with a neighboring tribe, using the red crystal as their source of power and wisdom. Mirami was forced to lead them into battle. Her people were defeated, and as punishment she was forced to eat a live snake. Later, she was pushed into a snake pit and quickly killed by the poisonous snakes.

Fear of Water

A forty-seven-year-old female administrative assistant for an engineering firm came to me to overcome her fear of water.

In a past life as a male in the South Pacific, he got into a fight with a man from another village over a girl. During the fight, he was knocked unconscious, signalling his defeat. His fellow villagers ostracized him and he drowned himself in shame.

In another life, my patient was the male sea captain of a large ship. On a voyage around the tip of South Africa, he encountered a severe storm. The crew was about to panic but the captain replotted the ship's course to avoid the storm. His calculations were in error and the ship sank. He and all of the crew drowned.

Stage Fright

A twenty-two-year-old female college senior came to me to help her overcome her stage fright. She was a theater major and apparently very talented. During rehearsals she could sing, act, and dance with absolutely no difficulties. However, during the actual performance she would develop symptoms of severe stage fright.

In a past life in Russia during the early 1900s, she was a member of an acting company. Her lover was also a member of the company. One day she discovered her lover was having a homosexual affair with the director. She was shocked and confronted him. He later committed suicide. The director discovered this, and my patient was arrested one night in mid-performance, to be shipped off to Siberia to live out a lonely and depressing existence. Her current drama coach at college was the Russian director in that earlier life.

A forty-five-year-old educator had a severe case of stage fright. She was regressed to a past life as a male preacher over 1,900 years ago. He disagreed with the Church and spoke out against their policies and interpretation of the teachings of Christ. One day, while preaching to the townspeople, he was attacked and killed.

Fear of Abandonment

A thirty-one-year-old female nurse came to me to help her overcome an oppressive fear of abandonment pervading all her relationships with men. For years, during a past life in Philadelphia in the 1890s, she had been involved with a married man. One day he very coldly broke off the relationship. She felt betrayed, hurt, abandoned, and ultimately drowned herself.

In another life in imperial Rome during the reign of Nero, she belonged to an upper-middle-class family. Her father arranged for her to marry a Roman soldier who beat her and pursued a multitude of extramarital affairs. She later converted to Christianity, left her husband, and hid from the Roman authorities. She took care of the sick among the other Christians who were then living in caves, where she finally died of starvation.

Shyness

A twenty-eight-year-old female accountant came to me to help her overcome a shyness problem.

In a past life in Germany in the 1890s, she was a retarded male child locked up in an institution. He was mute and suffered chronic mistreatment at the hands of the other inmates. Over the years he became more and more frustrated and fearful of people. He couldn't even complain about this abuse because he could not speak. At the age of sixteen, he finally committed suicide.

In another life in ancient Rome, she was stoned to death after being accused unjustly of adultery.

Jealousy

A forty-four year-old female radiologist came to me to help her overcome a case of intense jealousy. Ever since she can remember, she had always been jealous of her boyfriends, and was now even more so with her husband of sixteen years.

In a past life in England in the early 1800s, she was a female writer. She was very jealous and possessive toward her husband. They later moved out to the country and she gave up writing to raise their children. Her jealousy persisted and her husband one night admitted to having affairs when they lived in London. They separated and she tried to go back to writing. She then suffered from writer's block and became an alcoholic. She died a failure and very depressed. Her husband in that hapless life is now her present husband.

In a past life in Spain during the 1600s, she was engaged to a sailor. One night some of her fiancé's shipmates kidnapped her, raped her, and spirited her aboard a ship bound for the Caribbean. Her fiancé eventually found out about this but didn't do anything about it. When they arrived in the Caribbean, he flaunted his affairs with the local girls to his fiancée. She hated him then and one night she killed him. She was caught, imprisoned, and hanged. Her fiancé in that life is her present husband.

Procrastination

A sixty-three-year-old female medical secretary wanted to overcome her tendency to procrastinate. In a Mexican past life as a male field worker with a wife and two children, he stole goods with his friends and sold them on the black market to save money to buy a farm. His friends cheated him out of the money and told the authorities that he was the only one who stole the goods. He was imprisoned and worked on a chain gang. Later, he was transferred to a fort where he saw his wife living with one of the soldiers. After he was released from prison he joined the army and became a good soldier. He was killed one day in an accidental explosion in the fort while staying late to complete an assigned task.

A forty-seven-year-old personnel manager came to me to conquer his procrastination over financial matters.

In a past life in Southeast Asia, he became the emperor's keeper of records for grain usage. He was successful, but later a soldier in the army charged with supervision over the granaries cheated the emperor by selling grain on the side, forcing my patient to fudge the records to cover his tracks. When this scam was finally discovered by the emperor, he believed the soldier's perjured testimony against my patient, who was immediately imprisoned. He eventually became record keeper (but now as a slave, not a free man) for the soldier who framed him. He procrastinated in his work and was ultimately executed for gross incompetence.

Arthritis

A male in his mid-forties came to see me for arthritis symptoms (traditional medical treatment had failed him for years—he is still seeing his M.D.) and for his recurring dreams of gross indebtedness.

In a past life in Europe, he manufactured beer. When business turned sour, he couldn't pay his rent or employees' salaries and eventually lost the brewery. He was imprisoned and felt useless, trapped, and guilty for being a failure. After his release from prison, he got a job in a factory and stayed debt-free. Two months after I began working with him, my patient's arthritis symptoms disappeared, along with the dreams of indebtedness.

Stomach Pain

A thirty-one-year-old radio personality suffered from stomach pains of unknown origin. In medieval England, she was a servant to an English lord. One of his mistresses accused her of having an affair with the lord and attacked her at night, killing her by repeatedly stabbing her in the stomach.

In a cave girl life, she was four years old when her parents were killed by an earthquake. The child starved to death while experiencing severe stomach pain.

Past life Possession

It is quite rare for a patient's past life personality to attempt to take over the current life body of the individual. When this does occur, it is usually due to extreme jealousy of the current lifetime. Such was the situation in Marsha's case.

Marsha is a good Christian woman in her early thirties. She always wears a cross around her neck. Marsha is dating a man named Dan, but is being stalked by her obsessive ex-boyfriend Hal. Lately, she has been exhibiting rather bizarre behavior: she is blasphemous toward the church, she acts like a prostitute with strange men, and she is having nightmares about being murdered on a tropical island. During her past life in Martinique, she was a young girl named Jacqueline, studying in a convent to become a nun. One night a drunken sailor raped her. She was comforted by the priest, but decided to run away from the convent. She ended up in a brothel working as a prostitute. The owner of the brothel was obsessed with her, beat her, and murdered her during a fit of jealous rage.

Dan is the reincarnation of the priest and Hal is the current life of the brothel owner. Past life regression and superconscious mind taps were the techniques used to confront Jacqueline and permanently remove her presence from Marsha's body. Marsha returned to her normal lifestyle and never heard from Jacqueline again.

CELEBRITY PAST LIFE EXPERIENCES

Jerry Springer

As part of the interview I did with him, Jerry was guided back into one of his previous lifetimes. This show aired January 7, 1994, and Jerry re-ran his taped past-life experience in October of that year.

As a knight in England during the 1600s, Jerry was severely wounded in a battle defending the honor of a noblewoman. He could no longer function as a knight, so the woman he saved employed him in the castle as a butler. This woman reincarnated as Jerry's current-life daughter.

Montel Williams

Montel was hostile, to say the least, to the very idea of reincarnation. However, this negative attitude didn't prevent him from experiencing a rather dramatic past life that he discussed during my interview on his talk show.

He described himself as a slave in the South during the Civil War, wounded and surrounded by four or five white farmers who were about to kill him. Later, on the air, he stated, "I felt very, very nervous and very, very scared." His death at the hands of the farmers is significant in that he is currently involved with many groups aiding underprivileged black children.

This was a very emotional past-life regression for this articulate black man, who strongly identified with the karmic significance of that past life.

Glenn Ford

Glenn lived as a piano teacher in Scotland in the early 1800s. In addition, he discovered a past life in the army of the French King, Louis XIV. Other lives revealed included a stint as a sailor in England during the 1600s, and a Christian named Flavius in imperial Rome who was thrown to the lions during the Circensian games in the Coliseum. The most important benefit he received from the regression experience was overcoming his fear of death. He stated, "It was as though a great eraser had scrubbed it from my life."

Sylvester Stallone

Stallone reported lives during the French Revolution and as a male American Indian. He was guillotined by the Jacobins during the former. When asked about this he replied, "It doesn't hurt. You don't feel anything except your head hits the basket."

As to his Native American lives he responded, "I can do American Indian dances, the eagle dance, for example. I feel a very strong kinship with wolves."

Loretta Lynn

This country-western singer reported lives as a Cherokee princess, a farmer's wife in America, a woman in Ireland, a bedridden old man, a waiter in the 1920s, and finally, a maid to one of the King Georges of England. She had an affair with the king, and was subsequently murdered by a male confidante of the king who was exceedingly jealous.

12

FUTURE LIFE PROGRESSION

Now that you understand the basics behind regression, let us discuss progression. Progression refers to forward motion in time. It is employed during regression to return the patient to the present. For example, let us assume you were regressed to the age of five. If I then wanted to move you forward to the age of eight, I would progress you three years on the count of five. Finally, I would progress you back to the present, just prior to concluding the session. This is called progression. You are never in danger of being trapped in either the past or the future.

Progression also has other uses. It can be used to see how a particular decision that a patient is contemplating will come out. For example, let us assume you are considering changing your job. You progress yourself two years into the future and you can learn if you actually did change jobs and whether it worked out to your advantage or not. Let me make clear that I am not referring to psychic experiences. I do not consider myself a medium or reader of the future. It is merely the use of hypnotic progression that enables me to help patients help themselves. I realize that there is no way to validate a progression experience other than to wait and see if a particular event occurs as seen in the progression.

Many people consider progression a form of wishful thinking. I will be the first to admit that the viewing of a scene in the future could possibly reflect the workings of the hopes and desires of the subconscious mind, except for one crucial fact: patients often view future scenes in which events occur over which they could not possibly exert control. An example of this would be the reading of a newspaper headline that exists five years in the future that describes a natural disaster or the election of a president or a war, and having that event occur five years later exactly as it was read in trance. No alternate explanation, in my opinion, even comes close to doing justice to this kind of data.

Suppose, for example, that you are in a helicopter above a major highway. You look down and see that traffic is stopped because of an accident. At this time you could radio someone in a car five miles behind the scene of the accident and inform the driver of the upcoming traffic problem. Since you are in a helicopter above the traffic flow, you are actually detached from the scene itself. The driver that you are warning is immersed within the flow of traffic. In a sense you are reading the future of this car. If the driver of that car keeps driving on that highway, he will encounter the congested traffic that you are now observing. The helicopter represents another dimensional plane, and on a different plane there is no time as we here on Earth (or on the highway, in this analogy) know it.

To extend the analogy further, note that from the vantage point of the helicopter you could also see what the traffic flow is like behind the car to whose driver you are talking. This would represent the past. The traffic ahead of the driver represents the future, and the traffic that the driver is experiencing now represents the present. You are, in effect, reading the past, present, and future from the helicopter. By leaving the earth plane or entering into hypnotic trance, you can read the past or future without the restrictions that occur in the waking, or beta, state.

The actual experience of a progression is rather difficult to describe. I have personally conducted thousands of progressions. Most people are afraid of the future and don't want to be progressed. Also, I have regressed myself into past lives and progressed myself into future lives, so that I can speak of these phenomena from personal experience. In a regression, the scenes can unfold in a logical and orderly fashion. The patient can recall the past in great detail, and these journeys into the past are often quite helpful to the patient in terms of understanding present karma and current behavior problems.

A progression, however, is far less stable. It is much more difficult to obtain information. When I perform progressions, I am essentially attempting to see how a patient's karma will be manifested in the future. This knowledge can very helpful to a patient in terms of the present.

It seems that when an individual is progressed into the future, he or she may be quickly removed from a particular scene and transferred to another without any instructions or cues from me. These sudden dislocations pose absolutely no danger to the patient, of course, but the continuity of the experience may be lost or fractured. For example, the patient could be describing a scene in some futuristic city. The next thing we know, the city has disappeared and a desert scene has replaced it. The patient may then describe a third and completely different scene, and act as if nothing unusual has happened.

The concept of "forbidden knowledge" is often mentioned by my patients. People ask me, "isn't knowledge of future events prohibited by the universe?" The answer is simple. If you are supposed to know something, such as your future, your higher self will see to it that you receive that data. If, however, you are not supposed to be aware of certain future events, then no person, place, or thing will give you that information (unless and until you are ready to receive it). Even with my highly sophisticated techniques and extraordinary success rates, I cannot arrange for you to receive information that you are not supposed to have. When the student is ready, the teacher will be there.

AGE PROGRESSION

The first series of cases I will present deal with the future of this life (age progression).

Yolanda's relationship with her lover, Bill, will be described more fully in Chapter 16 when I discuss the concept of "soulmates" at greater length. In this context, however, we'll explore the fact that she was able to use age progression with incredible accuracy to empower herself in her current life.

Compulsive overeating was Yolanda's main reason for coming to my office in 1989. She worked as an administrative assistant for an insurance company and had no outside interests. Yolanda was divorced, lonely, and her hobbies consisted of watching television and eating.

I guided her through a rather significant past life that will be presented in greater detail in Chapter 16. Following superconscious mind taps, she was instructed to go into the future of this lifetime.

After viewing her five frequencies, she decided on one that she found the most attractive. The following represents the most significant details of Yolanda's ideal frequency.

1. She would overcome a compulsive eating behavior pattern, lose weight, begin running, and enter marathons. Prior to this, she had done absolutely no running.
2. She saw herself getting married, but this marriage would not work out. She would eventually meet another man and have a fulfilling relationship with him.
3. A friend of hers would have a baby.
4. She would develop a business in designer T-shirts and do her own art work. She had no prior interest or training in art.
5. Her job would switch to group insurance.
6. Her life would finally come together.

Yolanda did lose weight and kept it off, as evidenced during a follow-up visit six years later. She also took up running as a hobby and regularly runs in the Los Angeles Marathon, among others. Her friend did have a baby, and Yolanda was transferred to the group insurance division of her company. Yolanda did take a painting class and established a designer T-shirt business, creating her own art work.

By far, the most significant "hit" on her list had to do with Bill. Yolanda first met Bill at her gym. She rarely worked out, so this event, by itself, is synchronistic. They began an intense love affair, but eventually Yolanda decided to break it off. The sole reason was that Bill was still married and couldn't bring himself to divorce his wife.

Several months later, Yolanda married a man she really did not love. This relationship did not last long and, as she perceived in her age progression a few years prior, she divorced him.

A few years later Bill called Yolanda to ask her to accompany him to a funeral of a mutual friend. He was now divorced and their relationship was rekindled. It is fascinating to note that their reunion was so heartfelt; it was as if they had never parted. Their love for each other was and is greater than it has ever been. Needless to say, Yolanda's life finally did come together.

Rosie worked as an executive secretary for an east coast public relations firm. In reality, she was just a regular secretary. Her boss, who owned this small firm, regularly abused her. She did all of his "dirty work" and was never acknowledged for her efforts.

This mousy-looking, shy, and very insecure woman wanted a new life. She was also having an affair with her boss and was afraid to end it. Her position did pay her more than she could earn elsewhere, and she desperately needed the money.

There was plenty of room here for empowerment. Rosie was trained with superconscious mind taps, then guided into her five future frequencies. The one she selected showed her moving to Florida and eventually buying into a radio station in that sunshine state.

I last saw Rosie in 1984. Four years later, she called my office and wanted to stop by to see me. She didn't have a problem but just wanted to say hello. I agreed to this meeting and could not believe my eyes when she came in.

This mousy woman had metamorphosed into an assertive, beautiful, and empowered soul. She had lost weight, changed her hairstyle and color, and now beamed with confidence. In fact, she came into town to visit her family. Rosie now resided in Florida and was part owner of a radio station there. She was a successful and fulfilled soul, well on her way to a very bright future. You might say her life turned out to be a "rosy scenario."

Andrea wanted to view the future of her current life in order to resolve issues concerning her relationship with her husband, psychosomatic illnesses, and their financial future. She suffered from rheumatoid arthritis, back pain, and insomnia. In addition, she was rapidly drifting apart from her husband (Roger).

Andrea was initially oriented and trained with superconscious mind taps prior to the age progression. During one of her progression frequencies, she was shot and killed in her hometown of Detroit. The frequency Andrea chose showed that she was to overcome her psychosomatic illnesses, while Roger would sell his business to become a highly paid consultant. Their relationship markedly improved on this path and they lived in Florida.

These age progressions were conducted in 1990, and according to my March 1995 conversation with her, these events transpired. Prior to my call, Andrea wrote me a rather nice letter notifying me of her move to Florida and updating me as to her progress.

One final sidenote here concerns the shooting that Andrea fortunately avoided. It seems that on the day she would have been shot (had she stayed on the frequency she was on when she came to my office), someone else was shot and killed in Detroit, and at the location she described. Andrea's higher self was working overtime in helping her help herself.

Joan had a real problem. This thirty-five year-old pharmacist was married to a man for six years, and the relationship was rapidly deteriorating. Another man (Harold) had expressed interest in her, and for the first time in her married life she seriously contemplated having an affair.

When Joan discussed this idea with her best friend Tonya, the advice was tempting. Tonya read quite a few books on reincarnation and concluded that Harold was her "soulmate." Tonya strongly recommended Joan leave her husband, Al.

Joan is a very conservative woman who does not believe in reincarnation. Furthermore, Tonya had the profile of someone who was immature and didn't always think things through before acting. To resolve this conflict, Joan called my office.

I recommended superconscious mind taps to train her to raise her soul's energy first, then proceeded with age progressions. Joan was quite relieved that I didn't insist on past life regression. She presented all five frequencies and discovered that those in which she chose to leave Al and move in with Harold resulted in disaster. Her ideal frequency was one in which she stayed with Al and worked things out.

Joan chose to stay with Al. Today she has a far better marriage than she had known for years. Al never did find out about Joan's dilemma. I was most impressed with Joan's maturity, intelligence, and open-mindedness, considering that she still rejects the concept of reincarnation. Fortunately, belief in this theory is surely not a precondition for making these experiences both valuable and effective.

FUTURE LIFE PROGRESSION

Next, we are going to explore future lifetimes from the twenty-first to the thirty-sixth centuries. The field of progression and hypnotherapy was developed back in 1977 when I asked a patient to go to the origin of her particular problem. A past life regression was my expected result. This patient decided instead to discuss the twenty-third century. My earlier book, *Past Lives — Future Lives*, is the first book ever written about future life progression hypnotherapy. For a complete spectrum of additional case histories, I would highly recommend that book.

The Case of Pete

Pete, a clinical psychologist, called me in August of 1984 for help with a handwashing compulsion. He knew all about compulsions, but could not help himself. Pete had spent years in therapy with no results. He would constantly wash his hands, day and night. He also changed his clothes two or three times a day, to "remove the dirt." There was absolutely no logic in his fear of contamination or his feeling that if he didn't go through his daily rituals he would become unable to function.

Another unusual aspect of Pete's psychological profile was the number 8. This number haunted him. He was born in August (the eighth month). Every time he obtained a new telephone number or a new address, the number 8 was always there. His grandmother had died in August, as had many other members of his family. In addition, the name Teresa seemed to haunt him throughout his current life.

In Pete's case, the most significant cause of his problem turned out to be centered in a future lifetime. At the end of the twenty-first century, Pete was a male technician in a nuclear research facility in Tulsa, Oklahoma. His name will be Ben Kingsley and he will have an obsessive-compulsive personality. When you add workaholic traits to this neurotic personality, there is a greatly increased propensity for an emotional breakdown.

Ben went on to tell me more about his position. He was in charge of the Teres-Alpha division, which dealt with researching ways to contain nuclear power and eliminate nuclear waste products more effectively. He was indeed a good supervisor—young, aggressive, knowledgeable, and totally dedicated. If you overlooked his emotional problems, he was perfect for the job. I couldn't ignore his psychological profile, and my concern for him was growing by the minute.

As I progressed him forward, he described his many activities at the facility. He sat in on board meetings, participated in planning major projects, correlated the data from his division, and handled public relations, among other things. In short, Ben had a lot of responsibilities. Considering his emotional state, I felt he was biting off more than he could chew. I asked him to go forward to the most significant event in that life.

Ben described working in the research facility one evening, trying to correct some of his calculations that were in error. His supervisor criticized him concerning his poor work performance, and Ben was quickly reaching his boiling point. Suddenly, he broke down and configured all the computers, causing a meltdown of the facility.

Ben had a nervous breakdown. Pete, sitting in my recliner, was in no danger. It was Ben who couldn't listen to reason. As a result of his actions, there was a complete meltdown of the research facility. The skeleton crew and Ben were killed. The nuclear contamination from Ben's miscalculations affected the entire Tulsa area. The water supply was contaminated. So were the food supplies, and so was everything else. I spoke to Ben from the superconscious mind level:

Dr. G: Ben, what did you learn from this?

Pete: I learned how to contaminate a major city by my stupidity. I learned nothing but how to hurt innocent people.

Ben didn't quite understand another connection from this future life. He died in August of the year 2088. The eighth month and the year 2088 were significant associations to the number 8. In addition, Ben worked in the Teres-Alpha unit. This spells out Teresa, a name that haunted Pete most of his life.

Pete was brought out of trance feeling drained and unsure of what this all meant. I told him that his future life was the real cause of his present contamination compulsion and explained the origin of his difficulties with the number 8 and the name Teresa.

But he was still confused. How could this future life help him now? He surely didn't want to experience that terrible life a hundred years from now. I agreed with him. Although I did effect some cleansing from the superconscious mind level, that wouldn't solve his problems. The answer lay in the application of the principles of quantum physics.

That future was just one of at least five major probabilities. Pete had perceived a negative frequency, or probability, though he had at least four others from which to choose. The solution to his problem was really quite simple. All I had to do was to have him perceive the other four choices and then, after he selected the ideal frequency, program that frequency to be his reality. By doing this I would help Pete to switch frequencies so his future would be quite different than it would have been had we failed to act on the knowledge provided during the progression.

You may ask how I do this. How can I change the future? What you must consider is that every time you make a choice you are, in effect, changing the future. In Pete's case, progressing him to the other parallel existences he would have at the end of the twenty-first century would accomplish that very goal.

Pete progressed nicely to four other lifetimes in that same time frame. After each life was reviewed, he carefully selected the one he felt was ideal, and I then progressed him to that frequency. The various environmental factors can be quite similar in these parallel frequencies, as was the case here. However, there will always be major differences, and each action by Pete in a certain frequency will have a specific effect on the total outcome of his life. He, as Ben, still worked in Teres-Alpha, but that name didn't act as a jinx. In fact, you might say it was a good-luck charm.

Pete made rapid progress after this session. He no longer feared the number 8 or the name Teresa. He understood what they really meant and why the contamination compulsion had been so deeply ingrained within his psyche.

Pete is totally recovered today. He accomplished this himself with a little assistance from progression therapy. I like this case because it illustrates the principle that *the future is now.* We can change the future, but we must first perceive it.

Life in the Thirty-sixth Century

Emily came to me in the summer of 1981. Her chief complaint was ulcerative colitis. This gastrointestinal disorder is described as a chronic, non-specific, inflammatory, and ulcerative disease of the colon, characterized most often by bloody diarrhea. This disease most frequently begins between the ages of fifteen and forty, and the cause is unknown. This syndrome is most uncomfortable, as it consists of an increased need to defecate, mild lower-abdominal cramps, and the appearance of blood and mucus in the stool. It is not uncommon for a patient to have ten to twenty bowel movements per day, often accompanied by severe cramps. A great concern is the possibility of colon cancer. Since we know stress brings on colitis attacks, tracing the source of the stress and reprogramming it out would literally solve Emily's problem.

The true origin of Emily's stress rested in the thirty-sixth century. She lived on Phonican, a planet in the Andromeda system. Her name was Sequestra and her people were enslaved by a fanatical group called the Aracatha. Sequestra was valuable to them because she was "keeper of the knowledge," and her mind stored priceless scientific data.

The Aracatha were pure energy, so they used Sequestra's people to experiment with the concept of being in a body for a time. Sequestra was assigned to head a research project to create genetically perfect bodies for the Aracatha to use at their pleasure. In reality, she led an underground resistance movement whose goal was to forever rid her people of the tyrannical Aracatha oppressors.

When I asked Sequestra what her plan was, she told me, "The karmic cycle is our only salvation. There are sixteen members of the Aracatha, and their goal is to occupy a human body at will. When I assist in the perfection of the technique, I know each member of the Aracatha will immediately play with their new toy. They will all enter a body and play."

The brilliance of her plan centered on a resonance frequency device she developed, which trapped the Aracatha one by one within the bodies they entered. Her plan was carried out and it worked like clockwork.

While the Aracatha occupied their respective bodies, they had already begun to illustrate the genius of Sequestra's plan. They participated in unusual sexual practices, murdered some of Sequestra's people for sport, and generally incurred some heavy karmic debts. They were exiled to a small asteroid to live out the rest of their lives. Emily truly benefited from the progression aspect of my therapy. She is now free of colitis and has a new lease on life.

Jerry Springer's Future Life

Jerry Springer's attitude toward his past life regression, described in the previous chapter, can best be summed up by the term "healthy skeptic." However, at the outset of progression therapy, he did not think he would be capable of viewing the future, an opinion he soon recanted.

In the latter part of the next century, Jerry will be a rancher/farmer named Bobby, working in Montana. He is married and has four children. Bobby is involved with a government project designed to raise crops on our moon. He will be killed at the age of sixty when his craft crashes during a return trip to Earth.

Two interesting facts surfaced from this future life progression. First, Jerry's future-life wife is a girl he knew in high school named Robin. Secondly, he stated on his show that to this day he is afraid to dive into a pool. This phobia has led to much embarrassment during past vacations.

A Future-Life Rebel

Sabrina is a quiet and reflective woman. She is bright, attractive, and emotional. Her goal was to view herself in a future life in order to get a glimpse of her soul's purpose.

During the twenty-fifth century on another planet, Sabrina is a female revolutionary named Commander K. She lives in an underground city with her boyfriend, B. Her society outlawed any expression of emotions, and had nearly perfected surgical and genetic procedures to achieve this goal.

This society also had a quota of children (artificial insemination and test tubes were their means of procreation). Children in excess of the government's quota were killed. Commander K and B secretly rescued some of these children and cared for them in an underground facility. These children were also taught to love, which was punishable by death.

One day, the secret police discovered their facility and Commander K, along with B and many others, were put to death by injection of a yellow fluid. The karmic test of being controlled by others was most evident in this future life.

Sabrina had very little control over her current life. Through subsequent superconscious mind taps and by her own efforts, she was able to empower herself in her current lifetime. This automatically nullifies the necessity of having to repeat this course again 500 years from now as Commander K.

In conclusion, by having patients perceive their future options in this life as well as in future lifetimes, they are empowered to take control of their own destiny by selecting their ideal frequencies and programming them into dominance. I personally find this most rewarding. The fact that each and every one of my patients can control their own destiny is fulfilling to me beyond measure.

13

BEREAVEMENT

I have had an increasing number of what I refer to as pre-bereavement patients during the past ten years. Pre-bereavement is defined as a patient exhibiting the classic bereavement symptoms over someone who is still alive. One additional characteristic is a sense of impending doom and panic that their loved one is about to cross into spirit (die). There is no logic or rationale to this syndrome, merely an oppressive feeling that a loss is about to occur.

Jennifer's case is a perfect example of pre-bereavement. She came to my Woodland Hills office in the spring of 1993. Apparently, she had a vision in the form of a dream that her mother (Betty) was going to die before her birthday in December. This was no ordinary dream. Jennifer had no history of precognition, and the feeling so overwhelmed her that it became the dominant force in her life.

Betty was Jennifer's best friend, in addition to being her mother. To lose Betty at this time would be devastating to Jennifer, who did not have much of a social support network. What is interesting to note is that Betty had visited her physician a few months prior to Jennifer's dream and had checked out as normal.

My assessment of Jennifer's vision was that it was possibly a superconscious mind tap, based on the fact that it was out of character for her to have such an experience. This would only apply if the content was accurate. Jennifer's background was rather traditional and quite conservative. You can imagine what her husband Ben's attitude was when she told him of her dream. Prior to her initial session, Jennifer exhibited on a regular basis panic attacks, depression, and other mood swings.

Superconscious mind taps and laying out the progression frequency map were the techniques I used to get to the bottom of the matter. Apparently, Betty had an undiagnosed kidney stone (according to Jennifer's superconscious mind), and this was the main problem. We explored the other frequencies in the future of this life, and Jennifer chose one in which her mother remained healthy and lived beyond the year 1993.

To know Jennifer is to be exposed to a rather assertive woman. She cajoled Betty into returning to her physician to check out her kidney. Betty's doctor found a three-centimeter kidney stone and immediately ordered surgery. Betty survived the operation and was informed that if she had waited much longer, there was a large probability that she would have died of renal (kidney) failure. Jennifer saved her mother's life by listening to her subconscious mind.

I have had the pleasure of meeting Betty. As this chapter is being written in June 1995, Betty is alive and well. Furthermore, Jennifer has completely resolved her pre-bereavement issue in relationship to Betty.

As pre-bereavement cases are not that common, let us now turn our attention to a classic example of bereavement. Lloyd was a very successful businessman. He had two daughters and a devoted wife. Life was good. One day in the summer of 1989, Lloyd's world was shattered. His oldest daughter, Maria (age 18), was killed in an automobile accident near Lloyd's home.

There is no way to do justice to what happened over the next seven months. Lloyd's life fell apart. He and his wife bickered constantly, and both experienced severe depression as a result of their bereavement. Lloyd suffered from insomnia and cried on and off throughout the day. He literally could not work, and he stayed home quite often. Fortunately, he was self-employed, but the financial problems stemming from his absenteeism didn't help.

According to Elizabeth Kübler-Ross in her book *On Death and Dying*, the grief process consists of five stages:

1. Denial and isolation.
2. Anger.
3. Bargaining.
4. Depression.
5. Acceptance.

Kübler-Ross states (p. 275), "There is a time in a patient's life when the pain ceases to be, when the mind slips off into a dreamless state, when the need for food becomes minimal and the awareness of the environment all but disappears into darkness."

The first step I performed with Lloyd was a superconscious mind tap. In addition to training him to access his own higher self and thus raise the quality (frequency vibrational rate) of his subconscious mind, he was instructed to heal Maria's soul.

Maria was on the astral plane and was a troubled spirit. Her traumatic death was still unsettling. That is why she communicated with her father through his dreams, but she was causing nightmares as a result of this contact. A recently departed soul will often communicate this way with those they felt closest to when they were on the earth plane (for a detailed description of the plane concept, see Chapter 24). In Maria's case she felt closest to her father, Lloyd.

By sending out a white light, loving energy to Maria, Lloyd enabled her to stabilize her feelings and finally enter the white light. This path would take Maria to the soul plane where she would choose her next life. In addition, Lloyd was able to see a future life during which he was a scholar and Maria reincarnated as his granddaughter.

Although this resolved Lloyd's bereavement issue, it should be pointed out that he could still contact Maria's soul if he desired. A remnant of the soul's energy would be available for communication during a superconscious mind tap, even though her soul proper resided on the soul plane, preparing for its next lifetime. This type of "seance" is healing as well as informative

Alice's case is most intriguing as it deals with bereavement, an "angelic" experience, and a surprise soul contact. This thirty-five-year-old, highly successful businesswoman had exhibited bereavement over her late father for the past five years.

Her father left her mother shortly after her birth, and Alice blamed herself for her father's abandonment of the family. Since she was the youngest of fifteen children, this guilt exhibited itself as a lifelong depression.

When her father died five years ago, the bereavement served to compound her depression. Alice now thought that she could never find out the real reason for his departure. On December 2, 1994, Alice saw my interview on NBC's daytime talk show "The Other Side." During my appearance, I guided the entire studio audience into the future of this life (age progression), a future lifetime (future life progression), and a superconscious mind tap. I discussed how anyone could contact the soul of a lost loved one through the latter technique.

Alice was a motivated and excellent patient. During the superconscious mind tap, she was able to contact the soul of her late father. His spirit informed her that he left the family solely because he could not provide for them, as he was disabled and could not work. His departure had nothing to do with Alice's birth.

A most interesting and unexpected event happened while Alice was contacting her higher self during this session. The spirit of her husband's late sister came through and informed Alice that she had died as a young child, so her parents could have two additional children.

As Alice came to my Los Angeles office from out of state, these sessions were held daily. She quickly overcame her bereavement issue concerning her late father and felt better in general. The morning of the last session was quite strange. Alice reported what many call an "angelic" experience on her way to my office. (I will more fully discuss encounters and healing with "angels" in Chapter 15.)

While Alice was driving to my office from her hotel, she was about to miss her turn. Suddenly, two cars coming from different directions nearly hit her. They were not driving very fast and Alice swerved her rental car to avoid them. When she looked back to note their location, they had disappeared from sight. It was quite impossible for them to turn off since there were no driveways or intersections for them to enter. These two cars literally disappeared into thin air. Alice then got her bearings and was able to make it to my office on time, safe and sound—quite confused, but safe nonetheless.

Miryana's case is significant in another way. She lost her grandfather, a dentist whom everyone in the family called Dr. John, when she was six years old. At that age, children don't quite understand the concept of death. Miryana was saddened and she greatly missed Dr. John.

This melancholy state persisted through most of her life. When she came to my office (she had seen me on the 11:00 news on her CBS affiliate on May 17, 1994, following the airing of my television movie "Search for Grace"), she wanted to access her higher self. The news segment showed one of my patients going through a superconscious mind tap as part of the interview.

Miryana contacted Dr. John. He informed her that the reason he died when he did was that it was his time to go. He told Miryana that he had learned all he could spiritually as Dr. John, and it was simply time to move on.

Words cannot express the look on my patient's face following this session. She cried, laughed, and felt better than she had in years. Dr. John was the one primarily responsible for Miryana's soul healing. This is most unusual, because generally it is the patient who tries to calm down the departed soul and guide them toward the white light.

Dr. John must have been quite a man. I only regret that I personally didn't have the pleasure of meeting him when he was alive. Lastly, Dr. John did comment on the fact that I was a dentist (I retired from dentistry at a rather young age in 1989), and he felt comfortable with my presence during the sessions.

Angie was a recent patient who lost her husband Jim to a heart attack two years ago. They had a great marriage but were only together for fifteen months. This was Angie's second marriage. She had divorced her first husband after seventeen years of wedlock. That first marriage was one of convenience.

When I worked with Angie, the problem was bereavement over Jim's death. She was angry at the fact that she stayed with her first husband for seventeen years in what she described as a loveless relationship. When she finally meets her "soulmate," he dies in only fifteen short months.

I guided Angie into a past life to see if there was a karmic tie with Jim. In a Dutch past life in the early 1800s, she was married to Jim. Jim's name was Erik, and he ran a small farm. They were very happy. After only one year of wedded bliss Angie, then named Johanna, was about to deliver her first child. Unfortunately, she died during childbirth.

When I guided Angie to the superconscious, she was able to survey that past life. Angie did contact Jim's spirit and he reaffirmed his love for her. He told her that it was his time to go, that he would share a future life with Angie, and at that time they would spend many years of love and happiness together.

After two sessions, Angie was satisfied. She overcame her bereavement and thanked me for my efforts with tears of joy running down her face. She was not interested in exploring a future life with Jim. When I asked her why not, she responded, "Jim was always a man of his word. If he says we are going to be together in 300 years, that is good enough for me."

That answer, along with the spiritual growth and soul healing exhibited by Angie, was "good enough for me" as well.

Joy's history was most unusual for a bereavement case. She was a twenty-six-year-old teacher when I worked with her. Three years earlier, her fiancé Michael was killed while piloting a small plane.

To add to this heartbreak, Joy broke up with him just prior to the fatal crash, because she had discovered that Michael had had an affair with her "best friend." Joy felt guilty over possibly being responsible for his compromised mental state during his flight. She also missed him, and became very depressed.

During her superconscious mind tap, Joy contacted Michael's soul. He assured her that she was not in any way responsible for his death. He confessed that he really wasn't ready for marriage and would have broken up with Joy anyway. Just prior to his flight, Michael informed Joy that he'd had too much to drink and was in no condition to fly.

Thus, it was Michael's irresponsibility that led to his death. He drank that day not to get over losing Joy, but because he had a drinking problem long before he had ever met her.

A combination of events, data, and the experience of tapping into her higher self had helped Joy overcome her bereavement and go on with her life.

The superconscious mind tap helps to quickly resolve bereavement issues by:

1. Training the patient to raise the quality of their own subconscious mind's frequency vibrational rate.
2. Contacting and communicating with lost loved ones.
3. Overviewing past and future lives with that loved one.
4. Finding out exactly why the loved one chose that time and method of dying (crossing into spirit).

Age progression greatly adds to the patient's empowerment by allowing them to scan the five frequencies (options) and select their ideal path for themselves. Lastly, future life progression gives the patient an opportunity to perceive being together again with their lost loved one in a future lifetime. This not only helps them overcome their bereavement, but removes any fear of death, thereby fostering their belief in God and the beauty of the universe. As Lao-Tse, the sixth century B.C. Chinese philosopher, so elegantly put it, "Death is not an end and birth is not a beginning."

14

THE HEALINGS OF EDGAR CAYCE

Born on a farm near Hopkinsville, Kentucky, on March 18, 1877, Edgar Cayce never enjoyed the benefits of a formal education. He was to spend most of his years in Virginia Beach, Virginia, which under ordinary circumstances would have made for an insular life without significance in the larger scheme of things, but Edgar Cayce was one of the world's most influential and best-known psychics and soul healers, possessing the remarkable innate ability while he was in a hypnotic trance to medically diagnose individuals he had never even met. This startling achievement was but the preamble to an even more profound gift: Cayce would follow each diagnosis with a proposed course of treatment which proved to be correct in ninety-nine per cent of the cases brought before him. A representative case could begin with something as simple as Cayce's receipt of a letter from an unknown patient. Knowing only the patient's name, Cayce was able to discern both the correct diagnosis and treatment strategy, despite having no knowledge whatsoever of the precepts of modern medicine. (There is some irony in the fact that Cayce resisted the concept of reincarnation almost until the end of his life.)

Cayce's remarkable achievements were scrutinized in a research paper compiled in 1910 by Wesley Ketchum, a young physician who forwarded his work to a Boston research society for publication. The story was picked up by *The New York Times*, which carried it on October 9 of the same year. Like a spreading flame, news of Cayce's achievements opened the floodgates, as sick and suffering people across the country inundated him with pleas for help. Ketchum made the observation that

> Cayce's subconscious is in direct communication with all other subconscious minds, and is capable of interpreting through his objective mind and imparting impressions received to other objective minds, gathering in this way all knowledge possessed by endless millions of other subconscious minds.

Edgar Cayce understood healing as a unifying process that balanced and merged the physical and mental realms with the world of the spirit, and it was Cayce's unique gift that he was peculiarly attuned to this balance and could perceive the oneness of soul and body at the elemental level. The soul in its natural state rests completely in its oneness with God and with the universe. By this standard, all of us fall short of wholeness and stand in need of healing.

Achieving wholeness by way of holistic healing involves a sequence of balanced, integrated, and carefully timed "applications toward wholeness" which embrace the physical, mental, and spiritual realms. A healing sequence was composed of deliberately articulated steps that ran *ad seriatum,* the timing of each step embodying in itself a critical element of balance and its restoration. For example, Cayce would often instruct the patient to discontinue a given application after a narrowly defined interval (e.g., three weeks), whereupon a new application was substituted for the old with an equally well-defined terminus. The nature, intent, and significance of these time-sequential application patterns bespeak the potency of temporal structuring, and as such deserve our serious attention, for holistic approaches to healing can ill afford to omit considerations of timing and sequence in light of such overpowering evidence in their favor.

It was Cayce's contention that a spiritual approach to healing requires more than the acknowledgement that the Source of all healing is God—in the sense that a river needs not only a source from which to spring, but a channel in which to travel. For Cayce, this meant recognizing that all healing comes *through* the Spirit from within our own being—thus completing the picture by pointing out the necessary dynamic that undergirds the holistic approach to healing. Thus conceived, healing is seen not as the result of external application or medical manipulation, but rather of "attuning" to the Spirit within (superconscious mind), through which healing can finally flow. This concept can be independently deduced by considering the two motives driving the desire for healing: the will to *change* patterns that incur illness, and the will to *better serve* God and others. As our desires, purposes, and ideals approach oneness with the Spirit, they likewise become a channel for the flow of the Spirit, which invariably initiates spiritual healing as a natural consequence of such "attuning."

The time-honored and ancient practice of laying-on-of-hands is commended by the readings, which rank it among the other applications and regulate it accordingly (e.g., by governing application durations to maximize the quickening and attuning process). In like manner, music, said to "span the space between the finite and the infinite" (2156–1 [see note re: reference codes, p. 148]), must necessarily form an integral part of any well-ordered holistic approach to healing. The vast richness and depth of music's healing effects have yet to be rediscovered in our century; the same can with justice be predicated of the human voice.

A dominant refrain in the readings is the recognition of the power of suggestion. Hypnosis and self-hypnosis are somewhat less frequently recommended to quicken and focus the healing process, but remain a nonetheless important part of the holistic arsenal. [N.b. When conducting a hypnotherapy session in my office, I employ metaphysical music to weave a background fabric of sonic embroidery calculated to relax my patients, enabling them to more readily achieve contact with their superconscious mind. The results are so impressive that I've made such music a principal part of the cassette tapes provided to my patients.]

Osteopathy is affirmed to be the proper basis of all physical healing according to the readings. The core tenet of osteopathy is the notion that normal bodily function stems from a pattern and force arising from within the body. Osteopathy does not limit its attention merely to the spine and its adjustment, but regards the circulatory system as equally important, inasmuch as blood distributes nutrients and oxygen to the cells while removing toxins and waste products—the key to optimal cellular function.

The Edgar Cayce readings evince a concern with thorough as opposed to superficial healing. A revealing exchange between patient and healer underscores this emphasis. When promised a complete cure, the patient asked how much longer it would take to finally realize total health and wholeness. The perceptive reply rings out, "if it's a day or a year, what's the difference if it's accomplished?" (281–5). Impatience is inimical to the healing process. In fact, the idea that applications are to be performed with "persistency and consistency" dominates the physical readings, so frequently do these terms appear.

It follows that where patience goes undeveloped, soul growth and true healing are precluded. No condition is too severe to be healed, provided our will is made one with our internal *pattern of wholeness.*

The Edgar Cayce readings document the precise physical effects that the patient's attitudes can impose on their body.

> To be sure, attitudes often influence the physical conditions of the body. No one can hate his neighbor and not have stomach and liver trouble. No one can be jealous and allow anger of same and not have upset digestion or heart disorder (4021–1).

Cayce's own telling of the origin of his gift of soul healing merits our attention:

> All healing comes from the divine within, that is creative. Thus, if one would correct physical or mental disturbances, it is necessary to change the attitude and to let the life forces become constructive and not destructive. Hate, malice, and jealousy only create poisons within the minds, souls, and bodies of people (3312–1).
>
> There is much more to be obtained from the right mental attitude respecting circumstance of either physical, mental, or spiritual than by the use of properties, things or conditions outside of self, unless these are in accord with the attitudes of the body (5211–1).

The readings bear witness that fear lies at the root of the majority of humankind's ills.

> ... fill the mental, spiritual being, with that which wholly casts out fear; that is, as the love that is manifest in the world through Him who gave Himself the ransom for many. Such love, such faith, such understanding, casts out fear. Be ye not fearful; for that thou sowest, that thou must reap. Be more mindful of that sown! (5459–3).

The readings clearly propound the idea that all subconscious minds are in mutual contact one with another. Dreams, working through the subconscious, are able to bring us into a perceptive alignment with those in either the physical or spiritual planes. We may find ourselves the objects of night visitations by a host of incorporeal entities for any number of reasons: they may come to us intending to assure, to inform, or to influence—and it falls to us to discern how useful or beneficial their input actually is. Some cases are self-validating, such as the recorded dream reports of deceased relatives instructing their heirs concerning the whereabouts of lost objects, such as a will.

Events experienced in the third dimension should be conceived as a "past condition," because the conventional spatial universe is a projection or correlative of what is actually being built at an altogether higher level of existence. Consequently, tuning in to the higher levels, as dreaming can enable us to do, awakens us to the more profound, underlying reality of what is actually being built, and can alert us to what may soon be projected into the physical realm in the future. *Every important occurrence in our lives is foreshadowed in our dreams.* This assertion should not become burdened with unwarranted extrapolations, however, for it is nowhere asserted that all dreams are precognitive, nor that present events are prefigured in precise detail in the minutiae of one's dreams. "Foreshadowing" works at a deeper level, providing a cognitive framework for recognizing the spiritual things we are presently building that may pass into three-dimensional reality in the future—in short, we possess a built-in early warning system. Such dreams are more aptly termed "procognitive" or "prophetic." In contrast, dreams focusing on the physical body and its symptomology are characterized as "prodromal."

Parallels between Cayce's soul healing approach and my process (see Chapter 4) can be multiplied, particularly as concerns the conceptual foundations of both systems. Note, for example, Cayce's allusion to the superconscious mind: "The Spirit of Forces as come from those on high, speak as often ... as such forces did of old" (294–34). That his conception clearly antedates modern theory makes the parallel all the more significant—a common archetype must underlie these respective models.

Cayce draws important distinctions between praying *for* another, versus praying (and meditating) *to* another. In the one case, we seek to suffuse an individual with light, bidding the influences about him to be reconfigured in harmony with that light; in the other, we seek to redirect the energy originating and arising from an individual or entity, usually with the intent to effect a healing. There are those who recoil at this distinction, thinking that it impugns the efficacy of their prayers, or vitiates their legitimacy if unsolicited by their object. These fears are unfounded, and are not corollaries of the distinction made above—for which reason a careful exposition of the truth is warranted.

We may use prayer to cast a protective hedge around anyone and everyone; such prayers may be highly potent indeed, and of immeasurable help to their object. Conversely, prayer and meditation for another (e.g., a prayer for healing) should never be offered in the absence of a direct solicitation—in other words, the individual who is the proposed object of prayer *must request such healing*. Healing requires total unity of purpose between the person praying and the person being prayed for, lest prayer be offered at cross-purposes and healing rendered void. Clearly, if a smoker suffers from emphysema, prayer offered on his behalf to alleviate his breathing pathology while he remains unwilling to change his habits would not be fully lawful. An unsolicited prayer for protection might help the smoker to better resist the influence of advertisements, but the impetus to abandon smoking altogether must arise from within the individual, not without.

Every individual possesses an internal source of energy from the indwelling spirit of life, as well as an innate pattern defining the standard of perfect functionality. Recall that the basic law of spiritual healing maintains that all healing comes from the Spirit working within and through the individual. Evidently, prayers provide a more coherent, higher signal through which healing is sympathetically effected by the spirit. This signal may quicken—resuscitate—both the life-pattern and impetus toward wholeness that dwell within the individual. Once the life-pattern is revivified by prayer and energized by the spirit flowing through the recipient of prayer, the indwelling power is sufficient to effect a healing, which may in fact follow. When someone desires change and asks for our help, prayer and meditation can become invincible, and should rank first among the weapons we choose to battle illness and infirmity.

The readings propose that physical healing is premised on the proper balancing of the rotary forces of the atom. Once balance is achieved, our atoms are healthy. From healthy atoms arise healthy molecules, healthy cells, healthy tissues, healthy organs, and a physical system that is properly constituted from its most elemental components as an integrated whole. Although counterintuitive from the narrow standpoint of modern physics, this holistic formulation properly recognizes the unity of nature, whereas the physicists' limited instrumentation breaks down at these ultrasmall scales, forcing them to advance an "argument from silence." We might charitably add that this "silence" is inadvertently self-inflicted—and stems from the de-emphasis of a holistic worldview.

The readings further indicate that the human body is naturally predisposed to heal and renew itself. Each and every organ has its own cyclical timetable for self-renewal; when these overlapping cycles are composited together for the body as a whole, we discover that the body renews itself entirely in a seven-year cycle. This important fact points up the critical significance of the phrase, "consistently and persistently," for treatment pursued in such a manner, if applied in cognizance of this seven-year cycle, may result in a thorough healing as a consequence of the renewal process transpiring in conjunction with the treatment.

The element of empowerment that forms a subtheme winding throughout Cayce's text deserves separate attention. Consider the following:

> Turn within. ... For, remember, thy body is the temple; there He has promised to meet thee. Therefore ye may commune with Him—NOT outside! That from the outside must answer to that within. What is thy relationship to Him? (2067–6).

Much of Cayce's work anticipated the future, serving as a premonition of things to come, for he was aware that somatic illness often originated in the mind as the result of emotional frustrations, resentments, and anger. It was not unusual, therefore, for him to counsel one woman to cleanse herself physically and mentally. "Keep the mental in the attitude of constructive forces. See in every individual that which is hopeful, helpful. Do not look for others' faults, but rather for their virtues, and the virtues in self will become magnified. For what we think upon, that we become."

Cayce was humble, a religious, God-fearing man who read the Bible daily throughout his life. He never turned anyone away, even though conducting more than two readings a day imposed considerable strain upon him. Moreover, he never conducted a health reading unless expressly requested, and he never made treatment contingent upon an individual's ability to pay. Far from being an intimidating presence, Cayce set everyone at ease who came to see him.

When Cayce's recommendations were diligently followed, his record as a healer was virtually infallible. Ironically, his advice was frequently disdained or ignored, sometimes because of unwillingness to invest the necessary time and effort to fulfill Cayce's prescriptions, and sometimes because the patient's search for a therapist to implement the treatment came up empty.

Dr. William O. McGarey, a respected M.D., also devoted study to Cayce's achievements. He stated:

> One striking concept has come out of the Cayce health readings, the concept that each cell has a consciousness of its own. Apparently, Cayce was able to identify clairvoyantly with the consciousness of

these cells, to look at every gland, organ, blood vessel, nerve, and tissue from inside the body. His unconscious seemed to communicate with the autonomic nervous system, traveling through the sympathetic and parasympathetic systems, which it controlled, into each and every cell.

Throughout his life, Cayce was plagued by self-doubt concerning his work. He abandoned his psychic mission and returned to the field of professional photography several times. His wife, Gertrude, gently prodded him to use his gifts, and not to shirk his metaphysical calling. Gertrude was herself a beneficiary of Cayce's healing powers, as was the couple's son, Hugh Lynn. Her husband's gift was not a mere abstraction, for she had felt its power firsthand. The story bears retelling here.

Gertrude's lungs were often struck by episodes of spasmodic hemorrhaging. Her doctors warned her that the next hemorrhage would be her last, for she would not survive it. Cayce naturally intervened, conducting the first reading he'd ever done for a member of his own family. In trance, he prescribed a preparation to permanently stanch the hemorrhaging in his wife's lungs. A specialist who sat in at the reading, while impressed, remained pessimistic. The apothecaries were doubtful that the prescription would even compound. It did, and Gertrude responded to the treatment immediately. The hemorrhages never returned. While she convalesced, Cayce instructed her to inhale from an empty cask of apple brandy, providing additional soothing relief. Gertrude's recovery was several months long, but her lungs thereafter remained healthy.

As a child, Hugh Lynn suffered a serious eye injury. He had been playing with his father's flashlight kit when some of the powder suddenly flared up into his eyes. The doctors' prognosis was poor: the boy's eyesight might never be restored. They recommended surgery, maintaining that one eye had to be removed entirely. Cayce refused to permit them to proceed without first conducting a reading for his injured son.

Gertrude supervised the reading as Cayce spoke from his sleep. "Keep the boy in a completely darkened room for fifteen days, keep dressings soaked in strong tannic acid solutions on his eyes, frequently changing same. Thus will the sight be saved and restored." This prescription alarmed the doctors, who objected that the proposed salve would damage the boy's delicate eye tissues beyond salvaging (notwithstanding the fact that they had already dismissed the case as hopeless). They eventually complied with Cayce's instructions. When the final dressings were removed from Hugh Lynn's eyes twelve days later, sight had been completely restored. Both eyes were clear and bright. This was the sign Cayce had been searching for. From this point forward, he would devote himself to his soul healing without turning back.

At the outset, Cayce scheduled two readings a day, at 10 A.M. and 2 P.M., charging nothing for his efforts. After each reading, he awoke refreshed and hungry. Although he was clearly burning up considerable energy in the process, he suffered no symptoms of depletion or fatigue.

Cayce was approached by C. H. Dietrich in the summer of 1902. Dietrich, the Hopkinsville school superintendent, petitioned Cayce to help his five-year-old daughter, Aime, who had suffered severe retardation from an illness that struck her when she was just two years old. At this juncture, Cayce had not yet become aware of his power to perform a physical reading at a distance. Accordingly, he traveled to Hopkinsville on a weekend, seeking out the Dietrich family. Once in a trance, Cayce intoned, "The trouble is in the spine." The details came as a shock to Dietrich. "A few days before her illness, the child slipped getting out of a carriage and struck the base of her spine on the carriage step. This injury weakened the area, and led to the mental condition." Dietrich was ambivalent about Cayce's diagnosis, but was struck by the fact that Cayce had put his finger on an almost forgotten incident in the child's life, one dismissed at the time as inconsequential. How could Cayce have known about the fall from the carriage?

Some of Aime's vertebrae were indeed out of alignment, causing subluxation pressures on nerves. Layne, an osteopath, realigned the vertebrae that Cayce had pinpointed. Three adjustments performed in the span of five days greatly improved the young girl's condition. In a matter of months, she had enrolled in school with classmates her own age, completely cured of her retardation. Dietrich's gratitude toward Cayce was inexhaustible. His heartfelt testimonials reached Dr. Wesley H. Ketchum, who came to employ Cayce as a psychic diagnostician, eventually to steer him into a professional career that would fill the rest of Cayce's life.

When George Dalton, a wealthy contractor, shattered his leg in a fall, an entourage of doctors, including Ketchum, were called in for consultation. Conventional medicine, represented by five veteran physicians from the South, advised conventional splinting while remaining pessimistic of the outcome. Ketchum had never treated a compound fracture before, and in those days treatment was often administered at home or at the doctor's office—there were no hospitals. He consulted Cayce, who suggested a treatment quite radical for its time: boring a hole in the kneecap, nailing the bones back together, followed by immobilizing the leg in traction.

Ketchum's misgivings were understandable. Nothing of the kind had ever been tried, so far as he knew. "They used splints then," he recalled, "but metal screws were still in the future. However, I went down to the nearest blacksmith, and he made up an iron nail like a large roofing nail, with a big head on it." With another doctor and two nurses assisting, Ketchum bored through Dalton's patella and nailed it. The leg was placed in traction, with a pulley attached to the footboard of the bed.

During the following month, Dalton's leg healed rapidly. The nails remained in his leg until his death thirty years later. Such successes spurred further critical scrutiny of Cayce and his achievements. Cayce was continually tested by scores of doctors. Some had pricked him with pins while he was asleep to test whether or not he was faking. Others dedicated themselves to overthrowing Cayce as a fraud, hoping to expose his treatments as a ridiculous hoax. On one occasion, a committee of doctors thought they had the goods on Cayce. The case against the soul healer seemed airtight. Specialists had declared that a woman suffering from internal bleeding and abdominal pains required immediate surgery, whereas Cayce said her problem stemmed from an abrasion of her stomach wall, curable with a regimen of long daily walks and ingestion of a raw lemon sprinkled with salt. Cayce's pronouncements were so patently absurd that the doctors decided to exploit the situation in order to expose Cayce. They withheld the surgery they regarded as essential for the woman's survival, and waited for Cayce to take the fall. Three weeks later, the woman was hiking ten miles a day, unhampered by any abdominal symptoms whatever. She had been completely cured under Cayce's unorthodox regimen.

Ketchum brought Cayce to a banquet attended by lawyers from Kentucky, Tennessee, and Indiana. The guest of honor was the Attorney General of Kentucky. The occasion proved to be an excellent venue to showcase Cayce's power of universal knowledge. Several lawyers submitted written questions to Cayce that would clearly have been beyond his ken, i.e., questions requiring highly intimate knowledge of the questioner's personal life to properly answer. Again and again, Cayce shocked them with his detailed insights into their private lives. Each astonished countenance bore compounded witness to Cayce's accuracy.

Harold J. Reilly was a New York physiotherapist who often received prescriptions from people who had treatments prescribed by Cayce. Reilly's curiosity was piqued as the procession of Cayce's patients showed no signs of abating. He was struck by the fact that these patients invariably improved—that "Doctor" Cayce's competence as a medical professional was quite extraordinary. Regardless of the condition for which his prescriptions were intended, including bursitis, arthritis, nervous tension, and asthma, the end result was always the same. Cayce's patients were restored whole.

His curiosity getting the better of him, Reilly finally contacted one of Cayce's patients to question him. The patient shook his head, explaining that he had never even seen the "doctor." Reilly was incredulous, staring at the man in disbelief. The patient continued, "My wife sent in a request that he read for me, saying what was wrong. We had been to all kinds of doctors and they hadn't helped."

Reilly recognized that, his vast personal experience notwithstanding, he could not improve on any of Cayce's suggested therapies or treatments. The fact that Cayce could acquire the kind of medical information he did while in a trance was simply incredible. Even after two years of filling countless prescriptions for Cayce's patients, Reilly was unable to deduce the methodology of the man behind this steady flow of pharmaceutical business. He shared with his friends his consternation that "a man can go to sleep and give as good, or better, advice than I can, wide awake, in my own special field."

Cayce treated arthritis by prescribing warm pack treatments, castor oil being the dominant convection agent. An eight-inch-wide swatch of flannel was soaked in the warmed oil and then placed over the gall bladder, liver, or kidneys, as determined by Cayce's diagnosis. Lumbago called for the application of hot Epsom salt packs across the hips and back. Cayce sometimes augmented this treatment by calling for packs of Glyco-Thymoline, a therapy little known prior to Cayce's advocacy. Glyco-Thymoline served to increase stimulation through the skin, which shifted some of the organismic burden away from the kidneys, destressing them in the process.

The readings also recommended fume baths and occasional friction rubs. Fume baths served to both open up the pores and to tone up elimination within the respiratory system. Reilly settled on four candidates for fume baths which he felt provided the most soothing vapors: balsam, eucalyptus, pine, and Atomidine.

Fume bath formulations were tailored to individual malfunctions, but Reilly's general pattern was to decant one-half to one teaspoonful of the solution or oil in one to two quarts of steaming water. "If the person is not able to go to an institution for a fume bath, it is quite simple to fix one for himself." His instructions were straightforward.

> Sew together four blankets, or take a large piece of canvas and sew it together with an opening for the head, and an overlap at this opening—flexible, non-flammable plastic might be better. Next, take a stool and place it over an electric stove with a steaming pot on it. Fold towels on the seat of the stool and hang a towel in front of the stool to protect legs from the heat. The hotter the water, the more quickly the steaming takes effect. Then sit on the stool, wrap the covering close across shoulders and fasten it around the neck, after, of course, removing the clothing. A person with a cold can clear nasal or bronchial congestion, by leaving a small opening in the front where he can put his head down to inhale, closing off the opening when the inhalation becomes too strong."

Cayce's arthritis treatment consisted of four basic components: improvement of circulation by means of baths and salt pack applications; specific, localized massage using certain oils and resinous extracts such as myrrh and peanut oil; the adjustment of diet to alter the body's chemical balance and inhibit the intake of certain minerals; and osteopathic manipulation of the third cervical, ninth dorsal, and fourth lumbar vertebrae, the three regions most often mentioned in the readings. This four-pronged strategy alludes to the systemic range of Cayce's integrated approach to healing.

Reilly informs us that "Cayce specifically mentioned a yoga breathing exercise, the alternate breathing." The patient does this exercise with a closed mouth. Sealing the right nostril with the thumb, the patient inhales through the left nostril for a count of four, then retains the breath for a count of eight. Now sealing the left nostril with the thumb, the patient slowly exhales through the right nostril for another eight count. The next breath is drawn through the now-open right nostril in mirror symmetry with the first sequence, the full cycle generally being repeated three or four times as prescribed.

The role that massage played in Cayce's therapies merits separate attention. Cayce's frequent prescriptions of massage therapy with nourishing oils seem almost prophetic when viewed from the tail end of the twentieth century. Massage (as supportive therapy) forms a significant part of current medical treatment for multiple sclerosis. The opinion of the doctors concerning massage is telling in this respect. "It certainly helps to maintain the tone of muscles which have lost their normal innervation [active nerve network], the advantage being that when and if function returns, the muscle will not have atrophied and shortened."

Yet, modern medicine and Cayce are light years apart in their conception of the function of the oils. Contemporary medicine recognizes little more than a lubricating effect imparted by the oils, while Cayce insisted that the oils actually nourished weakened tissue. Cayce's view was reinforced by both his own patients' healings, and by Hotten in California, McGarey in Arizona, and Reilly in New York. The weight of the testimonial evidence favoring Cayce's perspective has gone essentially unrefuted, to the extent the record hasn't been ignored outright.

Oils were compounded in one of two basic blends, according to Reilly. "The simple mixture was usually a combination of equal parts of olive oil and peanut oil plus melted lanolin in the ratio: two ounces of olive oil, two ounces of peanut oil, one-quarter ounce of lanolin. The complex mixture had an olive oil base plus peanut oil, various combinations of Russian white oil, oil of cedarwood, oil of sassafras root, oil of pine needles, lanolin, oil of wintergreen, tincture of bensoin, tincture of myrrh, spirits of camphor, spirits of turpentine, mutton suet and/or oil of mustard."

The directions for preparation often varied. "In the majority of cases, it was suggested to massage from the spine to the distal [farthest] portions of the extremities, but in some from the tips of the extremities to the spine. Although the spine and extremities were mentioned most, the chest and abdomen were also suggested. A circular motion for the massage was recommended."

Cayce once advocated that people test themselves with litmus paper. If the litmus paper turned blue, all was well. If it turned pink, they had an acid condition, generally a harbinger of an imminent cold. It was Cayce's contention that "a body is more susceptible to a cold with an excess of acidity. An alkalizing effect is destructive to the cold germ. An extra depletion of the vital energies produces a tendency for excess acidity. At such periods, if an individual comes in contact with one sneezing or suffering with cold, it is more easily contracted."

The mechanisms by which colds invade the body were a continuing object of Cayce's explorations. Cayce separately considered drafts, sudden temperature shifts, unusual changes in clothing, and wet feet as either vectors in themselves, or enabling agents for other vectors. "All of these affect the circulation by the depletion of the body-balance, body temperature, or body-equilibrium. Then if the body is tired, worn, overacid—or more rarely, overalkaline—it is more susceptible to a cold, as, too, from being in a warm room, overheated. When overheated there is less oxygen, which weakens the circulation of the life-giving forces that are destructive to any germ or contagion."

Cayce regarded no ailment as incurable, so long as the patient was ready to be healed and the therapist was knowledgeable. Cayce, familiar with incurable migraine headaches, differed with the medical establishment as to their cause. The majority opinion was that migraines were the result of a nervous, tense disposition, but Cayce saw migraines as a symptom of an altogether deeper dysfunction, which Cayce's treatment for migraine makes clear.

> Most migraine headaches begin from congestions in the colon. These poisons cause toxic conditions which make pressures on the sympathetic nerve centers and on the cerebrospinal system, and these pressures cause the violent headaches, and almost irrational activities at times.
>
> These should respond to colonic irrigations. But first, we would x-ray the colon, and we will find areas in the ascending colon and a portion of the transverse colon where there are fecal forces that are as cakes.
>
> There will be required several full colonic irrigations, using salt and soda as purifiers for the colon; and we will find that these conditions will be released. The first cleansing solution should have two level teaspoonfuls of salt and one level teaspoonful of soda to the gallon of water, body-temperature. Also in the rinse-water, body temperature, have at least two tablespoonfuls of Glyco-Thymoline to the quart and a half of water (3400–2).

Cayce was not averse to employing radiation against illness, recommending the use of a radioactive appliance in conjunction with an hour of meditation designated for self-analysis. "Keep the attachment plates very clean, polishing them with the emery paper each time before attaching to the ankle and the wrist, and polishing them each time when taking them off."

Osteopathy occupied a significant place in Cayce's unique suite of therapeutic approaches. He often prescribed adjustments to relax the neck area, and recommended corrective manipulation of the sixth dorsal in the midback, and the lumbar axis of the lower back. Said Cayce, "Do these and we should bring help for this body."

Headaches accompanying menstrual cramps were also targeted for therapeutic relief by Cayce. His discussion includes an extended and illuminating discussion of the underlying mechanism he is attempting to redirect:

> These are part of the clogging that is a part of the general eliminating system. There are channels or outlets for the elimination of poisons, that is, used energies, where there is the effect of the activity of the circulation upon foreign forces taken in breath, taken in dust, taken in particles of food or those activities which come from such as these—from odors of the like. These all, by segregating of same in system, produce forces necessary to be eliminated. We eliminate principally through the activity of the lungs, of course, and the perspiratory system, the alimentary canal, and the kidneys. Then, as in the case of women, as here we find that such periods of the menstrual flow cause congestion in certain areas until the flow is begun, or until there is beginning of the let-up of same. This then, clogs some portions of the system. The headaches are the signs of warnings that eliminations are not being properly cared for. Most of this, in this body, comes from the alimentary canal and conditions that exist in portions of the colon itself, as to produce a pressure upon those centers affected from such periods. Hence the suggestion for the osteopathic corrections, which aid but which do not eliminate all of those conditions which are as accumulations through portions of the colon. Consequently, the colonic irrigations are necessary occasionally, as well as the general hydrotherapy and massage.

The greatest of the American psychics has not left posterity without an important witness for those following in his footsteps, whether researchers studying psychic development or individuals possessing in some measure the kind of gift Cayce had in superabundance. Once, while in trance, he revealed that the psychic force that traveled through his subconscious functioned through certain glands. "In the body we find that which connects the pineal, the pituitary, the Leydig: these may be truly called the silver cord." The force was more active in women, feeding the tempting conjecture that this disproportion arose as a natural consequence of their less highly developed conscious powers, which is counterbalanced by an enhanced subconscious development compared to men. The higher subconscious levels were accessible only when a spiritual outlook prevailed, an outlook unblemished by any focus on the material realm. Contemporary psychics with an appetite for notoriety would do well to heed Cayce's lesson. "One fed upon [that which is] the purely material will become a Frankenstein that is without any influence other than material or mental," he warned.

Cayce could not conceive of the psychic force as being unusual or out of the ordinary. He felt it was a natural component of the array of innate talents with which we are all born, being no more extraordinary than the powers man employed to make human flight a reality. He likened it to the inspiration for great works of art, poetry, and mathematics, and when so defined, the psychic force finds a fitting analogue in the impulsive insight at the core of the theory of relativity, a theory that Einstein recalls came to him "mystically."

Like other doctors who had studied the Cayce readings, Dr. McGarey was impressed with the results when he employed Cayce's approach with his own patients. McGarey was highly esteemed in the medical community, and operated a clinic with his wife, Gladys, who was also an M.D. McGarey was surprised by the efficacy of castor oil packs in treating assorted abdominal complaints such as stomach ulcers, appendicitis, colitis, and gall bladder conditions. Being classically trained, he was reticent to apply the packs unless conventional approaches had been tried and found wanting.

Many healing professionals have gone through Cayce's remedies with a fine-toothed comb, seeking therapeutically useful clues concerning his treatment of such mystifying ailments as arthritis and cancer. The Cayce files record a multitude of "cures" for arthritis, evidenced by testimonials filed years later by those whose arthritis went into remission. What is significant is Cayce's "broad front" approach to the disease. He understood clearly what modern medicine is just now coming to realize, that arthritis is the combined reaction of both body and mind to multiple wrongs and abuses.

Cayce was asked if his readings could possibly lead to cures of presently incurable diseases and conditions, and his response is a model of clear, consistent application of his thoroughly tested core principles.

> We find that all conditions existent in physical bodies are produced by that which may be met. There are in truth no incurable conditions. For each ailment is the result of the breaking of a law. Healing will of necessity come when there is compliance with other laws which meet the needs. No healing is perfected without some psychic force exerted. In regard to healing of any kind, the counteracting force, whether operative or medicinal, or self-producing, is nothing more nor less than the active force exerted in psychic force.

Well before the modern conception of cancer had been codified, Cayce had delineated the essential difference between benign and malignant growths. "Ulcer is rather that of flesh being proud or infectious, while cancer is that which lives upon the cellular force by the growth itself." Cayce felt that sarcoma "was caused by breaking of tissue internally which was not covered sufficiently by the leukocytes [germ-killing white corpuscles] due to the low vitality in the system." Cayce had occasion to wage battle against quite a few cancers in his career, having prescribed treatments for authenticated "cancer" cases directed to him by a host of doctors. Follow-through examinations conducted by the A.R.E. over the years showed that those treated by Cayce had enjoyed significantly improved health in the aftermath of psychic therapy.

In May of 1934, he gave an emergency reading for a ten-year-old girl admitted to Mount Sinai Hospital in New York. Cayce had not been briefed on any details of the girl's condition, and yet promptly announced that she was suffering from infantile paralysis. He elaborated further, focusing on the "wasting of those centers of bulb gland or plexus forces along the spine, attacking principally the locomotory centers." One component of the therapy he recommended involved a "transfusion from a body that has been cured or relieved of that known as infantile paralysis." Cayce was, in effect, advocating gamma globulin transfusion to bolster the girl's resistance to the infection. His recommendation is not exceptional in itself, until one considers that he made it decades before such techniques were ever developed and incorporated within modern medical praxis. Cayce seemed to be reaching well into medicine's future each time he articulated a new therapy.

It is understandable that even open-minded medical practitioners found Cayce's gifts baffling. His knowledge of human anatomy, disease, and drugs was encyclopedic in scope. He spoke with authority on dietary matters, often preparing detailed lists of meals for his subjects which were fine-tuned to the very last calorie, vitamin, and nutrient. He not only prescribed drugs, but often directed how they were to be compounded. His therapies were rarely limited to diet and drugs alone, often including massage, manipulation, and therapeutic baths. A fully documented report of one of his most extraordinary cases is a marvel of medical detail. The report is so analytically explicit as touching diagnosis and treatment that it would have taxed the capacity of even the most erudite physician to prepare—and yet, it was written by a man who had never progressed beyond grade school.

The work of Edgar Cayce is enjoying somewhat of a renaissance today, as more doctors are now studying his work than ever did when Cayce was alive. Given his track record, it is understandable that a growing contingent of physicians would be carefully scanning his work, looking for the key to unlock the mystery of the many diseases that have remained impervious to conventional research and treatment.

At the time of his death in 1945, Cayce had given more than 14,000 telepathic-clairvoyant readings. Of these, 2,500 were so-called "life readings" that traced the past lives of individuals, restoring a lost historical context in which to frame and understand the problems plaguing the individual at the present time. Fortunately, these discourses have been preserved for us and are on file at the library of the Association of Research and Enlightenment at Virginia Beach (A.R.E., Inc., P.O. Box 656, Virginia Beach, VA 23451). The A.R.E. was specifically chartered to preserve these Readings, the *raison d'être* for its founding in 1932. Being an open-membership research society, the A.R.E. has continued the massive task of collating and indexing the historical data, initiates investigations and empirical inquiries, promotes conferences, seminars, and lectures, and markets books and audiotapes concerning the achievements of Cayce and other soul healers.

Each reading in the A.R.E. library is carefully indexed, supplying the name of the stenographer, the individual conducting the session, and the names of all witnesses present at the reading. Additionally, each reading is supplemented by background information, if any, along with any extant follow-up correspondence with the patient, the patient's physician, and the patient's family. As a final note, I would highly recommend that you read the story of Edgar Cayce's life, as well as any other books corroborating the remarkable story of America's most famous psychic healer.

Do I dare to add that if you want to know what new insights will be published in the *New England Journal of Medicine* next year, read Edgar Cayce today? That's not so bold a claim as one may think at first blush, especially when one realizes that the odds and track record are still heavily weighted in Cayce's favor!

15

ANGELIC HEALING

A *TIME* magazine poll taken in 1993 suggests that most Americans believe in angels. Sixty-nine per cent stated that they believe in the existence of angels, while forty-six per cent believe they have their own guardian angel.

There have recently been many books written on experiences with angels. Various forms of soul healing most certainly occur during and following these events. Before I describe some clinical cases of such healings, a discussion of the theological views of angels would be appropriate.

Angels are universal. Sometimes they are referred to as *Kami* or *peri* or *fravashi.* They are always messengers, protectors, and guardians. These entities are beings, creatures as we are, but significantly different. Angels have their own society and values, hierarchy and activities. They have consciousness and will and purpose. They are organized to achieve goals and to grow in consciousness.

According to theologians, angels are not a society of glorified human beings. They do not represent the ultimate growth potential of the human spirit. Not a single human being has ever become or will become an angel. We humans and the angels are on parallel tracks as far as our respective development is concerned. Angels do not live in the same physical universe as we do. They enter through a type of doorway to make themselves known to us. They are pure spirit, as god is spirit, without any corporeality (physical body) at all. Angels do not have wings. They can be anywhere they want in an instant. An angel is going to appear to us in whatever way it believes is best suited for drawing our attention; such appearances are calculated to maximize our response to their message, spurring us to action. They communicate by telepathy.

According to Sophy Burnham, one of the foremost authorities on angels, angels "come as visions, dreams, coincidences, and intuition, the whisper of knowledge at your ear." "Sometimes a stranger may come up and give you just the information or assistance you need. Sometimes you yourself are used as an angel, for a moment, either knowingly or not, speaking words you did not know you knew."

Angelic society is an ordered one, characterized by cooperation and love. Angels are not affected personally by the pain and evil that still exist on earth. Their hierarchy consists in descending order of rank:

1. Seraphim, cherubim, and thrones—these act as a heavenly council and render worship around the throne of god.

2. Dominions, virtues, and powers—they govern the function of the cosmos.

3. Principalities, archangels, and angels—these act as guardians to humanity.

All angels worship God. Angels often come to earth on special missions to bring messages from God. Every person who has ever lived has had an angel watching over them. This is common to all religions. Angels do not disturb our free will. We can ignore them if we want to. The only creed an angel has is love.

There are four factors that determine whether we will have a face-to-face contact with our angels:

- Such contact must be part of God's plan.
- We must truly understand what angels are and do, as well as what they will not or cannot do.
- Our motives for wanting such an encounter must be pure.
- We must be prepared for an encounter.

Angels will use whatever medium is most likely to attract our attention. Very often they will utilize our dreams to help us.

Some key characteristics of angelic experiences include the following main points:

- Their message leaves us confident, never anxious.
- Angels don't try to force us to do anything.
- Angels don't leave us confused.
- Angelic messages are designed to give us freedom to choose.
- An angelic encounter leaves us changed for the better in some way.

If your encounter with an entity does not meet these criteria, then it is simply not an angelic experience. There are entities in the universe (troubled spirits) that attempt to influence us. Fortunately, white light protection techniques and superconscious mind taps can protect you from these negative and dysfunctional beings. Any being you can summon at will, with or without rituals, is probably not an angel. We must always test any kind of spiritual encounter. Angels have no message of their own. All of their communications emanate from God. Angels are created beings. They are servants, tutors, and guides. They never linger when they are on a mission.

The preceding information is the classic theological interpretation of angels. For many years I have stated that angels did not exist as separate entities, but rather were manifestations of one's superconscious mind (higher self) or masters or guides (entities who are not part of your energy or soul but who have perfected their soul and have chosen to help others rather than ascend to the higher planes). Kenneth Ring apparently agrees with my assessment as do many others. Ring states in *Life At Death* (p. 244):

> I am inclined to conclude, therefore, that the guardian angel interpretation, rather than constituting an alternative to the one based on the concept on the higher self, is actually an alternative manifestation of the latter.

AN ANGEL IN UNIFORM

Marissa was eighteen years old when she had an angelic intervention that saved her from a most traumatic experience. She was a virgin and a devout Christian. Marissa's best friend Carla was quite the opposite, and repeatedly tempted Marissa into "broadening her horizons" with sex and drugs. Carla slept around, smoked pot, and occasionally used cocaine. Marissa had never tried drugs and wouldn't even drink alcohol. The only reason Marissa associated with Carla was because Marissa had no other friends. One day Carla invited Marissa to a party at her home in Los Angeles. Carla's parents were in Palm Springs for the weekend, so they had the place to themselves.

When Marissa arrived she was shocked. In addition to the presence of over 150 people at the party (she had been told only a dozen or so were invited), there were drugs all over the place. People were smoking pot, popping pills, and even syringes were in use.

Todd and James were two of Carla's best friends. They quickly led Marissa to the den to show her something Carla had made for her. As Carla painted for a hobby, this was not a suspicious request.

While in the den, Todd and James tore Marissa's blouse off and announced they were going to rape her. Marissa froze and prayed for a moment. A loud knock at the front door changed everything. A man announced, "This is the police—open this door!" Marissa noted his name, badge number, and patrol car number, and then left the party. She did not file any charges against Todd or James.

A few days later Marissa called the precinct to express her gratitude to the officer. She was amazed to learn that the police had no record of an officer with his name. The patrol car number and badge number were not on their records either. Lastly, no official call was made or reported to Carla's house that night.

When Marissa told me of this incident four years later in my office, she asked me who this man could possibly be. I informed her that it was probably her "guardian angel." Today, Marissa is married and the proud mother of a baby boy. Yes, she did remain a virgin until her wedding night as she purposed. She also married a man of like qualities and they are both very happy.

This case illustrates a different type of healing. This form is preventative. Marissa's angel (or manifestation of her higher self or guide) saved her from a most physically, emotionally, and spiritually traumatic encounter. I do not doubt for one moment that she would have been severely compromised by the rape and other abuse Todd and James would have perpetrated upon her.

This experience has resulted in a further strengthening of Marissa's belief in God and in the power of faith.

THE HOLLYWOOD ANGEL

Since my practice is located in Woodland Hills, California (a suburb of Los Angeles), a certain percentage of my local patients remind me where I live by their experiences. Sam was a salesman living in Hollywood, California. His neighborhood was a rough one where crime was rampant and drug deals were consummated on local street corners and alleys.

It was Sam's habit to walk to a local convenience store to get cigarettes in the evening. Although he lived in this dangerous neighborhood for several years, Sam never had any problems with criminals. One fateful evening in September of 1994, he was approached by three would-be muggers on the way to his favorite convenience store. One of his potential assailants pulled out a knife and demanded Sam's wallet. The other laughed and told Sam that they were going to "hurt him badly."

The next thing he remembered was the appearance of a tall, thin man in his early thirties who stood between Sam and the muggers. The muggers looked at this stranger and stood motionless. Sam ran to freedom, but upon looking back toward the tall stranger, he was shocked. The stranger just disappeared into thin air while the muggers stood almost frozen.

To this day Sam still can't explain what happened. This "angel" clearly saved Sam's life. I call that the ultimate form of healing.

AN ANGEL ON THE FREEWAY

Most cities in America have highways. In California they are called freeways. There are so many accidents and deaths on California freeways that the CHP (California Highway Patrol) has trouble counting them. This is a case of one of my patients who almost became a statistic.

Eva came to my office in 1994 for a past life regression. She reported an incident that occurred three years ago that saved her life. It seemed that Eva was driving on a freeway in Los Angeles during a very heavy rain. As she was not a very skillful driver, she had problems steering and seeing through the downpour.

All of a sudden, Eva felt a force jerk the steering wheel to the left. She stopped the car and waited for the rain to stop. Eva was nervous and frightened. As soon as the rain stopped Eva opened the car door and checked out where she was positioned.

The guard rail was damaged and had the "force" not jerked the steering wheel Eva would have fallen over fifty feet to her death. Her angel had saved her life.

LINDBERGH'S ANGEL

Charles A. Lindbergh did not report his angelic encounter during his famous flight to Paris in his first book, *We, Pilot and Plane*, published in 1927. However, in his subsequent book, *The Spirit of St. Louis*, published in 1953, he did describe the following account:

> While I'm staring at the instruments, during an unearthly age of time, both conscious and asleep, the fuselage behind me becomes filled with ghostly presences—vaguely outlined forms, transparent, moving, riding weightless with me in the plane. I feel no surprise at their coming.... Without turning my head, I see them as clearly as though in my normal field of vision. There's no limit to my sight—my skull is one great eye, seeing everywhere at once.
>
> These phantoms speak with human voices—friendly, vapor-like shapes, without substance, able to vanish or appear at will, to pass in and out through the walls of the fuselage as though no walls were there. Now, many are crowded behind me. Now, only a few remain. First one and then another presses forward to my shoulder to speak above the engine's noise, and then draws back among the group behind. At times, voices come out of the air itself, clear yet far away, traveling through distances that can't be measured by the scale of human miles; familiar voices, conversing and advising on my flight, discussing problems of my navigation, reassuring me, giving me messages of importance unattainable in ordinary life.
>
> I'm on the border line of life and a greater realm beyond, as though caught in the field of gravitation between two planets, acted on by forces I can't control, forces too weak to be measured by any means at my command, yet representing powers incomparably stronger than I've ever known (pp. 389–390).

THE MONK AND THE PAINTER

When Joseph Aigner, who became a well-known portrait painter, was eighteen years old, he tried to hang himself but was prevented by the mysterious arrival of a Capuchin monk.

This took place in Vienna in 1836. Four years later in Budapest, Aigner again tried to hang himself and was again prevented by the sudden appearance of the same monk. Eight years went by and Aigner, who had espoused a revolutionary cause, was sentenced to the gallows for his political activities. He was reprieved, however, at the instigation of a monk—the same Capuchin. Was the Capuchin actually Joseph Aigner's "guardian angel"?

AN ANGEL CURES CANCER

This case was reported in *TIME* in their December 27, 1993, issue in an article titled *Angels Among Us*, written by Nancy Gibbs. Ann Cannady was diagnosed with uterine cancer. Her husband Gary had lost his first wife to this same disease and could not handle another loss. Ann prayed obsessively during the next two months. Three days before her scheduled surgery a very tall black man named Thomas rang her doorbell. Thomas told Ann that her cancer was gone. He quoted from Isaiah 53:5: "And with his stripes we are healed." Thomas also stated that he was sent by god to help Ann. As Nancy reports on page 60:

> Next, Ann recalls, "he held up his right hand, palm facing me, and leaned toward me, though he didn't touch me. I'm telling you, the heat coming from that hand was incredible. Suddenly I felt my legs go out from under me, and I fell to the floor. As I lay there, a strong white light, like one of those searchlights, traveled through my body. It started at my feet and worked its way up. I knew then, with every part of me—my body, my mind and my heart—that something supernatural had happened."

Ann tried to cancel her surgery, but her skeptical surgeon would only agree to perform another biopsy to mollify Ann before beginning the procedure. When the test came back negative, the surgery was canceled. There has been no recurrence of the cancer.

HOUDINI'S ANGEL

Harry Houdini (1874–1926) was the most famous magician the world has ever known. Even now, several decades following his death, Houdini's name is still instantly recognizable: it has become synonymous with mystery, illusion, and suspense.

Houdini (born Elrich Weisz in Pest, Hungary) was very close to his mother (Celia). She was the most important person in his life, and theirs was a model mother-son relationship.

On December 27, 1906, Houdini performed one of his most dangerous tricks. Wearing two sets of handcuffs, he jumped from a bridge in Detroit through a hole in the ice covering a frozen river. The trick consisted of escaping from the handcuffs and emerging through the hole to safety.

After three minutes the crowd surrounding the riverbanks saw no Houdini. After five minutes, the reporters declared him dead. Finally, eight minutes later, Houdini climbed out of the hole to the warmth and safety of blankets and hot coffee.

When asked how he survived, Houdini recounted an angelic experience. The river's current had swept him away from the hole. By the time he got his cuffs off, he was disoriented and couldn't find the opening. To further complicate matters, his body was freezing (hypothermia) and he knew he would drown. The secret of this trick was to use the pockets of air that were trapped between the river and the ice. Houdini's problem was that he lost his sense of direction and didn't know where to swim.

Suddenly, Houdini heard his mother's voice directing him to the hole. Keeping his breathing shallow, he swam toward the sound of his mother. He also felt his body warming up inexplicably, and he finally emerged from the hole eight minutes after his jump. The angel appeared in the form of Celia's voice to save the life of Harry Houdini.

An interesting medical note is that according to the *Merck Manual* (fifteenth edition) "if near-drowning takes place in very cold water, the victim may be hypothermic" (p. 2376). "As body temperature drops, the patient proceeds from fatigue, weakness, incoordination, apathy and drowsiness" (p. 2393).

The next two angelic experiences come from Sophy Burnham's book, *Angel Letters*.

AN ANGEL ON A TRAIN

In 1938, a sixteen-year-old boy named Charles was trying to return home. He had been traveling for over four months. Charles was in the railway yard in Hayti, Missouri, waiting to hitch a ride in a boxcar.

It was not wise to board this car while the train was still in the yards because the men who oversaw the loading of freight would forcibly eject and beat up potential "freeloaders."

Charles' plan was to jump onboard when the train began moving. As he began to execute his plan he ran into a problem. He only got halfway into the boxcar. His legs were dangling out the door with the upper half of his body lying flat on the boxcar floor.

Since there was nothing for Charles to hold onto, he was unable to pull himself completely into the boxcar. He knew that if he fell off he would be killed under the train's wheels.

Charles began to pray by saying, "O God, please don't let me die here." Suddenly, a large black man appeared and pulled Charles into the boxcar. When Charles turned around to thank him, the black man was gone. The train was moving too fast for him to have jumped out and survived.

AN ANGELIC DIAGNOSTICIAN

While vacationing in Hawaii in 1986, a mother named Teddy showed concern over her youngest daughter Taryn. Teddy brought Taryn to a medical clinic and the doctor could not find anything wrong. An "inner voice" informed Teddy that Taryn was in medical danger. Three more visits to this same clinic brought the same negative results.

The next time Teddy heard this voice, it directed her to bring Taryn to a hospital on the other side of the island. The pediatrician examined Taryn and said she was fine. Teddy now demanded x-rays and blood tests be run on Taryn.

The tests came back and Taryn was rushed to the intensive care unit, as she was diagnosed with mycoplasma (a type of pneumonia). She was using less than one third of her lung power at this time. Eventually, Taryn returned to normal health.

Intriguingly, Taryn was born on All Saints Day. Not surprisingly, her name means "Earth Angel."

16

SOULMATES – RELATIONSHIP HEALING

Love relationships are by far the most rewarding of all karmic entanglements. Couples quickly find out that they have been together before in many past lives. They will also be reunited in future lifetimes. When there is a problem in a relationship, past regressions can often pinpoint its exact cause. One partner may have deserted his wife in a past life, thus incurring a karmic debt. In the life prior to that one, the wife may have deserted her husband, or perhaps she accidentally caused his death. Thus, a cycle of karmic debt and retribution becomes established. In relating to significant others, there are two fundamental challenges. One is to understand oneself, and the other is to know the soul of the other. The better you get to know your significant other, the more profound your understanding of yourself will become.

Before I begin describing cases of soulmates, a classification system needs to be mentioned. Since 1974, I have worked with over 11,000 patients. More than 33,000 past life regressions and future life progressions were conducted on this large statistical population. In my experience, three totally separate kinds of soulmates were observed.

The first type is what I call the true soulmate. This category consists of souls which have originated from the same oversoul at the exact same time. Others call this type the twin flame, or the twin soul. You and your true soulmate can be traced back to the same energy source, and are therefore perfectly compatible. My research has established that you will not meet up with this soulmate until the very end of your karmic cycle. It is at this time that your soul's energy will be perfected and, assuming your counterpart has perfected him/herself, you are eligible for this merging as you both—now united as one perfect soul—ascend to the higher planes (see Chapter 24). If you were to meet your true soulmate prior to this point, it would spoil any other relationship. No other soul could possibly match your true soulmate's qualities.

Second, we have the boundary soulmate. This is a positive relationship, but you have known this soul only in a limited number of past lives. There are differences and some minor problems with this person (soul) but, all in all, the relationships are positive experiences.

Last, we have the retribution soulmate. This is the only type that may be negative. You feel irresistibly drawn to this person but the results are almost invariably hard and traumatic. This soul has been in a few or more of your past lives, usually exhibiting similar destructive patterns. If your relationship with a significant other has been both positive and negative in previous lives, this category would apply.

My experience suggests the validity of the "Miss or Mr. Right Now" approach, as opposed to the notion of keeping the same mate on a permanent basis. This does not preclude the possibility that you could have a fulfilling life together with one person, but merely recognizes that your growth, and that of your partner, is very likely to have a time limit. After that term ends, it is to both of your advantages (if you want to grow spiritually) to part and find another "soulmate" (preferably one functioning at a more evolved level).

The case of Carl and Martha was described in detail in my book, *Past Lives – Future Lives*. Carl came to see me several years ago. He was bothered by what is referred to as secondary impotency, meaning that he is able to function sexually at some times but not others. There was nothing physiologically wrong with Carl, but psychologically he exhibited several problems.

Carl described three past lives with his current wife Martha. During the Middle Ages he was a soldier named Hans, living in a German castle. Hans had wanted to take over this castle ever since the lord died. The lord's wife (Martha) had no plans to move. Hans organized a rebellion within the army, but the lord's wife amassed her own troops and put down the insurrection. Hans was killed, swearing to wreak his revenge on Martha.

It was in France about 300 years later that Carl reincarnated as Ladin, a fisherman who was married to Jeanne (Martha). Jeanne died while giving birth to their son. Ladin affirmed quite succinctly, "I'll never go through that again."

Their third lifetime together was quite different. Both of them were male and living in Maine in the early 1800s. One day Carl accidentally shot his best friend Sam (Martha) while hunting. Carl wasn't able to find a physician until it was too late. When Carl finally arrived with the doctor, Sam said "Don't touch me!" Sam made Carl feel guilty and useless. This incident became imprinted on Carl's subconscious mind, and his present impotency was a direct result of these past events.

This case illustrates the principle of changing sexes. Martha was a male in her last life as Sam. Although most of your lives will be lived as one sex, the karmic cycle requires you experience lives as both sexes.

When Carl was Ladin, in the eighteenth century in France, he blamed himself for Martha's (Jeanne's) death. She died in labor, and Carl promised himself that he wouldn't go through that experience again. He didn't want to have any more children. In his next life as the hunter in Maine, he would never marry again. One might say that he indirectly caused the death of Martha as Ladin, but as the hunter he directly caused Martha's (Sam's) death by accidentally shooting him. The amount of guilt that Carl brought with him from these past lives was enormous.

In his lifetime as Hans, Carl forced Martha (the lord's wife) out of the castle. Martha was ultimately victorious, causing Carl's death in the process. Carl swore that he would get back at her if it was the last thing he ever did. He was true to his word as he indirectly sought karmic retribution during his next two lives as Ladin and the hunter. His present life might have ended in the same way. Fortunately, Carl was able to see the cause of his sexual difficulties. He and Martha are retribution soulmates.

It doesn't matter who started the conflict. All that really matters is that the problems get resolved. Today, Martha and Carl have no sexual problems. They love each other very much and have finally learned to live together in peace. It takes many lifetimes for most couples to finally resolve their difficulties.

My most dynamic case of a retribution soulmate relationship is reported in my previous book, *The Search for Grace: A Documented Case of Murder and Reincarnation*. The patient—I'll call her Ivy—was obsessively attracted to John. John literally tried to murder Ivy on three separate occasions, but Ivy was unable to break away from this relationship. The soul of John had murdered Ivy in twenty of her forty-six past lives uncovered during hypnosis. She wanted desperately to break off the relationship and end the recurrent nightmares from which she awoke screaming in terror every night, being murdered over and over again by the same mysterious man—but she just couldn't seem to pull herself free.

Ivy lived in Buffalo, New York, in the 1920s as a woman named Grace Doze. She was a cold and calculating woman who had little respect for her husband Chester, whom she held in contempt. Grace had many affairs during her marriage. She was a real "Roaring Twenties" party girl. Grace was responsible enough not to abandon her son, Cliff, but beyond that concession to maturity her lifestyle was hedonistic.

One evening in the early May of 1927, Grace met a bootlegger named Jake at a speakeasy. They saw quite a bit of each other during the next two weeks. She decided to leave Chester and move in with Jake, having rented an apartment on Purdy Street. This event was to occur immediately following Grace's regular Tuesday night swimming session on May 17th at the local high school.

When Jake picked up Grace on that fateful evening at about 9:45 p.m., he was drunk. When Grace mentioned that her son Cliff would be living with them, Jake became abusive. He was quick to anger even when he wasn't drinking, and during the drive their discussion rapidly escalated into a heated argument. Without warning, Jake punched Grace with his right hand. She was conscious but in pain. Jake then strangled her until she died. CBS aired this case as a television movie on May 17, 1994, exactly sixty-seven years to the hour since Grace Doze was murdered.

I have to wonder if the subconscious force that motivated Ivy to so strongly want to be regressed into this life had to do with the deep synchronicity that brought us together, and brought her story through me to CBS, and thus to the public at large. Perhaps Grace Doze's unhappy spirit could not rest without clearing up the mystery of her death. Ivy gave me over two dozen facts that were verified by an independent researcher. She was finally able to break this karmic bond and go on with her life.

Ivy's case illustrates many aspects of soul healing. In addition to overcoming her obsession with John, she improved her self image, overcame her fear of choking, and became an empowered soul. She took control of her life and is a happier person today as a result of her energy-cleansing experiences. When I conduct past life regressions on married couples (all sessions are done separately) I find that approximately twenty per cent of the couples have been together in previous lifetimes.

The case of Marie is fascinating because it deals with a healing of a phobia as well as a soulmate experience. Marie had a great fear of not being able to escape from a locked room. It could even be in her own home: as long as a door was locked, her fear would be evident.

In a previous life, during the early 1900s, she had been a teenage girl raised on a farm by very strict parents. One night there was a fire in the house and her parents were killed. The farm was destroyed, and she moved into town and became a teacher. Later, she met Andrew and was very happy. The only problem was that she couldn't have children. Andrew had a mistress, so she left him and moved to St. Louis where she met and married Paul, a wealthy man with children from a previous marriage. She was happy and spent the rest of that life with Paul. Paul later reincarnated as her current-life husband. Marie overcame her phobia as a result of re-experiencing the death scene with her parents in the past life.

Yolanda met her current significant other (Bill) at her gym. They began dating and soon developed a very special relationship, but Bill was not yet divorced. Yolanda broke up with him because of that and later married someone else. This marriage did not work out, and in February of 1994 Bill asked Yolanda to go to a funeral with him. He was still not divorced, but they began dating again. It was as if they had never parted. This is by far the most significant relationship in both their lives.

In a past life during the Middle Ages in Holland, Yolanda was Mary Weiss, the daughter of a castle lord. Mary was in love with a peasant named Shelem, but her father forbade this relationship and sent Shelem away when he discovered their affair. Mary Weiss was married to a man she detested. He was old and very cruel to her. When she was middle-aged she was alone; her husband had died and her children had moved on. She met Shelem again, but all she could muster was a friendship with him because he was mute (his tongue was cut out) and retarded. This resulted from the torture he went through under the orders of Mary Weiss' father. In Yolanda's current life, Shelem is reincarnated as Bill.

Yolanda is black and Bill is white. They are also from different religious and environmental backgrounds, as was the case in their past life together. Additionally, Bill had had his tongue cut out in the past life as Shelem. In his current life he is a song writer. He thus overcame a communication block. In both lives Yolanda is reunited with Bill, but the present one is far more fulfilling.

Ann and Phil illustrate soulmate ties extending from past lives to over one thousand years in the future. This couple had many lives together, and it seems that whenever they were apart their separate lives became miserable. Happiness and fulfillment characterized their lives when together.

One of their happiest past lives together took place in England approximately 150 years ago. Phil was a university professor and Ann was his loving wife. What is interesting here is that Ann independently corroborated much of the data Phil give me, because I worked with them separately as a matter of therapeutic policy.

It will be during the thirty-first century that Phil will be female and married to Ann (she is male). They will work as scientists aboard a space station. This case illustrates changing sexes as well as future life progression. For a more complete explanation of both concepts I refer you to my first book, *Past Lives – Future Lives*.

When I first worked with them, their problem revolved around their marriage. There were several issues sabotaging this union. Superconscious mind taps were conducted following the past life regressions and future life progression to initiate their soul healing. Today their relationship is successful because they strive to make it work from the deepest depths of their souls.

Elizabeth Barrett Browning said it best:

How do I love thee? Let me count the ways.
I love thee to the depth and breadth and height
My soul can reach, when feeling out of sight
For the ends of Being and ideal Grace.
I love thee to the level of everyday's
Most quite need, by sun and candle-light.
I love thee freely, as men strive for Right;
I love thee purely, as they turn from Praise.
I love thee with the passion put to use.
In my old griefs, and with my childhood's faith.
I love thee with a love I seemed to lose
With my lost saints, — I love thee with the breath,
Smiles, tears, of all my life! – and, if God choose,
I shall but love thee better after death.

There is a tendency in life to create your own reality. In fact, quantum physics and holographic memory theory (see Chapter 23) establish this. The energy you receive from others is a function of the energy you send out. What goes around comes around. Relationships can be quite karmic, with origins going back thousands of years. The next time you are introduced to someone who has a powerful effect on you, be sure to ask them, "Didn't we meet in a past life?"

17

NEAR-DEATH EXPERIENCES – HEALED BY THE LIGHT

Approximately forty per cent of the people who relate their near-death experiences describe what is known as a core experience. This begins as a feeling of overwhelming joy and happiness. A lack of pain and other bodily sensations becomes evident. Occasionally a transitory buzzing sound is noted. A brilliant white light is usually seen.

At this time the individual appears to be hovering above his or her physical body. Both hearing and vision are highly developed, more so than normal. Clarity and alertness dominate the mental state, and this experience is most definitely interpreted as being real.

A dark void or tunnel now appears to be pulling at their astral body, and they eventually enter this tunnel. A presence of a loving being is felt as the individual emerges from this tunnel. Time is meaningless now and this person's life is played back in rapid episodes. The individual appears to be immersed in white light at this time.

A highly evolved spiritual being or beings now give the individual a choice of going on in the light, or returning to the physical body. In some cases there is a direct urging to reenter the body. Once the decision to return is made, this experience quickly ends and there is no recollection as to the process of returning to the physical body. It is impossible for the recipient to accurately relate the quality of this experience to others.

The legal definition of clinical death in many states is a flat electroencephalograph (EEG) reading. Electrical activity is required for the brain to function. Even a hallucination produces this electrical activity, which would appear on the EEG.

Many NDEs have been recorded on patients who exhibited flat EEGs. These patients were medically dead, and if their NDEs were mere hallucinations, why didn't their EEGs register them? The answer is quite simple. These NDEs are real and enlighten us about what occurs after our physical body dies.

Some patients in an operating room report instrument readings that are documented by their medical records. What is crucial about this phenomenon is that the patient is under general anesthesia and could only see these instruments if they were awake, turned around or were hovering over their physical body. Dr. Ray Moody described an elderly woman's account of her near-death experience so accurate that she even correctly reported the colors of the instruments used on her. What is especially impressive about this example is that she had been blind for over fifty years. Cultural conditioning can be eliminated as a factor since over twice as many of non-NDEs were familiar with the work of either Ray Moody or Elizabeth Kübler-Ross back in the 1970s, as compared to those who did report an NDE.

SUMMARIZING NEAR-DEATH EXPERIENCES

- NDEs cannot be explained adequately on the basis of drugs, hallucinations, or cultural conditioning.
- Religion, race, and age are also unrelated to NDEs.
- Ninety-five per cent of NDEs are positive and literally transform the personality of the recipient. Many patients do not want to return to their physical body because the NDE experience is so positive.
- A Being of Light often conducts a panoramic life review of the patient during a NDE. Not only is every action observed, but the effects on others are noted. Telepathy is the mode of communication.
- The patient sometimes gets information about the future. Some of these precognitions have been documented.

- NDEs have been described by Plato, Swedenborg, The Tibetan Book of The Dead, and the Bible. Biblical accounts appear in the Old Testament, in Isaiah 26:19 and Daniel 12:2; and in Acts 26:13-26 of the New Testament.

> At midday, O king, I saw in the way a light from heaven, above the brightness of the sun, shining round about me and them which journeyed with me.

- The overnight personality changes that occur, including a greater zest for life, improved self-confidence, healthier eating habits and increased compassion, simply cannot be explained by hallucinations or any other conjecture proposed by the skeptics critical of this experience.

Case Studies

Near-death experiences have redirected lives, created saints, inspired religions, and shaped history. They have given us rather impressive evidence of life-after-death, empowered individuals and they are responsible for a very special form of soul healing. Howard Mickel of Wichita State University reported a Colorado man's spontaneous remission of leukemia, which is one of the longest, recorded cases of this type of remission. This man had a near-death experience just prior to his remission.

In one case, Janine came to my office recently to deal with certain routine issues by the use of the superconscious mind tap technique. Upon providing her history, she reported a most unusual benefit from a NDE.

In 1980 Janine was a thirty-year-old divorced teacher with a seven-year-old son. She was involved with a manipulative and dysfunctional man who had swindled her out of many thousands of dollars (practically all of her life savings), and was verbally and physically abusive toward her. Janine was so shy and insecure that she felt she must have deserved to be in this relationship.

However, Janine could not emotionally handle all of these stresses. During a two-week period she began experiencing delusions, feeling that "evil forces" were trying to take over her body. Being a devout Christian, this was even more traumatic for her. We refer to this syndrome as brief reactive psychosis, and for the duration Janine was psychotic.

Janine was scheduled for a hysterectomy. Being free of her delusions the day before, she went through with the operation. During the procedure complications arose, and Janine was clinically dead for about three minutes. She had a classic NDE, and as a result her delusions disappeared and never again returned.

Janine's NDE effected an energy healing that helped her keep her sanity. In addition, it facilitated her psychic development. Seven years later her then fourteen-year-old son drowned and Janine was able to receive communications from his spirit. This greatly helped her deal with this loss, thereby significantly softening the bereavement she experienced.

Coreen worked in a factory and was very depressed. This forty-two-year-old patient was married to a very abusive man. Her depression became worse, and she entertained many suicidal thoughts.

Finally, she decided to end it all by taking an overdose of Valium, along with vodka. Her best friend found her and called 911. Coreen was taken to a hospital immediately. Her heart stopped twice in the operating room, and she was clinically dead for a short time. She was revived through electric shock treatment.

Her NDE consisted of the following events:

1. She rose up to the ceiling to observe her body on the operating table. She recalled the exact conversation the doctors had while working on her. This was confirmed later by her physician.
2. She experienced a beautiful, peaceful state and did not want to return to her body.

Following her NDE:

1. Her depression lifted. She never attempted suicide again.
2. She divorced her husband. Prior to the NDE she was too weak to let him go.
3. She developed a love of life she had not previously enjoyed.

Coreen came to see me to find out if she had known her husband in past lives. As it turned out, he was involved with Coreen in three previous existences, all of which were traumatic to her. She had experienced a great deal of soul healing as a result of her NDE that had taken place years before she ever entered my office.

A most unusual case of a NDE in a future life was reported to me and presented in Chapter 21 of *Past Lives – Future Lives*. During the thirty-first century on a small moon in the Shyron system many light years from earth, my patient Melodea is a medical technologist.

She is married to a surgeon (Romer) and very depressed because of his excessive involvement with his work.

A virus has been killing many of her people. Due to Melodea's body chemistry and blood type, she was to be used to develop a serum to kill this virus. During these experiments Melodea falls into a coma and has a NDE. She eventually recovers, and the serum is mass produced and distributed to her people. As a result of this experience, Melodea and Romer become very close and her depression lifts. Melodea's thirty-first-century NDE proved to be a most soul healing one at that.

When Melodea answered my questions, her responses were framed from the perspective of an actual NDE. There was, however, no danger to the patient in my office in describing these future events.

In 1973, Bernie was driving a truck in Texas and had taken amphetamines to keep awake. He then went to a hospital to have a wart removed from his nose. Shortly after his surgery, he had a severe reaction caused by the interaction of the general anesthetic and the pep pills. Bernie was clinically dead for a few minutes and his body turned gray. Bernie saw himself rise out of his body. He did not want to return, but suddenly, a force pushed him back into his body.

Since then, Bernie has had many classic out-of-body experiences. He has traveled while out of his body to the Egyptian pyramids. He has seen Jesus, the Virgin Mary, and others. When his soul returns to his body, it makes quite a bit of noise.

As a result of this 1973 NDE, Bernie has been able to heal people while in this altered state. In the mid-1970s Bernie went to visit his construction foreman, who was in the hospital. By doing a laying-on-of-hands healing, he helped his foreman's recovery. Bernie has received letters from people who were ill, and has, by telepathy, healed them through the use of thought energy and white light projection.

The energy produced by Bernie is so strong that once, while concentrating on the water in a plastic cup, he partially melted the cup, leaving his fingerprints behind on the cup.

One of Bernie's healings involved projecting his energy to a bedridden woman in Holland, and his efforts paid off—Bernie lives in Texas! He has had many psychic precognitions and once foresaw the drowning of a friend's teenage son that occurred one winter. The lad fell through the ice while playing hockey, as Bernie predicted.

Mark had a NDE shortly after his birth that resulted in a very significant healing. As a baby born six weeks premature and under three pounds in weight, his prognosis was not good. To further complicate matters, Mark's father was in the Navy, stationed in the Philippines at Sangley Point Naval Base.

The thermostat in the hospital incubators was broken and Mark experienced his first out of body experience (OBE) and only NDE. As he states: "I found myself floating above my isolet, looking at this red, prune-like thing with tubes attached, wondering if there wasn't some mistake. This couldn't be the body I was supposed to be in. Something was wrong here, and I didn't like it."

"As I was hovering near the ceiling of this room shaped like an L, I was aware of both hot and cold sensations, with heat coming from directly above, the cold emanating lower down around me. I also remember the walls being a purple color, and my isolet was off in the short end of the L, separate from the other babies down in the long end of the room. The 'Voice' that wasn't a voice said I should go back into that body, and that everything would be fine, not to worry."

Mark's life was saved by this "voice." Although he has had many other OBEs since, this was his only NDE. An interesting footnote to this case is that thirty years after his NDE Mark met the navy doctor who delivered him. The doctor acknowledged that, in fact, Mark was delivered in an L-shaped room which was painted mauve. This paint was left over from the redecoration of the Admiral's quarters. No one was supposed to know about the paint as it was not the typical battleship gray characteristic of military bases. The doctor also informed Mark that he was placed in the corner of the room near the closet. This was done to protect him from being further compromised by the germs of the other infants.

The doctor told Mark: "I've done some research on this and can't find a smaller surviving baby on the record the year you were born. I don't know why you're here, but you're definitely here for a reason."

Aren't we all?

NDEs are also reported among children. Their characteristics do indeed coincide with those reported by adults. One adult element of NDEs that is absent in children is the panoramic life review.

Visions of the future (age progression) are occasionally reported in NDEs and some have been documented. The eruption of Mount St. Helens and the Three Mile Island accident are examples of some better-known incidents.

The previews are presented conditionally as something that will happen if the person continues to live. Experienced as a vivid memory rather than as a forecast, the previews often are highly detailed.

They often occur as an extension of the panoramic life review. Those who have had a near-death experience are adamant that it was anything but dreamlike.

"Any adequate neurological explanation," writes Kenneth Ring, Ph.D., "would have to [show] how the entire complex of phenomena associated with the core experience (out-of-body state, paranormal knowledge, the tunnel, the golden light, the voice of presence, the appearance of deceased relatives, beautiful vistas, and so forth) would be expected to occur in subjectively authentic fashion as a consequence of specific neurological events triggered by the approach of death."

To this day, neurologists have been unable to meet Ring's emphatic challenge—there simply is no contrary explanation.

Dr. Michael Sabom, an Atlanta cardiologist, interviewed twenty-five people who had undergone resuscitation but who did not have a near-death experience to compare their "educated guesses" as a control against actual NDE patients. He found that twenty-three of twenty-five of these patients made major errors in describing the resuscitation procedures. None of those who did have a NDE made such a mistake. Formerly a skeptic to the field of NDE, Sabom has become one of its most enthusiastic supporters.

NDEs are different from an out-of-body experience that is not associated with clinical death, in that in the latter we do not find reports of white lights, beings of light, or panoramic life reviews.

Finally, in reference to the "presence" that is felt, or the "voice" that is often heard during a NDE, Ring believes that it is the higher self. He rejects the notion that these are merely an extension of the personality. My assessment parallels Ring's.

18

SOUL HEALING THROUGH RELIGION

Soul healing through religion involves a departure from ordinary human experience and activity. Jewish, Moslem, and Christian mystics tend to agree that credit for these soul-healing miracles belongs exclusively to God, as manifested in His blessedness, grace, and/or mercy. The average person might forego such elevated language, preferring to describe these mystics as people who "were carried away," as if "something came over them."

Some manifestations of soul healing through religion are:

- Levitation.
- Out-of-body experience.
- Movement into extraphysical worlds during hypnosis, lucid dreams, and deep meditation.
- Deliberate influence imposed by a mind upon living tissue at a distance (telergy).
- The creation of a special joy or presence in their place of worship by mystics and saints.

According to the *Historia Monarchorum* (Russell, 1980), soul healing was practiced by monks in the early Christian era. John of Lycopolis restored eyesight to the blind wife of a Roman senator. Eyewitnesses recorded that Elias, Apollo, Macarius, John the

Hermit, and Abba Or performed a variety of healings. In an era marked by brief lifespans, many of these men lived to a ripe old age. Abba Or and John of Lycopolis died in their 90s, while Elias passed the century mark.

BIBLICAL ACCOUNTS OF HEALING

The first Book of Kings (17:20–24) describes Elijah's meeting with a mother whose son had died. Turning to God, the prophet asks:

> O Lord my God, hast thou also brought evil upon the widow with whom I sojourn, by slaying her son?
>
> And he stretched himself upon the child three times, and cried unto the Lord, and said, "O Lord my God, I pray thee, let this child's soul come into him again."
>
> And the Lord heard the voice of Elijah; and the soul of the child came into him again, and he revived.

In a similar story (2 Kings 4:18–37), the prophet Elisha resuscitates the Shunammite's son, who had died suffering from pain in his head. The Book of Isaiah (35:5–6) describes the coming King of Righteousness who will show God's power:

> Then the eyes of the blind shall be opened, and the ears of the deaf shall be unstopped.
>
> Then shall the lame man leap as an hart, and the tongue of the dumb sing.

According to the four Gospels, the individuals that Jesus healed comprised a virtual role call of suffering humanity; a cursory enumeration would include the following healings:

- Four cases of blindness: Bartimaeus (Mark 10:46–52; Matthew 20:29–34; Luke 18:35–43); the blind man of Bethsaida (Mark 8:22–26); two blind men (Matthew 9:27–31); and the man blind from birth (John 9:1–34).
- A man with dropsy (Luke 14:1–6).
- A centurion's servant with paralysis (Matthew 8:5–13; Luke 7:1–10).
- A wounded slave of the high priest (Luke 22:50–51).

- The sick of Capernaum (Matthew 8:16–17; Mark 1:32–34; Luke 4:40–41).
- Two cases of fever: Peter's mother-in-law (Matthew 8:14–15; Mark 1:30–31; Luke 4:38-39); and the official's son (John 4:46–54).
- Eleven lepers: a single leper (Matthew 8:1–4; Mark 1:40–45; Luke 5:12–16); and on another occasion, ten more (Luke 17:11–19).
- A deaf-mute (Mark 7:31–37).
- A woman with a hemorrhage that failed to respond to eighteen years of traditional medical care (Matthew 9:20–22); Mark 5:25–34; Luke 8:43–48).
- A multitude from Tyre, Sidon, and Galilee (Matthew 12:15–21; Mark 3:7-12; Luke 6:17 19).
- Those by the shore at Gennesaret (Matthew 14:34–36; Mark 6:53–54).
- The sick at Bethsaida (Matthew 14:14; Luke 9:1–11); and those suffering at Tiberius (John 6:2).
- The crowds Jesus encountered while entering Judea (Matthew 19:2).

Jesus claimed that his soul-healing powers bore witness to his being an agent from God. He was even able to heal the sick from a distance. The healings conducted by Jesus that involved the laying on of hands are similar to those performed by Saint Francis of Assisi, Valentine Greatrakes, and numerous other ascetics. These ancient soul healers established a reputation that understandably inspired confidence. Modern soul healers have since embraced such ideas and techniques, conforming as they do to the gospel accounts that have been handed down to us.

HEALING IN THE MIDDLE AGES

Soul healing later came to be associated with the many shrines that the early church dedicated to its martyrs and saints. The lists of miracles compiled by medieval monks shows that the shrines, many of which housed relics of their patrons and namesakes, catalyzed an immense range of cures (Gardner, 1983). Such lists, called the "medical journals of the Middle Ages" by French medievalist Luchaire, provide richly detailed evidence for the effectiveness of soul healing. Historian Ronald Finucane (1973) examined two such compilations, one detailing miracles occurring at the shrine of Saint Godric in northeastern England, the other recording occurrences radiating from the tomb of Thomas Becket in Canterbury. These two shrines are credited with 600 cures between them. The patients healed included nobles, knights, yeomen, ecclesiastics, craftsmen, and the poor. Conditions cured at both locations included blindness, deafness, paralysis, and other afflictions likely to have been psychogenic in origin; organic infirmities such as broken bones, epilepsy, leprosy, and gout; and overt mental disturbances. "For many reasons ... the two cults exhibited unique characteristics," Finucane wrote, "yet the behavior of pilgrims cured at both shrines was similar—indeed, was repeated at every other saint's shrine in medieval Europe—and can still be observed in some parts of Christendom today."

After having analyzed 1,500 cures attributed to such healing centers of antiquity, Finucane reconstructed the typical rituals employed by pilgrims seeking relief at the shrines. Certain devotees, for example, were led to a particular place through dreams; others made choices based on the casting of lots, or were sent to the healing center by order of a physician. Having arrived at the shrine, the infirm sought purification through confession, oblations, and prayers to the presiding saint or martyr to enjoin their intercession. The supplicants were generally accompanied by a tumultuous crowd of fellow victims. When these were miraculously cured, the electrified atmosphere and excitement inspired new confidence in those who witnessed it. Like the sick at the temples of Aesculapius, some slept within the shrine's church, with vigils extending for several days. For those who required proximity to the healing power of the saint, niches near the bones and relics were occasionally provided.

The prayers of pilgrims were often accompanied by tears, moaning, swooning, vomiting, the cracking of bones, writhing, shrieks, or profuse bleeding, all of which contributed to a heightened atmosphere of intense expectation and enthusiasm. For example, a deaf woman praying before Becket's shrine "felt a surge of pain, and within her head it seemed as if many twigs were being snapped into tiny bits. While she was thus afflicted she cried as if an interior infection had burst, a great deal of pus flowed from her ears, after which blood came out, and, after the blood, her hearing returned." A blind woman led to Becket's shrine felt "as if she were engulfed in the raging heat of a furnace." Ripping the veil from her head and tearing her garments across her breast, she collapsed upon the floor and lay very still for an hour, after which she opened her eyes, stood up, and exclaimed, "I can see!" (Finucane, 1973).

Some pilgrims enjoyed only partial relief at a certain shrine, only to be completely healed elsewhere. Finucane describes a blind woman whose eyes were partially cured during a visit to Becket's tomb. Upon arriving at Godric's tomb, where she spent the night, her vision recovered completely. Not unlike the pilgrims at Lourdes in our own century, the people whom Finucane studied were motivated by an insuperable confidence that they would surely be healed. They were then subsequently caught up in the emotionally charged atmosphere of the crowds at the shrine. Like many who are cured in similar circumstances in our own day, those early pilgrims felt that they had made contact with a transcendent wholeness, an entity or energy beyond comprehension, that restored them whole in a manner that seemed miraculous.

VALENTINE GREATRAKES

Valentine Greatrakes, the "Irish stroker," was born in 1629. His family, of English descent, had settled in county Waterford. His is a remarkable story, but some background is needed to fully understand the significance of "stroking" as a therapy.

Scrofula (tuberculosis of the cervical lymph nodes) was called the King's Evil in seventeenth-century England. This affliction could sometimes be cured by the royal touch. In fact, healing powers were ascribed to certain kings and queens of Europe. Such powers tended to make the "divine right of kings" all but self-attesting—who could argue with the miraculous? During his exile in Holland, Charles II of England demonstrated his God-given right to govern England (and dislodge Cromwell) by touching, or "stroking," thousands of sufferers. After his restoration to power, he touched 22,982 such individuals, as reported in the records of his reign (Laver, 1978).

Greatrakes, however, did not limit his healing powers to this single affliction. He cured people suffering from a wide range of infirmities throughout Waterford and nearby counties. He eventually attracted sufferers from England, where the Plague was raging. By the summer of 1665, his fame had spread to London, where it reached the ear of Viscount Conway of Ragley Hall. The viscount's wife had been suffering incapacitating headaches since her youth, and the viscount was desperate to help her. He approached Greatrakes, who traveled to Ragley Hall but was unable to cure the viscountess. However, he healed hundreds of others, and was eventually invited to London by the king himself, where he treated many thousands of people, including royalty, scientists, and men of letters. The English chemist and physicist Robert Boyle attested to seven of Greatrakes' cures that he had personally witnessed, although he was inclined to attribute them to "a lucky commotion in the blood and spirits conducive to healing [stimulated] by exalted imagination and strong passions" (Laver, 1978). Despite his wide-ranging successes, however, the Irish healer encountered heated opposition, most notably in the person of David Lloyd. Lloyd, a chaplain to Isaac Barrow (a prominent British scientist), wrote and distributed a pamphlet that was scathingly critical of Greatrakes and his claims. Greatrakes responded by composing an autobiography, which he hoped would establish his authenticity and sincerity. Within its pages are signed testimonials by John Wilkins (founder of the Royal Society), the Cambridge Platonists Ralph Cudworth and Benjamin Whichcote, the poet Andrew Marvell, several physicians, and many other prominent figures. It is beyond dispute that the extant records prove that Greatrakes had made a deep and lasting impression on the people of London, from the least to the greatest.

Like celebrated healers of other eras, Greatrakes responded to the sick in dramatic, spontaneous ways. He would stroke them, massage them, occasionally wield a knife to lance boils, offer his urine to drink or to rub onto wounds or lesions, or spit into eyes dimmed by blindness. He forthrightly insisted that he was merely an instrument of God, a claim that must have reinforced his effectiveness among the devout. "The resemblance in phenomena induced by [Greatrakes'] stroking to those elicited by Franz Anton Mesmer and his immediate successors nearly a century later were remarkable."

Greatrakes' patients often exhibited convulsive crises, not unlike many of Mesmer's patients. They sometimes sank into anesthetized states, at least temporarily, the depths of which could be probed using pins and knives. Like Mesmer, the Irish healer sometimes drew pain out at the toe and cast it out like polluted water. Moreover, objects associated with these two men were sometimes used to accomplish cures even when their owners were absent, a phenomenon reminiscent of the powers attributed to the bones of the saints, and other such religious relics. By reputation and personality, Mesmer and

Greatrakes were empowered to create an overwhelmingly powerful aura of belief that ultimately catalyzed the self-restorative powers of those they treated. Whereas Mesmer credited the infusion of magnetic fluid for his cures, Greatrakes regarded the grace of God as the source of his healing power. However divergent their perspectives, both of these men stimulated countless thousands to raise their center of personal energy, thus producing soul healing.

NEW THOUGHT AND CHRISTIAN SCIENCE

Faith healing has been nurtured in the United States by organizations affiliated with the New Thought movement. Phineas Quimby (1802–1866) was the primary inspiration behind this movement. Quimby, a watchmaker by trade, had developed a mind cure that hearkened back to the theories championed by the French mesmerists. Among Quimby's many converts, the most influential was Mary Baker Eddy. He had cured her of several lifelong afflictions that were largely psychosomatic in origin.

Mary Baker Eddy pored over Quimby's teachings with reverent care, and then created her own brand of New Thought, which was later codified in *Science and Health*, which was published in 1875. (N.b. later editions of this systematic volume were titled *Science and Health with Key to the Scriptures*, the title most recognizable to modern ears.)

Until her death in 1910, Mary Baker Eddy promoted her teaching through the Christian Science Church, which quickly spread throughout the United States and beyond. "Matter is nothing more than an image of mortal mind," she wrote. "Evil has no reality. It is simply a belief, an illusion of material sense. Nothing but God is real and eternal, and sickness is an error." The devout Christian Scientist typically treats health problems with similar maxims, and with prayer, maintaining a steadfast denial of the "mistakes" that produce the sickness. A trained practitioner may also help suffering individuals, perhaps even at a distance, by guiding their thoughts and emotions into harmony with the Divine Mind. Strict believers do not accept standard medical treatment beyond rudimentary hygienic precepts (Paulsen, 1926).

Christian Science attaches great weight to the power of suggestion, regarding negative thought with an almost superstitious abhorrence. Its dogmatic denial of disease and misfortune has been criticized by physicians, who argue that such ideas have deleterious consequences for those who accept them, i.e., that adherents would likely decline treatment for conditions for which standard medicine has a proven cure. On the other hand, psychologists have been concerned that the tenets of Christian Science encourage followers to suppress emotional issues that simply aren't susceptible to resolution by suggestion alone. The enormous success enjoyed by Christian Science seems to indicate that reliance upon prayer and upon affirmations of the ultimate good demonstrably promotes health and well-being for a great many people.

SPIRITUAL HEALING IN THE TWENTIETH CENTURY

Pattison, et al. (1973), published a study in the *Journal of Nervous and Mental Disease* intended to debunk contemporary faith healing. These researchers studied forty-three pentecostal believers who had experienced faith cures, concluding that these individuals exhibited "denial, repression, projection, and disregard of reality" in the normal functioning. The study proposed that the primary function of the cures was "not to reduce symptomatology, but to reinforce a magical belief system that is consonant with one's subculture."

Criticisms of this kind do not, however, negate the positive results of soul healing. Even when denial and repression are evident in their ranks, healing cults often produce legitimate, real cures. Religious healings have occurred far too often, among too many different populations, to be dismissed as a stunted response to adversity. This fact is in evidence at Lourdes, which is visited annually by thousands of physicians of every imaginable religious stripe—Catholic, Protestant, Jew, Moslem, Buddhist, and agnostic—who often testify concerning dramatic cures they witnessed at the site.

HEALING AT LOURDES

As part of its tireless efforts to establish the authenticity of religious phenomena, the Catholic church founded a Medical Bureau at Lourdes in 1883, twenty-five years after Bernadette Soubirous had experienced her famous visions of the Virgin. The bureau was chartered to determine the nature of the cures that proceeded from the famous shrine. Since 1954, the bureau has sent dossiers on cases deemed scientifically inexplicable to the International Medical Committee of Lourdes, a group of physicians and medical researchers from several nations charged with reexamining the cures submitted for review for the purpose of authentication. I described the case of Vittorio Micheli in Chapter 6 as an example of a Lourdes cure.

The Medical Bureau at Lourdes and the International Committee have produced a wealth of material dealing with spiritual healing. Their collective archives—which include x-ray pictures, photographs, biopsy records, and summarized lab tests—are a valuable resource for studying the regenerative capacities of human beings.

Prominent visitors to Lourdes have also supplied persuasive testimony regarding cures at the shrine, as well as perceptive insights into their causes. Alexis Carrel (1950), a Nobel Laureate in medicine and a medical director of the Rockefeller Institute, related the story of his first visit to Lourdes in 1903 in intimate detail. Having arrived a curious skeptic, he attached himself to a woman with tubercular peritonitis. As he watched, her sickly features changed so dramatically that he felt he might be "suffering an hallucination." Then, before his eyes, a large abdominal tumor that had filled her navel with pus disappeared within a matter of minutes. To Carrel's astonishment, the woman seemed to be free of all pain. He visited the woman in the local hospital later that day. She was sitting upright in bed, eyes gleaming, her cheeks full of color, her abdomen normal and without a trace of the horrid tumor Carrel had seen just hours before. This case, and others like it, convinced him that many of the cures at Lourdes were authentic, whether they were miraculous in origin or not. One thing was certain: these cures could not be attributed solely to the relief of functional disorders.

Various afflictions Carrel had witnessed had seemed intractable prior to being cured at Lourdes. As both a rationalist and a scientist, Carrel confessed that his Lourdes experiences had forced him to admit that human beings clearly possessed mysterious capabilities that science would be wise to explore as thoroughly as it had done with germs and new surgical procedures.

The wide range of organic disorders healed at the shrine, or by ingestion of water extracted from its springs, can be illustrated by several cases culled by Aradi (1956), as follows.

Francis Pascal

Born a normal child, Pascal was afflicted with meningitis when he was three. The disease left him blind and partially paralyzed. In August of 1938, when he was four years old, he was immersed twice at Lourdes and was instantly healed. Members of the Medical Bureau and other medical experts confirmed that Pascal's blindness and paralysis were truly organic, not functional in etiology. The archbishop of Aix-en-Provence declared the cure to be miraculous in 1949. Pascal lived to be a normal adult.

Gerard Bailie

When he was two and a half years old, Bailie was stricken with bilateral chorioretinitis and double optic atrophy, an eye disease deemed incurable under normal circumstances. He lost his sight completely after an operation was attempted. In September 1947, at the age of six, his eyesight was completely restored during a visit to Lourdes. His condition was thought to be incurable because his optic nerves had atrophied, but reexamination by the Medical Bureau established that his ability to see objects clearly was restored in its entirety.

Delizia Cirolli

In 1976 Silician-born Delizia developed a painfully swollen right knee that was eventually diagnosed as a case of Ewing's tumor. Her parents refused to have her leg amputated. Her mother took Delizia to Lourdes, but x-rays taken a month later showed no signs of improvement, prompting the family to prepare for her death. Friends and sympathizers continued their prayer vigils on Delizia's behalf, beseeching the Virgin of Lourdes to restore the girl whole. Delizia was given water from the shrine on a regular basis during this time. Three months later, without any warning whatsoever, the tumor had vanished. X-rays showed repair of the bone that had metastasized. Four subsequent trips to the Medical Bureau (in 1977, 1978, 1979, and 1980) proved that the cure had been complete.

Serge Perrin

In 1970, Perrin of Lion d'Angiers was cured of organic hemiplegia with ocular lesions caused by cerebral circulatory defects. Physicians who examined him were certain that his afflictions were organic, and their diagnosis was later confirmed by the International Committee. Perrin's cure was deemed scientifically inexplicable, in part because of its sudden onset and unqualified totality.

Among the many cures at Lourdes, there have been complete remissions from ulcers with extensive gangrene, anterolateral spinal sclerosis (ALS), tuberculous peritonitis, leg and abdominal tumors, dorsolumbar spondylitis, blindness originating in the cerebrum, bilateral optic atrophy, multiple sclerosis, and sarcoma of the pelvis.

To put the healing power of intercessory prayer to the test, physician Randolph Byrd (1988) randomly divided patients in a coronary care unit at San Francisco General Hospital into a target population of 192 and a control group of 201. Neither patients, staff, doctors, nor Byrd himself knew which patients would be the targets of prayer, and the people who prayed were given nothing more than their subject's first name, diagnosis, and general condition. Every subject was assigned three to seven intercessors, each of whom was asked to pray daily for their patient's rapid recovery. Byrd collected information about all his subjects without knowing who were targets and who were controls.

Congestive heart failure, cardiopulmonary arrest, and pneumonia occurred less often in the group receiving intercessory prayer than they did among subjects in the control group. Fewer patients in the prayer group required ventilatory support, antibiotics, or diuretics. In the prayer group, eighty-five per cent were considered to have a "good hospital course" after admission, versus seventy-three per cent in the control group. Finally, a general analysis of the differences between targets and controls in terms of their recovery from disease showed a high degree of statistically significant divergence between the two groups.

JEWISH MYSTICS

For most Jewish mystics, the greatest adventures of spirit occur in the common tasks of life, when zohar, the splendor of existence, becomes manifest. "Any event can awaken our higher faculties," wrote Edward Hoffman (1981), a student of Kabbalism and Hasidism, "for the transcendent can be found in everything and everywhere." In spite of its focus upon the goodness of everyday life, Jewish mystical literature describes soul healings not unlike the charisms of Catholic saints and the siddhis of Indian yoga. For example, the Baal Shem Tov, founder of Hasidism, was said to have actualized a supplicant's wishes in a way that incontrovertibly proved his extraordinary powers of mind over matter. He also predicted future events and read the history of various persons and objects. The Rabbi Dov Baer of Mezritch (the Maggid) and the Rabbi Zalman of Liady (founder of the Lubavitcher sect flourishing today) frequently exhibited extrasensory abilities.

SOURCES

Aradi, Z. *The Book of Miracles*. Farrar, New York: Straus and Cudahy, 1956.

Byrd, R. "Positive Therapeutic Effects of Intercessory Prayer in a Coronary Care Unit Population." *Southern Medical Journal,* 1988, 81:826–29.

Carrel, A. *Voyage to Lourdes*. New York: Harper, 1950.

Dowling, St. J. "Lourdes Cures and Their Medical Assessment." *Journal of the Royal Society of Medicine*, 1984, 77:635–36.

Finucane, R. "Faith Healing in Medieval England: Miracles of Saints' Shrines." *Psychiatry*. 1973, 36:341–346.

Gardner, R. "Miracles of Healing in Anglo-Celtic Northumbria as Recorded by the Venerable Bede and His Contemporaries: A Reappraisal in the Light of Twentieth-Century Experience." *British Medical Journal*, 1983, 287: 1927–1933.

Hoffman, E. *The Way of Splendor*. Boulder, CO: Shambhala (pp. 122, 179–180). 1981.

Laver, A. B., "Miracles No Wonder. The Mesmeric phenomena and organic cures of Valentine Greatrakes." *Journal of the History of Medicine and Allied Sciences* (Jan), 1978, 33: 35–46.

Mouren, P. "The Cure of M. Serge Perrin." Report to the International Medical Committee of Lourdes. Bureau Medical, Lourdes, France.

Paulsen, A. E. "Religious Healing." *Mental Hygiene*, 1926, 10:541–95.

Pattison, E., et al. "Faith Healing." *Journal of Nervous and Mental Disease*, 1973, 157:397–409.

Russell, N. *The Lives of the Desert Fathers: A translation of the Historia Monachorum in Aegypto*. New York: Mowbray, 1980.

19

SHAMANIC HEALING

I briefly alluded to shamans in Chapter 2, but an entire chapter is needed to do justice to this ancient form of soul healing.

Strictly speaking, shamanism is a religious phenomenon restricted to Siberia and Central Asia, where it is known as *Saman*. It is defined as a technique of ecstasy. In the surrounding regions, Saman has been transliterated into Yakut as *ojuna* (*oyuna*); Mongolian as *bügü, bögä* (*buge, bü*), and *udagan*; and Turko-Tartar as *kam*. Later, parallel phenomena of a magico-religious nature were observed in North America, Indonesia, and elsewhere.

The shaman is both magician and medicine: he cures the afflicted, like any other doctor, but also performs miracles in the tradition of the fakir. He is a psychopomp (i.e., he guides souls). He might wear other hats as well, serving as priest, mystic, and even as poet. In many tribes the sacrificing priest co-exists with the shaman, an important fact when it is remembered that every head of a family is also the head of the domestic cult. The shaman remains the dominant figure.

Magic and magicians can be found across the globe, whereas shamanism manifests a specific magical specialty: "mastery over fire," "magical flight," and so on. Though a shaman is surely a magician (and more), not every magician qualifies as a shaman. Every medicine man is a healer, but the shaman's method is his exclusive domain, unique and beyond usurpation. The shaman specializes in a trance during which his soul is thought to leave his body to either ascend into the sky or descend into the underworld.

In Central and Northeast Asia, shamans are recruited either by hereditary transmission of the shamanic profession from father to son, or by spontaneous vocation (answering the "call" to become a shaman). A shaman is not fully "credentialed" until he has received two kinds of teaching: ecstatic (via dreams, trances, etc.), and traditional (shamanic techniques, names and functions of the spirits, mythology and genealogy of the clan, secret language, etc.). This twofold course of indoctrination, conducted by the spirits and the old master shamans, is tantamount to a formal initiation. It is only through this two-fold initiation—ecstatic and didactic—that the candidate is transformed from a possible neurotic to a shaman of note within his social group.

The "call" upon an unwitting candidate for shamanism often involves an encounter with a divine or semi-divine being. This being appears to the "called one" in one of several vehicles, including dreams, sicknesses, or other circumstances, and informs him that he has been "chosen," exhorting him to follow a new rule of life hereafter. More often than not, the messengers approaching the candidate with the good news of his appointment to humanitarian service are actually the souls of his shaman ancestors.

The shaman has a working relationship with his "spirits." These entities are also called "guardian," "helping," or "assistant" spirits. He prays to these beings. His influence is restricted to a few select souls. Additionally, shamans have divinities peculiar to themselves but unknown to the masses, divinities to whom they alone offer sacrifices.

Animal skulls and bones found in sites of the European Paleolithic period (before 50,000–ca. 30,000 B.C.) can be plausibly interpreted as ritual offerings. Most of the spirits that shamans address possess animal forms. They can appear as bears, wolves, stags, hares, and many kinds of birds (most notably the goose, eagle, owl, crow, etc.).

The shaman is "protected" by a "spirit of the herd" during his ecstatic journeys. A spirit in the shape of a bear accompanies him on his descent to the underworld, while a gray horse is with him in spirit as he ascends to the sky. All through Asia, North America, and elsewhere (e.g., Indonesia), the shaman performs the function of a doctor and healer. He announces the diagnosis, goes in search of the patient's fugitive soul, captures it, and makes it return to animate the body that it has left. It is the shaman who conducts every dead person's soul to the underworld.

The technique of ecstasy is characterized by the shaman's soul leaving his body and descending to the underworld or rising to the sky in search of lost souls. It is the shaman's "guardian spirits" that protect the souls he has recovered on these journeys. Only a trained shaman can chart these dangerous territories.

As suggested previously, the principal function of a shaman in Central and North America is magical healing. Disease is attributed to the soul's having strayed away, or having been stolen. Treatment naturally leads to a search for the lost soul, which must be captured and persuaded to return to its rightful place within the patient's body.

In some parts of Asia, the cause of illness can be the intrusion of a magical object into the patient's body, or even "possession" by evil spirits. In these cases, therapy consists of either extracting the harmful object or expelling the demons. On occasion, disease could actually have dual causalities. For example, someone may be both possessed by evil spirits and have had his soul stolen. In such a circumstance, the shaman must not only find the missing soul, he must also expel the demons that have taken up residence in the patient's body.

Only the shaman can undertake a cure of this kind. Only he can "see" the spirits. Only he knows how to exorcise them. Only he can perceive that the soul has fled. Only he is empowered to overtake the soul, in ecstasy, and return it to its proper body.

Cures often involve various sacrifices, and even these are mediated and regulated by the shaman, who determines not only their form, but whether or not they are even needed. Physical health is restored only upon restoration of balance among spiritual forces. It is often the case that illness follows on the heels of neglect or omission of duties owed to the infernal powers, which themselves belong to the sphere of the sacred.

Everything concerning the soul's adventure here on earth and in the beyond is the exclusive province of the shaman. Through his preinitiatory and initiatory experiences, he learns the drama of the human soul, its instability and precariousness. In addition, he knows the forces that threaten it, and the regions to which it can either willfully flee or be involuntarily conveyed by evil spirits. Shamanic cure involves ecstasy precisely because illness is understood to be a corruption of the soul.

The main shamanic technique entails passage from one cosmic region to another—for example, from earth to sky or from earth to the underworld. The shaman knows the mystery of the breakthrough between planes. This communication among the cosmic zones is made possible by the architectonic structure of the universe.

The universe in general is conceived of as having three levels—sky, earth, underworld—connected by a central axis. This axis passes through an "opening," a "hole." This hole serves as a multi-purpose vestibule: gods pass through it to descend to earth, the dead use it to reach the subterranean regions, and the soul of the shaman journeys through it in either direction while in ecstasy.

The role of the Eskimo shaman is healing and treating sterility in women. Sterility is thought to be caused either by violating a taboo, or by having one's soul stolen by one of the dead.

If it is determined that taboo violation is the cause of sterility, the shaman "cleanses" the impurity using collective confession. On the other hand, if the soul has been stolen, the shaman takes an ecstatic journey into the sky or the depths of the sea (confronting the Mother of the Sea Beasts) to locate the patient's missing soul and return it to its body. The patient's soul may have fled due to any number of causes: dreams may frighten it away, or dead persons reluctant to enter the land of shades may prowl the camp looking for another soul to take with them. It is even possible that the patient's soul may have strayed of its own volition.

Injurious objects are usually projected by sorcerers. These can be pebbles, insects, even small animals. The sorcerer inserts them into the patient using the power of his mind. Such objects may also be sent by spirits, who often take up residence in a body in their own right. In either case, once the shaman has discovered the cause of the illness, he simply extracts the magical objects using suction. The requisite seances are conducted at night, usually in the patient's own home.

If the shaman discerns that an embedded magical object is causing the patient's illness, he proceeds to suck that part of the body that is the seat of the illness (as determined by the shaman during his trance). The shaman usually sucks on the skin directly, although some suck the sick through a bone or a willow-wood tube. After sucking the blood, the shaman spits it into a small hole and repeats the ceremony. He then draws a few puffs from his pipe, dances around the fire, and sucks yet again, until the magical object has been successfully extracted. He shows the object (e.g., a pebble, lizard, insect, or worm) to the family, then disposes of it in the small hole in which the blood had been spat out, finally covering the hole with dust. The ceremony lasts all night long, ending shortly before dawn.

Shamans divide illness into six categories: (1) overt, visible accidents; (2) breach of a taboo; (3) terror caused by monstrous apparitions; (4) "bad blood"; (5) poisoning at the hands of another shaman; and (6) loss of the soul. The conception of disease as a loss of the soul that has either strayed away or been spiritually abducted is very widespread in the Amazonian and Andean regions, but the belief seems quite rare in tropical South America.

The shamans play an integral part in defending the community's psychic integrity. The war is against demons and disease, of course, but also against practitioners of black magic. Shamanism defends life, health, fertility, and the world of "light" against death, disease, sterility, disaster, and the world of "darkness." The lands that the shaman sees, and the beings that he meets during his ecstatic journeys, are described in detail by the shaman himself after returning from his entranced journey to the great beyond.

Dr. Jerome Frank, professor emeritus of psychiatry at Johns Hopkins University, reported a classic example of such soul healing in his book *Persuasion and Healing.* A German physician had three female patients who were all bedridden. Each had very different afflictions: the first suffered from an inflamed gallbladder and gallstones, the second had lost a great deal of weight during a difficult recovery from abdominal surgery, and the third was dying from uterine cancer.

The doctor felt that he had nothing to lose by trying soul healing on these patients, since all three had proven unresponsive to conventional therapy. A local healer attempted to cure these women, without either touching them or approaching them throughout the duration of the treatment. After twelve "sessions," the healer conceded failure: none of the women had improved. The doctor then told his patients a few key things about the healer. The women learned about his amazing gift, his many successes, and the benefits of his healing technique. The women were further told that the healer would be beaming his healing force at them that very day. In reality, the healer did nothing that day, but the results were astonishing nonetheless. The woman with gallstones recovered completely and returned home. The woman wasting away recovered and gained thirty pounds. The cancer patient did die eventually, but her suffering had become far less severe and more manageable in the aftermath of the supposed "beaming." Her body, which had become quite bloated, discharged its excess fluids, while her blood count improved and her strength returned. Her condition improved to the point that she could be discharged from the hospital, and her final three months were spent at home, unbothered by most of the symptoms that had previously wracked her body.

Dr. E. Fuller Torrey, a psychiatrist and anthropologist, has noted four areas where shamans and physicians find common ground. These four factors, which appear to have universal application, figure into the success of every treatment regimen, and include:

1. *The patient's expectations.* The farther the patient must travel to secure a cure, the greater the chance the cure will be effected. The presence of accoutrements such as amulets, stethoscopes, and degree plaques clearly intensify the patient's expectations.

2. *The doctor-healer's training.* All genuinely sincere healers, whatever their cultural heritage, undergo a rigorous initiatory program, years in duration, prior to entering full-time service as a practitioner of the healing arts.

3. *The naming process.* The placebo effect stemming from the use of a technical term should never be underestimated. The patient will experience cathartic responses (often emotional in tenor) that appear to facilitate the healing process.

4. *The personality characteristics of the healer.* For a soul healer desiring to expedite the healing process, empathy, genuine sincerity, and personal warmth are absolutely indispensable.

These four factors are applicable to a broad range of therapies. For example, the patient's confidence in a clinician will be directly proportional to that healer's personal warmth and professionalism. In like manner, the value of equipment and similar aids should not be underestimated: books, hypnodiscs, music, and candles enhance the patient's expectations for a cure. In my office, I prefer to use a hypnodisc, which creates the optical illusion of movement through a tunnel as it revolves. I opt to use it because it simulates nature so well, suggesting the dark tunnel that many patients describe when recounting near-death experiences.

Finally, the more documentation the soul healer can provide the patient in witness of his (the healer's) many years of successful practice, the greater the patient's security and confidence will become, in turn accelerating the healing process.

Additional sources that address the fascinating field of shamanic healing can be consulted with profit. For readers interested in pursuing this fascinating field, I recommend the following writers and their works.

Michael Harner, an anthropologist/author, wrote *The Way of the Shaman* and *Journeys Outside of Time*. Harner was the anthropology chairman at the New School for Social Research in New York, and has taught at the University of California at Berkeley, at Columbia, and at Yale. His Foundation for Shamanic Studies teaches a three-year advanced program in shamanism and shamanic healing.

Timothy White, founding publisher of *Shaman's Drum: A Journal of Experiential Shamanism*. The editors of this publication describe their mission in a nutshell:

> We see shamanism not as a religion or a cultural tradition, but as a spiritual way of life based on the direct experience of the natural spiritual life forces around us. Shamanism provides teachings and techniques that can help ensure the healing, survival, and well-being of both the individual and the community.

20

SOUL HEALING THROUGH ACUPUNCTURE

Sole credit for the discovery of acupuncture belongs to the pioneers of ancient Chinese medicine, who developed this unique therapy on the foundation of their native folk medicine. Other branches of Chinese medicine have obvious counterparts in adjacent Oriental cultures, most notably Indian herbalism and Persian medicine. But acupuncture, the stimulation by needle, heat, or pressure of precisely defined points on the patient's skin, is wholly Chinese in origin and practice.

Remarkably, the seminal text on the theory and practice of acupuncture was penned over *forty-five* centuries ago. Credited to Huang Ti, the so-called Yellow Emperor of legend (c. 2697–2596 B.C.), the *Classic of Internal Medicine*, or *Nei Ching*, continues to exert authority, even down to our own day, as the definitive text on acupuncture.

The Chinese had exceptionally keen powers of observation. Their diligent research revealed previously unseen patterns in the human body's response to various organic dysfunctions. They discovered that very specific regions of the skin (called points) became sensitized when a given organ's function became impaired. This correlation between the sensitized points on the skin and abnormal organ function, far from being merely a random coincidence, was discovered to be a binding roadmap, demonstrating that each organ and bodily function had a corresponding "signature" on the surface of the skin. The results of acupuncture research, compiled from decades of ancient research, have established the validity of the relationships the Chinese had developed. Because the evidence pointed to a systematic relationship between the points on the skin and the internal organs of the body, the Chinese sought to do justice to their discovery by developing a framework in which to present and interpret the evidence they had so painstakingly compiled. Accordingly, acupuncture has been handed down to us clothed in metaphysical garb, in keeping with the Chinese philosophical heritage that gave it birth.

The pioneers of acupuncture soon realized that the patterns that evidently linked body function to specific patterns of points on the skin had actual predictive power: a given pattern of sensitive points would implicate a specific organ as the cause of the patient's difficulties. (Significantly, this level of precision in diagnosing illness was not to be reached by Western medicine until well into the twentieth century.) The Chinese soon realized that the patterns of points on the skin seemed to radiate in lines across the body surface. The imaginary line drawn through the points known to correspond to a specific organ was termed a meridian, providing a convenient shorthand for describing the patterns uncovered by the first acupuncture researchers.

Although many of the meridian identifications established by the Chinese appear straightforward from a Western point of view, some do not. We have no difficulty understanding that a given meridian is associated with the heart, or a lung, etc. But some meridians were linked to organs alien to the Western tradition of anatomy, such as the "heart constrictor" and the "triple heater." This circumstance becomes less unsettling when it is realized that the Chinese worldview is completely dynamic in outlook, for which reason organs are defined in terms of their function, not their physical structure ("morphology"). The notion that an action can exist without an agent was abhorrent to Chinese philosophy—a stance that undergirds their intriguing catalogue of organs lacking any clearcut Western analogues. (For their part, the Chinese today see Western anatomical definitions as clever but sterile abstractions that are almost comical in their one-dimensional approach to the human body, which was all that could be expected from researchers seeking information about living things by studying dead individuals.)

The Chinese soon realized an important implication of the meridian concept: lines that link point A to point B imply the notion of *transport*. Perhaps meridians were no less a pathway than were roads or rivers. Intuition and logic supported this new insight. In the process of time, the idea that meridians functioned as literal "energy pathways" in the human body became generally accepted in Chinese medicine.

The ancient Chinese doctrine of ch'i (spiritual and biological energy) is no less alien to Western medicine than are the meridian maps drawn by the pioneers of acupuncture. Early theorists proposed that every person born inherits a predetermined share of ch'i—that is, a fixed energy quotient indwells each person from birth. They held that ch'i was continuously *depleted* by the stresses and strains imposed on the body by the vicissitudes of daily living—whereas ch'i was *replenished* through energy obtained from food and air. (This biological model treats food holistically as an energy source, a more expansive concept than the narrow Western perspective that food is merely raw chemical fuel in the service of various metabolic processes.) A corollary of the ch'i model is the proposal that illness stems from energy imbalance. Excess ch'i is as harmful as too little ch'i, while the absence of energy altogether means death. The Chinese doctrine of disease can be reduced to a single sentence: *Energy imbalance is the root of illness.*

Ch'i flows from organ to organ, through the various meridians, in a fixed trajectory throughout the body. Its path extends from the innermost fundaments of the body to the boundary of the skin, weaving a path as beautifully complex as Western medicine's charts of the human circulatory system—and the ch'i energy paths are just as pervasive as their Western analogue. This constantly moving, churning energy is more akin to the Western concept of "nerve-energy potential" than to arteries and veins, however. It is even more closely related to the Indian doctrine of *prana* (life force). The common link between these Chinese, Indian, and Western notions is their conception of these biological energies as pure dynamic forces in continually active flux.

The foregoing summarizes the body-energy concept originated by ancient Chinese medical research. With this conceptual tool in hand, the Chinese were able to assemble a well-connected and systematic foundation for properly and logically developing the practical details of acupuncture therapy.

Although introduced to the West as early as the 1600s by Jesuit missionaries stationed in Peking, acupuncture was not accorded a serious hearing in scholarly circles until Soulié de Morant's research was published in the 1940s. De Morant, a French Sinologist and diplomat, wrote exhaustive analyses of acupuncture that offered a compelling and credible description and explanation of its theory and practice. Up until the publication of his research, acupuncture had made only temporary inroads into Western medicine; after de Morant had set it on a footing conformable to Western standards of logic and causality, acupuncture was never again pigeonholed as a mere curiosity.

The therapeutic significance of acupuncture comes into play when the acupuncturist adjusts the energy levels governing the function of impaired organs. Organ functionality can be "steered" by the practitioner, either boosting inadequate performance or trimming excess activity, by directly stimulating and guiding the energy flowing through the body's meridians. The human liver, for example, can often be revitalized when atonic, or calmed when irritated or congested, by means of specific acupuncture adjustments. Tachycardia (very rapid heartbeat, not to be confused with heart flutter or fibrillation) is exceptionally responsive to acupuncture therapy, evidencing almost immediate relief with the onset of treatment. Acupuncture's effectiveness in controlling the "action" of the stomach, intestines, bladder, and kidneys has been measured and documented. (In Chinese medicine, "action" and "function" are *not* synonymous terms. Action corresponds more to the mechanical activity of an organ considered in itself, whereas function embraces a far more comprehensive vision of an organ's purpose. The lungs, considered as a mechanical system, perform the task of inhaling and exhaling air—this constitutes the range of their *action*, but this *action* is in the service of a larger purpose altogether, the *function* of the lungs, which is inclusive of respiratory effects on the skin, the connection to human metabolism, etc. In short, Chinese terms, categories, and distinctions are freighted with significance, clarifying what would appear quite confusing when viewed through untrained Western eyes.)

Diversity characterizes each organ's response to acupuncture therapy. Among the internal organs, the liver is the most responsive to acupuncture, while the kidneys have proven difficult to control. On the other hand, the spleen and gall bladder do not lend themselves well to Western diagnostic methods, but their functions can be ascertained and regulated with ease when examined using Chinese pulse diagnosis and then treated by acupuncture.

Acupuncture achieves its highest potential when it deals with body energy, or ch'i. Every kind of pain dissipates immediately, and often permanently, when acupuncture is properly applied to the appropriate meridian point(s), provided no lesion is present. Contractures, no matter how chronic, are always relieved quickly. It is also possible to enhance muscular strength via acupuncture, since it improves vascular circulation and increases hemoglobin production, which both correlate with improved muscle tissue.

Acupuncture's efficacy has come under the most severe critical fire in cases where disease is attributable to microbial invasion, regarded by some as falling outside the scope of acupuncture's therapeutic range. Surprisingly, disorders of this kind do in fact respond quickly to acupuncture. China has many cases on record of cholera being cured within a matter of hours after the application of acupuncture therapy.

The efficiency of the sense organs can also be improved through acupuncture. Reported healings of blindness and deafness are so numerous, it would be imprudent to dismiss them out of hand. Of particular interest is the successful treatment of color blindness, which is quite important in Japan, since the disorder bars individuals with this condition from attending medical school and precludes acquisition of a driver's license. The mechanics of phenomena such as these are not readily explained in terms of Western medical knowledge—in fact, they are not susceptible to simple explanations even in the context of Chinese medicine. Nonetheless, the progress of illness and cure follows immutable physiological lines articulated in Chinese medical theory.

One significant discovery submitted to repeated empirical verification is acupuncture's propensity to increase red blood cell (RBC) production. Researchers in Japan and Europe have discovered that stimulation of a particular acupuncture point raises the RBC count of fully matured cells from a negative to a normal level within twenty-four hours. This level is usually maintained for four to six weeks, after which the treatment is repeated. These iterations continue until RBC production can be maintained, unaided by acupuncture, at a normal level. This point is reached when the underlying cause of the deficiency has been successfully treated.

The core concept behind acupuncture is the proposition that the body is self-healing, i.e., that living beings are brimming with vitality and are continually, subconsciously, rebalancing and regenerating themselves from within. This concept can be easily grasped. Cuts heal on their own, women have the creative power, once impregnated, to develop and produce children on their own, and the children in turn mature to adulthood, step by step, on their own. In much the same way, food is broken down, transformed, and separated into useful parts that are absorbed by the body, while the useless parts are evacuated. All this activity is performed automatically, without conscious direction or outside interference. In other words, there is a great source—and resource—within the body that continually maintains order, working for our benefit by vigilantly maintaining our health.

Acupuncture views the body as a self-rectifying dynamic whole comprised of a network of interrelating and interacting energies. Their uniform distribution and flow maintains health, whereas any interruption, depletion, or stagnation within this energy network leads to disease. Acupuncture is a system of medicine which seeks to aid these natural processes, helping the body rebalance itself by realigning or redirecting ch'i, the body's internal energy.

The concept of ch'i is difficult to define, even though everyone knows what it is at an intuitive level. It is often translated as breath, lifeforce, vitality, energy, or simply that which makes us alive. If there were no ch'i, there would be no life. A wilting plant lacks ch'i. A feeble person and a weak voice both exhibit a shortage of ch'i, while strong, lively, energetic people have ch'i in abundance. There is a lot of ch'i at a children's party. Ch'i is likewise overflowing in quiet strength. In illness, however, the ch'i is depleted, causing tiredness and depression. If ch'i is disturbed or agitated, it may cause irritability and over-reaction.

All of us know from experience what ch'i is, and can recognize when it is flowing smoothly. Acupuncture makes a detailed study of ch'i, dividing it into many different varieties as determined by their specific functions—for example, nourishment or protection. The proper quality, distribution, and even flow of ch'i is crucial to the underpinnings of organic health.

In addition to the idea of ch'i, acupuncture recognizes a subtle energy system by which ch'i is circulated through the body via a network of channels or meridians. The acupuncture points lie along these meridians, so that when the acupuncture needle is inserted, it affects the ch'i flowing within that meridian. This interlacing network of meridians is the *locus classicus*, the quintessential focal point, of traditional acupuncture.

The Chinese have compared the flow of ch'i throughout the body's meridians to water irrigating a landscape: feeding, nourishing, and sustaining the regions through which it passes. It is analogous in many ways to the circulatory and nervous systems, but unlike them is quite invisible to the anatomist's eye. However, the flow of ch'i can be determined from its effects, as trained practitioners well know, explaining why its course through the body had been so accurately charted more than 2,000 years ago. By needling the meridian points, the ch'i can be tapped or affected, influencing the state of the patient's health.

The Chinese have appropriated another analogy, describing the body as a musical instrument that constantly resounds with the flow of ch'i passing through the meridians, just as a flute will sound a tone when air passes through it. Good health equates analogically with a clear, pure tone emanating from the instrument, while illness is associated with discord. Stimulating different points or holes can alter the quality of intonation, changing a jarring dissonance to a pleasing consonance.

The notion of "tuning" (which we Americans most often associate with the engine of a car) and the associated concepts of the correct frequency and timing needed to make things run properly, are very useful—and meaningful—analogies for modern man. Incidentally, the fact that many of the theoretical principles of modern physics corroborate a worldview in harmony with the theoretical basis of acupuncture is no coincidence. Both disciplines are looking behind the scenes at the interaction of various energies. Acupuncture may be ancient in origin—but its principles have proven to be very modern indeed.

A new approach to health and disease arises naturally from a renewed understanding of the body as an energetic, vibrating whole. Modern Western medicine tends to be divisive, even fragmentary in its approach, focusing on one organ to the exclusion of the whole, of which that organ forms a systemic part. Acupuncture encompasses all the diverse signs and symptoms of ill health, distilling them without isolating them to create a basic pattern of somatic disharmony. This pattern includes the mental and emotional state of the patient as well as taking the physical symptoms into account.

These signs and symptoms are not seen as problems in themselves to be independently eliminated, but rather as warning signs pointing to ch'i imbalance in the patient. These imbalances can be corrected by inserting fine needles into predetermined acupuncture points lying on the relevant meridians.

Acupuncture, then, stimulates the body's own soul-healing powers. As the body returns to normal, the symptoms disappear. The aim of acupuncture is to restore the proper flow of ch'i, the life force of the body. This can be controlled at various points along the meridian system crisscrossing the body.

There is no substitute for the patient's own efforts to discover and remedy the cause of their illness. Acupuncture neither denies the ultimate responsibility of patients for their own health, nor offers itself as a panacea for every possible affliction, but until we learn to live more wisely, without prompting, there will remain a need for guides to point the way, and for systems of medicine to help restore bodily balance without adverse effects (*iatrogenesis*). Acupuncture is grounded in the theory of traditional Chinese medicine, inclusive of its practical and subtle understanding of health. Once one understands health, disease falls into place in its proper context—the clinician's task is therefore not to remove disease, but to restore health.

An acupuncturist who recently returned to the West after undertaking advanced study in China reported that his peers are now directing serious attention to a fundamental question. They do not frame their discussions in terms of which new disorders their science can cure, because Chinese medicine focuses on the patient, not the disease. This perspective notwithstanding, the widespread use of acupuncture has tellingly altered the way in which medical application of the discipline is set forth, for the search is no longer to discover which conditions respond to acupuncture, but rather to find which conditions don't respond.

The boast implicit in this approach underscores the confidence the Chinese have in their traditional medicine, based as it is on thousands of years of empirical study. This confidence is mirrored in the fact that the national health-care system of China has incorporated colleges and hospitals specializing in traditional Chinese medicine. These colleges and hospitals place traditional praxis on an equal footing with Western medicine, a circumstance the Chinese compare to the advantage of having two legs upon which to walk, since citizens can choose which therapy they prefer. It is interesting to speculate whether the Chinese—who regard traditional and Western medicine as complementary limbs of the same tree, of equal importance for maintaining a healthy nation—are puzzled by the West's apparent determination to concentrate on hopping along on only one leg.

In Western medical terms, we are accustomed to thinking of diseases as more or less specific entities. Consequently, we tend to judge the effectiveness of therapy in similar terms—it works if it gets rid of the disease. In the case of acupuncture, however, a different approach is required. An acupuncturist does not want to dodge the question if he or she is asked if acupuncture can cure cancer, arthritis, asthma, or psoriasis. The question would be more amenable to answering if phrased in a somewhat different manner. To an acupuncturist, such questions might present themselves thus: can the ch'i which is blocked, causing the immobility of arthritis, be moved again? Can the imbalance that is showing through the asthma be corrected? Rather than asking whether cancer can be cured, an acupuncturist will ask whether a particular person suffering from cancer can be brought back to health—or, if this is unrealistic because of the extent of the tumor's growth, can the patient's suffering be mitigated?

It is also important to recognize that acupuncture is only one part of the whole spectrum of traditional Chinese medicine. This also includes treatment with herbs, diet, massage, and exercise, which are often used in conjunction with acupuncture, or may even supplant it altogether. Acupuncture is not, therefore, an insulated system of medicine. It should be understood as one major method of treatment within a complete system that has a different perspective on health as compared to orthodox Western medicine. As the holistic approach to health gains more and more ground in the West, acupuncture use is becoming more widespread.

The common aim of all these traditional methods is to restore a person's health, balance, and harmony on all levels—physical, mental, emotional, and spiritual—by stimulating the body's own self-healing powers. The concept of holistic medicine, in which the person is seen as a whole rather than as a biomechanical machine afflicted by a series of unconnected symptoms, has been long familiar to the Chinese, although it is quite a new concept to Western ears. In contrast, the Chinese would be surprised that we would treat a patient's headaches in one medical department, their period pains in another, and their insomnia in a third. This fragmentation of medical theory is foreign to them.

A holistic viewpoint has always formed the basis of Chinese traditional diagnosis. Thus, asthma is merely a term, a label signifying a general theme—and people suffering from asthma will all show different variations on that theme. In one patient, an attack may be brought on by excitement or stress; in another by exertion; in a third, the onset of asthma may occur exclusively at night. An acupuncturist would look at each patient's background constitution, and would learn that perhaps one tends to sweat heavily, while another has very dry skin, and the third concurrently suffers from eczema. Questions on their general health would also be asked—family history, digestion, diet, bowels, etc.—to set the asthma within its historical context for a given patient. The patient may also be questioned about his or her emotional health. The Chinese hold that emotional stresses, such as a death in the family or other source of grief, can contribute to the advent of illness.

Because acupuncture is holistic in orientation, the disorder cannot be isolated from the patient. Because acupuncture utilizes a different framework for diagnosis, such analytic fragmentation is ill-suited for assessing the effectiveness of therapy. Nevertheless, it is difficult to show the depth and scope of acupuncture's potential action without using this Western perspective, and without giving examples in terms meaningful to Western medical practice.

Thinking within a Western framework, therefore, the following types of illness—some of which are diseases, some disorders, some merely symptoms—indicate the remarkably wide range of conditions for which acupuncture has proven effective:

- Bone, muscle or joint problems—including: arthritis, backache; inflamed, injured, or strained muscles; sciatica.
- Cardiovascular disorders—including: angina; high or low blood pressure; stroke; thrombosis.
- Childhood illnesses—including: catarrhal condition; colds; coughs; earache; skin problems; teething problems—acupuncture is remarkably effective in the treatment of children, although some practitioners prefer to use massage.
- Disorders of the head area—including: facial paralysis; headaches; migraine; trigeminal neuralgia; vertigo.
- Ears—including: deafness; otitis media; tinnitus.
- Eyes—including: conjunctivitis; glaucoma.
- Mouth—including: gum and tooth problems; ulcers.
- Nose—including: chronic catarrh; nosebleeds; sinusitis.
- Throat—including: sore throat; tonsillitis.
- Endocrine problems—including: hyperthyroidism; hypothyroidism.
- Gastrointestinal disorders—including: constipation; diarrhea; gastritis; duodenal and gastric ulcers; vomiting.

- Gynecological and obstetric problems—including: discomfort in pregnancy and as an aid to labor; menstrual problems (amenorrhea, dysmenorrhea, menorrhagia); morning sickness; thrush (candidiasis, moniliasis).
- Infectious diseases—including: dysentery; hepatitis; influenza; measles; mumps; whooping cough (pertussis).
- Liver and gall bladder disorders—including: gall bladder inflammation (cholecystitis); gallstones (cholelithiasis); liver enlargement.
- Mental/emotional disorders—including: addictions, depression, hysteria, insomnia, and phobias.
- Respiratory disorders—including: asthma; bronchitis (acute and chronic); cough (chronic).
- Sexual problems—including: frigidity; impotence; premature ejaculation; sterility.
- Skin disorders—including: eczema; psoriasis.
- Urinary disorders—including: cystitis, incontinence, kidney stones, retained urination.

Tests have shown that many types of sleeping pills reduce the Rapid Eye Movement (REM) phase of sleep, which is the time when most dreaming and soul healing occurs. All sleeping drugs tend to interfere with the natural sleeping patterns that are so critical to a person's psychological stability. Withdrawal from these drugs tends to increase Rapid Eye Movement sleep, which can lead to restless sleep and excessive dreaming, often including nightmares. Acupuncture can be helpful in alleviating these unpleasant effects, as well as helping the patient to re-establish a natural sleep pattern.

If a patient has problems sleeping, and feels unable to cope without resorting to sleeping pills, the acupuncturist can help reduce reliance on drugs while assisting with the regulation of the patient's sleeping patterns. Dependence on sleeping pills may be either physical or psychological, and the return to normal sleep may take up to six weeks to effect.

Some patients have discovered that acupuncture treatment has been of inestimable help in reducing or ending their nicotine addiction, so much that they cut back or quit smoking entirely. Acupuncture treatment tends to make the system more sensitive to toxins, and may therefore make the patient recapture a natural abhorrence for smoking. For the more serious addict, special treatments have been designed to clear and balance the lungs and to ease the effects of nicotine withdrawal. The patient must be firmly committed to quitting the habit, since acupuncture treatment can only provide assistance—it is not a miracle cure in itself.

Public awareness of the dangers of mood-altering drugs has grown over the last few years. The relative ease with which these potentially dangerous substances can be obtained is alarming in the extreme.

To the acupuncturist, the prescription of tranquilizers and stimulants to treat anxiety and depression is a matter of great concern. It represents perhaps the most disturbing example of the Western medical establishment's tendency to treat symptoms rather than their cause. There may be an occasional case where the use of antidepressants on a limited basis may help the patient cope with an overtaxing situation without apparent harm, but surveys linking extended use with ultimate addiction should alert all prescribers of such pharmaceutical substances that these drugs should be recommended and used with extreme caution. Like sleeping drugs, which are classified in the same category as depressants or sedatives, tranquilizers, and stimulants do not offer a direct cure, merely an alleviation of symptoms. Furthermore, their effect is generally short-term.

Withdrawal from all manner of addictive drugs can be helped by acupuncture treatment, although success will depend on the patient's determination and willingness to change.

In childbirth, the use of acupuncture can have two main effects: most commonly to reduce pain—less well known is acupuncture's ability to stimulate uterine contractions, ensuring a more healthy delivery. Reduction of pain without the use of drugs is of particular benefit, especially for the unborn child.

In China, acupuncture is also used to treat other problems associated with pregnancy, such as excessive morning sickness, or the malposition of the fetus. Traditionally, specific treatments are also given to the mother during the third and sixth month of pregnancy to aid development of the fetus. In general, conditions that conventional medicine would treat with drugs that could harm the unborn child can instead be treated with acupuncture, without the risk of any damaging effects to the unborn child. Even so, intervention is kept to an absolute minimum in all cases.

Acupuncture is finding increased use in the treatment of AIDS. This is a recent phenomenon, and the benefits are difficult to assess at this time. As with any treatment, effectiveness will depend on the severity of the individual condition, the amount of physical deterioration involved, and the specific medicine being used.

In the early stages of AIDS, acupuncture can be very helpful in reactivating the immune system. In every stage of the disease, it can help alleviate the large number of symptoms that tend to emerge. With rebalanced energy, the patient generally feels more relaxed and positive, maximizing the chances of a return to health.

Apart from limitations in the practitioner's knowledge and skill, and in a patient's willingness to heed advice, the most significant practical restriction is the need for the clinician to be present in order to administer acupuncture. In China, this problem is ameliorated by prescribing herbal remedies to be taken between consultations.

In the West, other limitations reflect the lack of practitioners. In particular, there is a need for hospital facilities, so that severe cases can be properly monitored, and emergencies dealt with effectively. Both severe asthma and emergencies such as appendicitis are treated by acupuncture in Chinese hospitals where immobile patients and the chronically ill can also be looked after and treated.

No acupuncturist would ever make the unequivocal claim that any identified disorder could definitely be treated successfully, for two reasons. First, treatment is not directed at the disorder itself, but at the person conceived of as an individual—and all people are different. Second, the names of the diseases, disorders, and symptoms listed on pages 202–203 reflect only a general classification scheme—to acupuncturist and Western physician alike. For example, there are several different types of eczema, and many possible causes for a bout of diarrhea or vomiting. Each case is considered individually and not in the disease-framework tabulated earlier. The scope and effectiveness of acupuncture is dependent in large part on the skill of the practitioner and the willingness of the patient to change. The practitioner needs perceptual acumen to assess the underlying causes that are giving rise to the disorder, and also must possess the ability to re-establish the flow of ch'i through acupuncture. The patient needs to be open to the idea of change so that soul healing can proceed.

Not surprisingly, it is far more demanding to practice an integrated viewpoint than to focus only on isolated symptoms. In the latter approach, each symptom can be dealt with in relative isolation, whereas holism requires that everything be related to the whole until the complete pattern of disharmony is correct in order to re-establish health. Although the holistic approach may be more difficult to practice, it is also more realistic in many ways. By taking in many different facets of a patient's condition, in the nature of the case, acupuncture offers a deeper understanding of the patient's health as a whole, providing a rounded and comprehensive picture. It emphasizes the uniqueness of each individual, ensuring that the patient is the object of treatment, not just some disease-label.

At what point do these two systems meet? In broad terms it can be affirmed that acupuncture lays its heaviest emphasis on restoring and promoting health, while Western medicine concentrates on eliminating disease. Although these aims might seem superficially similar, in practice the attitudinal differences this divergence of views generates are profound.

For example, consider the treatment of a sore throat. More often than not, a doctor will diagnose an attack in terms of a specific bacterium, whereupon he will prescribe a course of drugs, usually antibiotics, as treatment. The aim of the drug is to destroy the agents of infection. This approach usually works, and the sore throat disappears.

The same patient consulting an acupuncturist is given a lengthy initial examination. The whole case history is taken, including details not only of this specific sore throat, its onset, development, and present condition, but also the complete background (e.g., are sore throats unusual or common for this patient; the general health of the patient; the patient's emotional state; etc.). For example, assume that the acupuncturist has discovered that the patient has been prone to sore throats since a year ago, when his father unexpectedly died. Since then he has tended to get a sore throat very easily if exposed to drafts or cold weather. The therapist might make a diagnosis that the root cause of the conditions was the patient's lung ch'i being weakened under the stress of his father's death earlier. The lungs are now unable to resist penetration by wind-cold, which later turns to wind-heat. This has resulted in a propensity to get sore throats.

Treatment concentrates initially on the lung, large intestine, and three-heater meridians, with two primary objectives in mind. First, the wind-heat must be expelled in order to prevent further penetration into the lung and to relieve the sore throat. Second, the lung must be strengthened to improve its capacity for overcoming disease. In order to meet these objectives, however, the acupuncturist must assess why there was weakness in the first place, and then recognize how to rectify it. Through the strengthening of his or her lungs with additional treatment, the patient is better able to cope with the grief, moving through it to find that he or she is no longer prone to sore throats.

Acupuncture's aim is to build up the body's own inherent powers of self-defense, rather than bring in outside forces to help fight disease. By re-establishing the body's vitality, treatment makes the patient fitter, stronger, and more resistant to future infection. Although antibiotics can eradicate an infection, the fact that they operate externally may mask an underlying internal susceptibility, actually weakening the body's ability to resist disease in the future. Most people who have followed a course of antibiotic treatment for a relatively minor infection are familiar with the sense of weakness and debilitation associated with drug therapy.

While orthodox medicine seeks control over the symptoms of disease, often ignoring the cause in the process, acupuncture focuses its attention on the root causes of disease, relieving symptoms as a byproduct of solving the underlying systemic problem.

Historically, acupuncture is a major part of traditional Chinese medicine. As such, it is inextricably bound up with a unique theoretical system based on acupuncture points and meridians, combined with a theoretical and diagnostic framework wholly alien to anything encountered in Western practice.

In China, the training for traditional Chinese medicine requires five years of full-time study, two years of which are devoted to herbal medicine. Serious schools of acupuncture in the West have three-year, full-time courses.

An increasing number of family doctors are undertaking some minimal, part-time training in acupuncture. Although this increases somewhat the public and medical awareness of acupuncture and its benefits, the inevitable limitations of these courses can have a negative effect if they prevent an appreciation of acupuncture in its complete and integrated form. Such pseudo-acupuncture courses focus on the analgesic aspects of acupuncture and accupressure, ignoring the central role that holistic diagnosis plays in traditional acupuncture.

The research criteria laid down by Western medicine tends to restrict the type of acupuncture treatment that can be offered—while simultaneously restricting the assessment of its effectiveness. Success in Western medicine is measured in terms of relief of symptoms, whereas the acupuncturist's definition is infinitely more broad and encompassing. The aim of Chinese medicine is not merely to eliminate disease, but to improve the functioning and quality of life.

Patients receiving treatment will often comment that they feel better or are able to function more fully long before any distinct physiological changes become apparent. I hope that both orthodox and alternative medical research will give these important factors their proper weight and place in the future, seeing the patient as a whole being rather than a collection of independent symptoms.

In 1971 an American journalist witnessed major surgery being conducted using acupuncture as the sole means of anesthesia. He reported his observations in *The New York Times*, igniting a great deal of interest in the subject. Acupuncture was suddenly taken more seriously in the West, and a considerable amount of subsequent research has been conducted into the way acupuncture "works."

Early research suggested that the measured effects were purely neurological in origin (the so-called gate theory, or the reduction of pain sensations by stimulating alternate nerve pathways), whereas later research implicated various chemical mechanisms (e.g., endorphins transported via the blood stream).

Though this kind of research has gone a long way toward giving acupuncture the recognition it deserves in the West, it has tended to focus excessive attention on pain control, thereby deemphasizing acupuncture's wider range of therapeutic effects while ignoring the theoretical basis of Chinese medicine that created the system in the first place (the ch'i energy theory).

There are exceptions to the above rule, of course. A major conference organized by the World Research Foundation, called The Congress of Bioenergetic Medicine, was held in Los Angeles in November 1986. The conference aimed to bridge the gap between medicine and the latest discoveries in physics, and included detailed discussions of acupuncture and homeopathy. Particularly active researchers in these disciplines are Professor William Tiller of Stanford University, California, and Dr. Hiroshi Motoyama in Tokyo. Both scientists had been involved for many years in serious scientific study of the body's subtle energy systems. Dr. Motoyama invented a sophisticated diagnostic tool premised on the energy flow within the body's meridians which is now used in Japanese hospitals, and to a lesser extent in the United States, for early detection of organic imbalance.

The fact that this kind of research is still so rare demonstrates the difficulty of uniting the Western medical worldview with that of energy medicine. That this is not simply a problem of Eastern and Western thought disjunctions has been clearly shown by Professor

Tiller's research into acupuncture and the purely Western system of homeopathy. Fundamental to acupuncture's "orphaned" status is the medical profession's vague aversion to the concept of subtle energy.

Energy medicine accepts the existence of a subtle energy system within the body, holding that manipulating the body energetically can cause physical, material changes to take place. Matter and energy are understood to be completely interchangeable—in fact, they are regarded as being, ultimately, the same thing. These ideas are common coin among disciples of post-Einsteinian "energy physics," but the Western medical viewpoint remains rooted in an outdated, Newtonian worldview, the same one that has shaped Western conceptions of material reality for 300 years. This worldview has inculcated the notion that the body is a collection of component parts, not an integrated whole; a collection of individual organs and chemical reactions, not a dynamic being; and, perhaps most tragically, it sees the mind as being completely separate from the body.

Of course, the scientific method has had its successes and advantages, but as medicine moves forward technologically, we appear to be losing sight of the concept of health care, of the everyday maintenance of health, and the promotion of overall well-being.

The Chinese term for physics is *Wu Li*, which may be translated as "patterns of organic energy." Acupuncture is essentially an energy medicine, acting on the body's subtle energy system to bring about changes in the mind and the body. In order to begin to understand it in Western terms, we must accept the interchangeable nature of energy and mass, of mind and body. We must also accept the idea that the fundamental essence of nature is change and indeterminance.

The fact that the new physics corroborates these notions is surely exciting, but if the technology of this new science were to be employed in research into the subtle energies of the body and its intercalated meridian system, great advances into our understanding of "energy medicine" might be made. Historically, the kind of equipment necessary to detect such subtle energies has been unavailable, but recent technological advances may put acupuncture on a scientifically verifiable basis in the very near future.

Orthodox medicine—despite its use of ultra-modern equipment and its achievements in laser surgery and genetic engineering—is still deeply rooted in a mechanical world view. As the technology of modern medicine progresses, the treatment of patients has become ever more dehumanized and impersonal. The body is so subdivided into its constituent elements that all appreciation for the whole is atomized. The feelings and emotions of the patient are deemed irrelevant to the functioning of their body machine. This mindset tends to actively discourage patients from taking part in their treatment: they must occupy a passive position vis-à-vis their own healing.

The Chinese system of medicine refuses to see the body in mechanical terms. If acupuncture's role in Western medicine is reduced to the treatment of localized pain, however beneficial this may be in itself, it is no longer Chinese medicine in the full sense of the word. Only when grasped in the context of its ancient philosophy can acupuncture be seen as a vital part of a comprehensive medical system, embodying a true form of soul healing.

Let us hope that our Western world view will soon catch up with the discoveries of modern science, and that energy medicine will not be so alien a concept to the Western mind. Fortunately, our bodies seem to be able to understand energy medicine quite well.

A central idea in Chinese philosophy is the concept of the *Dao* (also called *Tao*), which was expounded in the classic text called the *Dao De Jing* (more commonly called the *Tao Te Ching* in the West). The Dao is the road, the path, the way, and by extension, the way we do things, or the way the Universe works. To maintain harmony with the Dao is to live in harmony with the way that the Universe works—keeping us in tune with nature and natural law. In Chinese medical terms, this idea of harmony amounts to a working definition of health.

Yin/Yang expresses a system of relationships, patterns, and functions. Everything in the Chinese view of the world and of life is related to a dynamic balance of Yin/Yang. Every thing has an inside (Yin) and an outside (Yang), a top (Yang) and a bottom (Yin), and there is continual interchange and intercommunication between the two. Life takes place in the alternating rhythm of Yin/Yang—day gives way to night, night to day; a time of light and activity (Yang) is followed by darkness and rest (Yin). Flowers open and close, the moon waxes and wanes, the tides come in and go out; we wake and sleep, breathe in, breathe out. Yin/Yang is a constant, continual flow through which everything is on the one hand expressed and on the other recharged. Yin and Yang are an inseparable couple. Their proper relationship entails health; a disturbance of imbalance between them leads to disease.

In medicine, Yin/Yang is used to describe and distinguish patterns of disharmony. Within the body, the back is considered Yang in relation to the front, which is more Yin; the lower parts of the body are Yin in relation to the upper parts, which are Yang; the interior of the body is Yin in relation to the exterior Yang.

In distinguishing illness patterns, weakness suggests Yin, strength Yang; fast, sudden onset suggests Yang; slow and lingering conditions are Yin; underactivity implies Yin, while overactivity bespeaks Yang.

The basic patterns of disharmony have been classified in Chinese medical taxonomy as the Eight Principle Patterns, and are grouped together under their basic Yin/Yang aspects: Interior/Exterior, Deficiency/Excess, and Cold/Heat.

These terms are frequently encountered in Chinese medicine, providing a fundamental diagnostic tool and heuristic framework for understanding illness.

Many books supply detailed lists of Yin and Yang phenomena, but such lists can be misleading. The important point to be gleaned is that nothing is ever entirely Yin or Yang. Everything contains the possibility of changing into its opposite. For example, the front of the body is Yin, in contrast to the back which is Yang. Looked at in another way, the chest is Yang when compared with the abdomen, which is more Yin. Similarly, the skin is Yang compared to the blood, which is Yin, but the blood becomes Yang in relation to bone marrow, which, being deeper and more interior, is more Yin.

This intermingling, changing pattern of Yin/Yang is beautifully illustrated by the symbol of *Tai Ji* (shown below), the great polarity. All things have a Yin and Yang aspect, represented here by the light (Yang) and dark (Yin) areas. They are in balance, but this balance is fluid and changing—a dynamic equilibrium between light and dark, constituting an active interplay and mutual exchange rather than a rigidly fixed and static quantity.

The small black circle within the light region, and the small white circle embedded in the black, convey the idea that nothing is either purely Yin or purely Yang, and furthermore implies that everything can be further subdivided into increasingly smaller levels of Yin and Yang. It is this that explains the endless variety of all life, the uniqueness of each individual. This is the key to understanding individual variation, and is crucial to acupuncture diagnosis and treatment. In modern scientific terms, a parallel can be made with genetics, in which the mother's (Yin) chromosomes combine with the father's (Yang) chromosomes to produce a unique combination within the child.

The symbol also illustrates the interdependence of Yin and Yang. The light grows out of the dark, while the dark grows out of the light.

This is the principle of mutual support which can be seen in any relationship. Mutual support is complementary to mutual control. There is a counterbalancing of Yin with Yang, and vice versa, from which a natural tendency to restore things to the norm can be inferred. Western medicine would call this *homeostasis*, and conceive of it in terms of hormone balances and nerve impulses.

At the height of Yang, Yin appears; when Yin is at its most intense, it transforms into Yang. This transforming of each essence into its opposite is constantly seen in health crises—for example, when a high fever breaks into chills and sweating. There are well-known cycles of a similar nature in cases of depression, where the patient swings from apathy and indifference to a dangerously false high or mania.

These primary concepts of the natural flow of life (Dao), expressed through the dynamic interchange of Yin/Yang, are at the root of Chinese medicine.

Until the 1970s, acupuncture practice in the United States was largely confined to the oriental quarters of major American cities. However, since 1971, development has been substantial. Books and articles have appeared by the dozens, practitioners have come from China, Japan, and Korea, and theorists and teachers have also visited from Europe. Americans in greater numbers have begun to study acupuncture, and schools of acupuncture have been established in various parts of the country. Many states now recognize the medical and therapeutic value of acupuncture. Acupuncturists are licensed for independent practice in fifteen states—California, Florida, Hawaii, Montana, Nevada, New Mexico, New York, New Jersey, Oregon, Rhode Island, and Washington. Four other states, Maryland, Massachusetts, Pennsylvania, and Utah, as well as the District of Columbia, license acupuncturists to work in collaboration with other physicians.

State recognition reflects the amount of research being carried out at noted centers of learning such as the University of California, the Downstate Medical Center in New York City, the Upstate Medical Center in Rochester, New York, the Lemuel Shattuck Teaching Hospital in Boston, and the University of Virginia.

Since 1981, the unifying force in American acupuncture has been the American Association for Acupuncture and Oriental

Medicine (AAAOM), which serves both as a forum for the profession and as an advocate for new thoughts and directions. In 1982, the National Accreditation Commission for Schools and Colleges of Acupuncture and Oriental Medicine was established as an independent body to monitor the performance, integrity, and quality of the acupuncture teaching establishments within the United States.

Acupuncture is growing steadily in the United States. There are some 4,000 practitioners currently at work, and at least 300 new ones are accredited each year.

Oriental systems of medicine—and nearly all alternative systems—stress the importance of the soul in their understanding of health and illness. To the acupuncturist, if the soul (Shen) is out of balance, the whole system lacks control and direction. It is no less important that the problems of the soul be treated through rebalancing, the removal of blockages, and the restoration of natural energy flow, and not by suppressing symptoms with potentially addictive and toxic medicines, as is often done for problems of the body.

In China, acupuncture is often used to heal emotional and mental disturbances. This is primarily because the Chinese see no reason to distinguish between physical and mental problems as we are prone to do in the West. Both kinds of disorders are treated at the same time by the same doctor, being viewed as different manifestations of the self-same pattern of disharmony.

Most patients find acupuncture treatment relaxing and calming. Long-term therapy has been shown to be as effective in treating problems involving emotional imbalance as it is in treating physical imbalance. Left untreated, emotional imbalance may result in physical symptoms, and is considered to be a major cause of disease by Chinese theorists. Emotions should be expressed freely, in moderation, and should never be suppressed nor over-indulged.

In summary, acupuncture is used daily in many countries around the world to treat people with both acute and chronic disorders, ranging in intensity from mildly discomfiting symptoms such as headaches to serious organic problems such as gallstones. It may be used to not only treat back pain, coughing, colds, and premenstrual tension, but also to influence the patient's soul for good. The Chinese regard the mind and body as parts of a continuous whole; both aspects may be affected by treatment. In all cases, treatment works by activating the acupuncture points, which stimulate the body's own restorative and recuperative powers so that the natural state of balance and harmony that is commonly called good health can be restored. An acupuncturist might say that treatment is analogous to removing a blockage impeding the natural flow of water, permitting the stream to clear itself and run freely in its re-opened channel once again. I would merely reply that it is, first and foremost, a form of soul healing.

For further information on acupuncture, I suggest the following contacts:

National Accreditation Commission for Schools
and Colleges of Acupuncture and Oriental Medicine
(NACSCAOM)
P.O. Box 954
Columbia MD 21044

National Commission for the Certification of
Acupuncturists (NCCA)
1424 16th Street NW, Suite 105
Washington DC 20036

American Association of Acupuncture and
Oriental Medicine (AAAOM)
783 Rincon Avenue
Livermore CA 94450

21

SOUL HEALING THROUGH MEDITATION

Some of the earliest of written records on the subject of meditation come from the Hindu traditions of around 1500 B.C. These records consist of scriptures called the Vedas, which discuss the meditative traditions of ancient India.

The sixth century B.C. saw the rise of various forms of meditation—Taoist in China, Buddhist in India—and even the Greeks delved into meditation.

The earliest known Christian meditators were the desert hermits of Egypt in the fourth century A.D. Their generic meditative practices strongly resembled those of the Hindu and Buddhist traditions.

In the eleventh and twelfth centuries A.D. the Zen form of meditation, called "zazen," gained popularity in Japan.

Finally, in the 1960s, a wave of meditative practice began in the United States in a form representing a "Westernized" style in the Hindu tradition. Called "Transcendental Meditation" (TM), it was brought to this country by Maharishi Mahesh Yogi.

In our Western culture, *meditation* refers to the act of thinking, planning, pondering, or reflecting. Our Western definitions, however, are not representative of the essence of the Eastern world's notion of meditation. In the Eastern tradition, meditation is a process by which one attains "enlightenment." It is a growth-producing experience along intellectual, philosophical, and, most importantly, existential (soul healing) dimensions.

Meditative techniques may then be categorized by the nature of their focal devices. Using this criterion, there are four forms of meditative technique.

1. Mental Repetition. This form of focal device involves dwelling on some mental event. The classic example of a mentally repetitive focal device is the "mantra." A mantra is a word or phrase which is repeated over and over, usually silently to oneself. We would include chanting under this category as well. TM uses a mantra format. The TM mantra is chosen from several Sanskrit words. Herbert Benson employs the word "one" as a mantra for the hypertensive patients he treats. A Tibetan Buddhist mantra in verse form is "Om mani padme hum" or "om" for short. The Christian prayer "Lord Jesus Christ, have mercy on me" is said to be a form of mantra as well.

2. Physical Repetition. This focal device involves the focusing of one's awareness on some physical act. An ancient Yogic (Hindu) style of repetitive meditation focuses on the physically repetitive act of breathing. Various forms of breath control and breath counting (called "pranayama") serve as the basis for one form of Hatha Yoga. The aspect of Hatha Yoga best known to the public involves the practice of postures (called "asanas"). The Moslem Sufis are known for their practice of continuous circular dancing, or whirling. The name "whirling dervishes" was given to the ancient practitioners of this style. Finally, the popularity of jogging in the United States has given rise to the study of the effects of such activity. One effect reported by some joggers is a meditation-like experience. This could be caused by the repetitive breathing or the repetitive sounds of the feet pounding on the ground.

3. Problem Contemplation. This focal device involves attempting to solve a problem with paradoxical components. The Zen "koan" is the classic example. In this case, a seemingly paradoxical problem is presented for contemplation. "What is the sound of one hand clapping?" is one of the most commonly known koan.

4. Visual Concentration. This focal device involves visually focusing on an image. It could be a picture, a candle flame, a

leaf, a relaxing scene, or anything else. The "mandala" is a geometric design which features a square within a circle, representing the union of man with universe. This is often used in Eastern cultures for visual concentration.

Practicing meditation for fifteen to twenty minutes, once or twice a day, is sufficient. Before lunch or before dinner are generally the best times to meditate, although practice in the morning may provide a relaxing start for the entire day.

When the focal device is successfully employed, the brain's order of processing appears to be altered. When the rational (analytic) mind is silenced, the intuitive mode produces an extraordinary awareness. This awareness is the goal of all meditative techniques.

This state of "extraordinary awareness" has been called many things. In the East, it is called *nirvana* or *satori*. A liberal translation of these words yields the word "enlightenment." Similar translations for this state include "truth consciousness" or "being-cognition." In the early Western world, those few individuals who understood it called it the "supraconsciousness" or the "cosmic consciousness."

Positive therapeutic growth can be achieved without reaching the ultimate supraconscious state. There are five steps in meditation:

1. Difficulty in Breathing.
2. Wandering Mind.
3. Relaxation.
4. Detached Observation.
5. Higher State of Consciousness.

Even the ancient Hindu and Zen scriptures on meditation point out that it is far more important to attempt to achieve the supraconscious state than it is to actually reach that state. Simply by taking time out to meditate, the individual is making a conscious effort to improve health. This effect, by definition, is the antithesis of the behavior pattern that leads to excessive stress. The importance of simply meditating, rather than achieving the supraconscious state, will remove much of the competitive, or success-versus-failure component in this process. The second hallmark of the supraconscious is a noticeable increase in relaxation.

The third hallmark of the supraconscious is that of detached observation. In the Indian scriptures, this hallmark is described as a state in which the meditator remains "a spectator, resting in himself" as he observes his environment. This state is an egoless passive state of observation in which the meditator simply "coexists" with the environment rather than confronting or attempting to master it.

The final step in the meditative experience is the "supraconscious state." This state appears to be a summation of all the previous states except in greater intensity. It has been characterized as:

- A positive mood (tranquillity, peace of mind).
- An experience of unity or oneness with the environment; what the ancients called the joining of microcosm (man) with macrocosm (universe).
- A sense of inability to describe the experience with words.
- An alteration in time/space relationships.
- An enhanced sense of reality and meaning.
- Paradoxicality, that is, acceptance of things which seem paradoxical in ordinary consciousness.

In his book *The Relaxation Response,* Benson describes four basic components in successful meditation:

1. A quiet environment.
2. A mental device.
3. A passive attitude.
4. A comfortable position.

Benson states that this "passive attitude is perhaps the most important element." With this attitude, the client "allows" the meditative act to occur, rather than striving to control the meditative process.

There are those who consider true meditation more of an active process. One of the goals of meditation is to attain a state of mind in which the soul is enriched by a more intense and unadulterated quality of love, intelligence, and strength than we have experienced before. It is this *enrichment* of awareness which is the true goal of meditation. The technical term for it is *transcendence*.

Transcendence always involves the act of entering into an enriched and active state of mind; it is not just an escape from something unpleasant or mundane. There are many steps which must be climbed before transcendence is achieved; it is not the simplistic act of "getting yourself out of the way" that many people want it to be. Indeed, some of the popular meditative systems, in describing the nature of transcendence, actually trivialize and distort it. A concentrated effort to forget our body, emotions, and mind, for example, can actually result in *disconnecting* us from our capacity to be aware and mentally alert. It unplugs us from our daily activities—and also from our capacity to receive the greater wisdom, goodwill, and strength of the higher self. It may serve to relieve some stress, to be sure, but the price we pay for the benefit is outrageous. It makes no more sense than does amputating an arm in order to cure a rash.

The purpose of transcendence is enrichment, not escape. If our expectation in meditating is simply to escape a dull and disappointing existence in the physical plane, we will have no chance of entering a legitimate state of heavenly consciousness. Instead, we will go directly to the fantasy department of our own emotions, where we will play with papier-mâché dolls of God and saints and angels—and maybe a demon or two. We will pretend to be meditating, just as children who play with dolls pretend to be grownups—and we will believe in our pretense, but we will not in fact be communicating with the higher self—just our wish life.

For these "active meditation" proponents, the goal of meditation is to transfer some of the life of the higher self into the personality where it transforms daily behavior and self-expression. As such, meditation is anything but a quiet, passive state; it is a dynamic process involving three distinct stages:

1. Contacting the higher self.
2. Transferring some quality, energy, or idea.
3. Using it to transform the life of the personality.

The first stage is similar to the activity of the actor trying out for a part. The director advertises the parts available; the actor responds and appears for an audition. To many, it might seem that winning the role is the hardest part of acting—but it is really just the initial stage. The same is true in meditating. Many people believe that contacting the higher self is the *entire* work of meditation. In reality, it is just the beginning.

For the actor, the next step is to learn the lines, walk through the paces of the role, and rehearse the part. It is much the same for the one who meditates. Having contacted the higher self, he or she seeks out the guidance or inspiration needed to act, and rehearses ways to express this in life.

Once the lines are memorized, then the actor faces the hardest task: mastering the state of mind, feeling, conviction, and movement of the role—and how the character must react to and interact with the others in the cast. The actor becomes the character and brings to life a believable portrayal of a human being. The third stage is also the hardest one for the meditator: having glimpsed the insight or love or plan of the higher self, he or she must now assimilate that greater life into his own expression. Old patterns of thought or behavior which will conflict with the new must be removed, and the meditator must move beyond them, establishing new habits, new patterns of thought and feeling, new definitions of self-image, new ethics, new skills, new values, or whatever is required to properly honor the inspiration and intention of the higher self. He or she must permanently improve his self-expression in some significant way while remaining flexible in order to grow some more in the future.

Meditation transforms. Meditators need to pattern themselves after the mythical alchemist, who sought to transmute lead into gold. Meditation is the alchemy of human consciousness, seeking to transmute our habits and feelings and thoughts into something more refined and noble—the wisdom, compassion, and skill which characterize the enlightened individual (soul healing).

True meditation goals are not merely cleaning up a few bad habits and then stopping, content with making modest improvement. The alchemy of transformation is meant to be a continual process, with each succeeding meditation adding a new layer of richness to our character and creativity. We are meant to take peak experiences of love and become so acquainted with them that they soon become our customary self-expression. When we do this, then we stand ready for even greater peak experiences than before. Just so, we are meant to convert awe-inspiring revelations into simple, common-sense attitudes and perspectives toward life. When we do, we stand ready to be inspired by even greater elements of the higher self.

The sure sign of the novice is the meditator who gushes about the wonders of his or her meditations. "Oh, wow—you should have seen all the white light." The experienced meditator has seen all the white light he or she wants to see; he or she continues to be moved by truly profound experiences, but they become progressively more subtle. Meditations move us not to talk and exclaim, but to act!

They move us to improve our character, learn new skills, make new commitments, contribute to life, and integrate the treasures of heaven into the rich opportunities of earth.

- A meditation that does not bring in the life of spirit is no meditation.
- A meditation that does not lead to growth of character or creativity is no meditation.
- A meditation that does not lead to soul healing is no meditation.

To understand this distinction, it is helpful to realize the difference between sensation and consciousness. Briefly stated, sensation is any perception made directly by the personality, either through its physical, emotional, or mental senses. Consciousness, by contrast, is the knowingness of the higher self. The capacity to sense is a projection of consciousness, but consciousness itself is much greater.

Many people who profess to meditate simply deal with a somewhat higher level of sensation than usual; they close their eyes to physical phenomena but keep them focused on emotional and mental phenomena. Except as a very introductory stage, this does not serve the work of meditation. We must make the effort to climb out of sensation and enter into the realm of consciousness.

- The goal of meditation is not just to get more ideas—it is to obtain the power to think!
- The goal of meditation is not just to get more good feelings—it is to tap the power to love! The goal of meditation is not just to slow down our heartbeat or breathe more deeply—it is to contact the power to act!

Consciousness *is* the staging ground of meditation. Meditation does not *alter* consciousness, as so many people glibly insist; nor does it *raise* consciousness. It turns our attention away from sensation and focuses it in consciousness. What may or may not happen to the physical body of the meditator is therefore inconsequential. It is what occurs in consciousness that is all important—and how successfully the meditator assimilates the power of consciousness into his daily self-expression.

In this regard, it is helpful to keep in mind that not all actors are successful in projecting the essence of their character to the audience. Some fill the stage only with emptiness, but the truly inspired actor magnetically charges the auditorium from the very moment he appears.

The work of meditation is to magnetically charge our awareness and activities with the dynamic presence of the higher self—the presence of consciousness. If we are using meditation effectively, then eventually everything we think and do and say will reveal the wisdom, love, and power of our spirit.

There are many worthwhile reasons for spending some of our meditation time helping others. Probably the most important is that the higher self itself is actively involved in healing the problems of humanity and promoting the evolution of consciousness in the human race. Since we are striving to value what the higher self values and act as the higher self acts, learning to help others is a natural way to honor the wisdom and love of the higher self. Some additional reasons for helping others through meditative activity include:

- It is part of our duty as a human being to help society grow and develop. The value of society and civilization to us individually is immeasurable. It has helped clothe us, feed us, protect us, educate us, and inspire us; it has given us a context in which to discover our individuality, find meaning in life, and grow as a human being. In turn, we have an obligation to help society.
- Humanity has a tremendous need for greater wisdom, love, and enlightened direction. If we can radiate even a small portion of these treasures of spirit into the mind and emotions of humanity, we perform a useful service.
- Using meditation to help others opens up a new opportunity for self-expression. Many people have an urgent need to increase their enlightened self-expression in life, thereby grounding intentions, ideas, and goodwill. Serving humanity and helping others is an excellent way of enriching self-expression.
- As we work in these ways, we realize more profoundly that we are, in a very real sense, a citizen of the universe. The work of helping others activates some of the most significant and powerful aspects of our individuality as a human being. It likewise helps us develop an awareness of the Aquarian spirit.

- The use of meditation to help others also gradually builds a rapport, physically and telepathically, with other people who are working with similar purpose and intent. This can greatly enrich the impact of the light and love which is radiated—and helps us find new friends and acquaintances who share similar interests and activities.

The focus of attention in meditation should always be on the *quality* of consciousness—not the *form* through which consciousness is being expressed, whether that is a chakra, a mantra, a color, a posture, a guru, or anything else. Our goal is to enlighten our understanding, enrich our emotions with compassion and goodwill, and mobilize our intention with dignity and skill.

Meditative techniques, as a form of soul healing, of the mantra type have been found useful:

1. In the treatment of anxiety and anxiety neurosis.
2. In the treatment of phobias.
3. For increasing "self-actualization" and "positive mental health."
4. As an adjunct in the treatment of drug and alcohol abuse.
5. As an adjunct in the treatment of essential hypertension.

22

SOUL HEALING THROUGH YOGA

In 1956 at the Institute of Mental Health in Bangalore, India, a frail forty-eight-year-old yogi named Shri Khrishna Ivengar stepped into a freshly excavated pit, which had been dug by a team of scientists who had come to witness what would happen. With prayer book in hand and chanting quietly, the yogi lit his incense and stepped into the pit, where he lay flat on his back. He was wired with electrical instruments to monitor his vital functions. The pit was then filled with dirt and covered with a wooden board. In order to survive, the yogi reduced his metabolism enough to sustain himself on the little air that seeped through the dirt. As the experiment progressed, the doctors, psychologists, and medical scientists from the World Health Organization waited anxiously, intently studying the monitors that registered the yogi's heartbeat, respiration, and other life signs. When the pit was uncovered more than nine hours later, the yogi was found alert and calm. He rose to his feet, smiled, and waved to the hundreds of spectators who showered him with garlands of flowers. The supreme irony lies in the fact that this extraordinary feat made no great impact in the annals of medical science.

In 1969, Swami Rama, age forty-two, came to the United States to demonstrate to Western medical scientists the benefits that yogic discipline could bring to the nervous system. He was willing to allow his yogic training of mind and body control to be monitored by modern medical instrumentation. This experiment took place at the Menninger Foundation in Topeka, Kansas. (Voluntary Controls Project: Swami Rama Research Department, The Menninger Foundation, June 6, 1970. Biofeedback for Mind-Body Self-Regulation: Healing and Creativity Research Department, The Menninger Foundation, October 30, 1971. Researchers of both projects: Elmer E. Green, Ph.D., Alyce M. Green, B.A., E. Dale Walters, M.A., D. W. Ferguson, M.D.)

The swami showed extraordinary differential control over the blood supply in his right hand. He caused two areas several inches apart on his right palm to change temperature gradually in opposite directions until they showed a temperature difference of about 10° F. The left side of his hand became flushed, while the right side turned an ashen gray. The swami wished to demonstrate how he could induce full cardiac arrest for a period of three to four minutes, but preparation for this feat required that he fast for a couple of days, taking only fluids. Since the swami had other pressing engagements, Dr. Elmer Green suggested that he stop his heart for just ten seconds, explaining that would be more more than adequate proof of the swami's powers of control.

The swami was wired for the demonstration. Before starting his "inner focusing," he requested that once his heart stopped he be informed via the control room intercom, using the phrase "That's all." This would signal him not to exceed the allotted time. He elaborated, saying he did not want to affect the functioning of his "subtle heart." Then he made a few tries at speeding and slowing his heart and suddenly announced that he was going to "create a shock," and that no one should be alarmed. Dr. Green thought the swami meant that he was going to give *himself* the shock, but he actually meant that the researchers gazing at his polygraph might be shocked by what he was about to do.

After seventeen seconds of motionless silence, someone intoned "That's all" over the control room intercom. The swami then pulled in his stomach muscles for a few seconds and relaxed. Almost immediately, the control room suddenly broadcast the news that the health record was not what had been expected, urging Dr. Green to take a look immediately. He did so, and reported to the swami that his heart rate had not dropped to zero, but had instead jumped from seventy beats per minute to almost three hundred beats per minute. The swami seemed surprised and disconcerted. "You know," he told Dr. Green, "that when you stop the heart in this way, it still trembles," using his hand to indicate a fluttering motion. The swami's cardiograph was examined later by Dr. Marvin Dunne, cardiologist and professor at the Kansas University Medical Center of Kansas City. The phenomenon depicted in the cardiograph was described as "atrial flutter," a state in which the heart tires at its maximum rate, during which blood fails to fill either chamber properly while the valves become totally ineffective. Dr. Dunne, who was not present at the demonstration, inquired whether the swami had passed out after this dangerous and phenomenal feat. Dr. Green told him that nothing of the sort had happened.

The medical reports indicate that the atrial flutter actually lasted for an interval of between seventeen and twenty-five seconds. The exact duration was indeterminate because the electrical impulse created when the swami drew in his stomach caused the EKG pen to fly off the edge of the paper; seconds after it returned, the heart rate had returned to normal. By drawing in his stomach, the swami had established a "solar plexus lock," allowing his heart condition to be maintained for a considerable amount of time, if he had so desired. In summary, the swami stopped his heart from pumping blood for at least seventeen seconds.

We will discuss how these feats were accomplished, and how yoga can bring about soul healing.

The basic problem of every living creature is survival in a hostile world. Countless generations ago, from the teeming human masses of the East where man lived in ever-present dread of famine, disease, flood, invasion, and vengeance of gods, yoga, a system or method of attaining physical and mental serenity under adverse and even horrible conditions, was introduced.

Man, in his essence, has changed little in the course of historic time. The philosophy of yoga and its practice, which enabled the Indo-Aryan to survive the stresses of his time, can also enable people of the modern Western world to achieve contentment and security in the face of perils in a rapidly changing world.

The word "yoga" cannot be translated into English. In Sanskrit, it derives from the root *yuja,* which is to join or weld together. Just as two pieces of metal are welded together to become one, so, in the philosophy of yoga, the embodied spirit of the individual becomes one with the Universal Spirit through the regular practice of certain physical and mental exercises.

Only the Indian form of yoga is well known in America and Europe, but there is strong evidence that yoga principles were known to the Egyptians and Chinese and that there were monastic societies among the Hebrew Essenes who were, from reliable historical evidence, groups of yoga practitioners.

Yoga means the union or linking together of man with God, or the disunion or separation of man from the objects of physical sensation in the material world. It is the science or skill which leads the initiate by easy steps to the pinnacle of self-realization.

To attain a condition in which the fullest relaxation is possible, it is essential to control the brain and the nervous system In old Sanskrit tracts we find the statement: "When the nervous system is relieved of all its impurities, there appears the perceptible signs of success ... the glowing color of health."

While speaking of the "brain," we must, to some extent, drop the Western traditional concept of the brain as the sole seat of consciousness. As far back as 2,500 years ago, the yogins were in conflict with the accepted Hindu medical science of the time. These ancient medical men held, as did the ancient Greeks, that the heart was the seat of consciousness. The yogins, on the other hand, stated that the brain, with its highly involved nervous system, was one unit which represented the true physical medium of human mental activity. There is an interwoven cerebro-spinal system and an autonomic nervous system. In the yoga system of histology, the cerebro-spinal system is said to consist of the *sahasradala,* the brain, and the *susumna,* the spinal cord, which are enclosed within the cavities of the cranium and the spinal cord or vertebrae. Linked together in the autonomic nervous system is a double chain of ganglia which are situated on each side of the spine and which extend from the base of the skull to the tip of the coccyx.

There are 72,000 *nadis,* or nerves, which form a countless number of nerve endings. Of the nadis, about a dozen have been thoroughly studied by the yogins. Three have been found to be of primary importance: The *ida* or left nostril, the *pingala,* or right nostril, and the susumna, the spinal cord. These are believed to exercise control over voluntary and automatic responses of the human body and can be brought under control by yogic methods.

Centuries before scientists recognized electrical force, yogins had evolved a theory of nerve-impulse transmission which has won acceptance from Western medical investigators in this century. If we substitute the word *prana* for electrical impulse, we find that the oldest yoga principles of neurology are now endorsed in the modern theory of nerve action. Obviously, the yogins anticipated the principles of electrical phenomena by discovering the positive and negative animal-magnetic currents, the nerve impulses, and that can be controlled and adjusted by yoga practice.

Every individual's physical and mental well-being depends on the fine adjustment of the nervous system, controlling even the secreting glands. One benefit of a yoga regime is the control or restraint of the various modifications which may take place in the nervous system. In addition to the beneficial effects of the physical aspects of yoga on the gross and finer muscles and tissues, yoga also establishes, through postures and attitudes and psycho-physiological practices, complete control over the nervous system. Only when the nerve impulses can pass in harmony through the spinal cord may *samadhi*, a state of suspended sensation, be reached.

Freedom from emotion is one of the tenets of yoga. Early modern psychologists discovered a strong relationship between the emotions and the body in terms of increased or reduced ductless gland secretion, respiration, circulation, and blood pressure. Yoga medical investigators have attributed diabetes, arteriosclerosis, nephritis, and other diseases to the effects of emotion on the glandular system and thence on the body organs. *Samatva*, or absolute freedom from emotions, is considered one of the prime essentials for the health of the nerves and brain. Even a minor emotional flare-up or a long period of subdued anxiety will affect the body.

One method of avoiding emotions and anxieties is to train or habituate the mind to concentrate on a selected object. This concentration is called *dharana*. Without purposeful concentration, the mind diffuses its energies in varied directions, while with strong concentration, the mind can be freed of distractions and can approach a state of detachment or nonawareness of extraneous matters. This is the essence of concentration. The habit of concentration is known to produce a sedative effect, similar to that induced by deep breathing, with manifold benefits to the health of the nervous system.

We will concentrate here on Raja Yoga, a system which has been found most applicable to the mental and physical conditions in which we live. Raja Yoga has eight principles. These are:

1. Yama—non-killing, truthfulness, non-stealing, continence, and non-receiving of any gifts.
2. Niyama—cleanliness, contentment, mortification, study and self-surrender to good.

3. Asana—posture.
4. Pranayama—control of vital body forces.
5. Pratyahara—introspection.
6. Dharana—concentration.
7. Dhyana—meditation.
8. Samadhi—super-consciousness.

Yama and *Niyama* constitute the moral training without which no practice of yoga will succeed. As this moral code becomes established, the practice of yoga will begin to be fruitful. The yogi must not think of injuring either man or animal through thought, word or deed.

Before continuing with our discussion of Raja Yoga, we should make a distinction between that school of thought and another, called Hatha Yoga.

Hatha Yoga deals entirely with the body. The sole aim of that school of yoga is to make the body physically strong. You can achieve almost the same effects as those given by Hatha Yoga by enrolling in a course at any health club. Hatha Yoga exercises are difficult and demand years of steady endeavor. Through this system, it is claimed that a yogi can establish perfect control over every part of his or her body. The heart can be made to stop or go as bidden, and the flow of blood and sensations of the nervous system can be controlled.

The result of this type of yoga is to make humans stronger and to prolong their lives; good health is its one goal. From the point of view of the Raja Yogi, the person who perfects himself or herself in Hatha Yoga is merely a healthy animal. This system does not lead to spiritual growth or give people the help to meet their need for relaxation that is found in Raja Yoga. However, certain aspects of Hatha Yoga have become part of the regime of Raja Yoga. These include some of its exercises, dietary aspects, and disease preventives, which provide the physical state of well-being enabling the proper pursuit of yoga.

The exercises, or postures, are called *asanas*. The series of exercises should be practiced daily until certain higher states are reached. They constitute the next stage in Yoga. At first, a posture should be adopted which can be held comfortably for a fairly long time.

The technique for this is as follows: stopping the right nostril with the thumb, with the left nostril, inhale according to your capacity.

Without pausing, exhale through the right nostril, while closing the left one. Now, inhale through the right nostril and exhale through the left. Practice this three or five times, at four times during the day—upon awakening, at midday, in the evening, and before going to sleep. Within fifteen days to a month, purity is attained.

Other Yoga Types

Karma Yoga. Karma Yoga means service (Seva) or selfless work, action done with an attitude of detachment for the fruits of the action. All misery and pain comes from attachment. If such selfless work is done, one gains freedom from all misery and pain.

Bhakti Yoga. This teaches how to worship and pray to God with love and affection. With this type of yoga, one learns to gain control over emotional instabilities and ultimately love the entire world.

Jñana Yoga. This form of yoga teaches the process of right reasoning and inquiry leading to thought-free meditation. With this practice, one learns with acuity of mind how to approach the ultimate truth.

Kundalini Yoga and Tantra. Kundalini Yoga teaches how to gain control over the dormant power of the Kundalini or psychic energy of transformation. Kundalini dwells at the base of the spine where the three psychic nerves (Ida, Pingala, and Sushumna) come together. Kundalini is emphasized in various Tantric practices, which include a number of yogic approaches like *Mantra Yoga, Japa Yoga*, and *Laya Yoga.*

Now, we may consider pranayama, or breath control. Breath is the most obvious manifestation of Prana. Along with the breath, we slowly enter the body, which enables us to discover the subtle forces and how the nerve currents are moving throughout the body. When we perceive and learn to feel these forces, we begin to get control over them and the body.

If possible, it is best to have a room devoted to your practice of yoga and to no other purpose. Do not sleep in that room; you must keep it holy. You must not enter the room until you have bathed and are perfectly clean in body and mind. Place flowers and pleasing pictures in the room. Have no quarreling, or anger, or unholy thought there. Allow only those persons to enter who are of the same thought as you are. Eventually, an aura of holiness will pervade that space, and when you are sorrowful, doubtful, or disturbed, entrance into that room will make you calm. If you cannot afford a room, set aside a corner; if you cannot do that, then find a place, either inside your house or outside, where you can be alone and where the prospect is pleasing.

Sit with a straight posture. The first thing to do is to sense a current of holy thought to all creation. Mentally repeat, "Let all things be happy; let all things be peaceful; let all things be blissful." Do so to the East, South, North, and West. The more you do, the better you will feel. You will find that the easiest way to make yourself healthy is to see that others are healthy, and the easiest way to make yourself happy is to see that others are happy. Afterwards, if you believe in God, pray. Do not pray for money, or health, or heaven, but for knowledge and light; every other prayer is selfish.

Pranayama may seem at first to be totally involved with breathing. However, breathing is only one of the many exercises through which we get to the real pranayama, or control of the prana. According to old Indian philosophers, the universe is composed of two materials, one of which is called *akasa,* the omnipresent, all-penetrating existence. Everything that has form, or that is made up of compounds, evolves from the akasa.

The akasa is manufactured into our universe by the power of prana. Just as akasa is the infinite, omnipresent material of our universe, so is prana the infinite, omnipresent *power* of this universe. At the beginning and at the end of a cycle everything becomes akasa and all the forces that are in the universe evolve back into the prana. In the next cycle, out of this prana is evolved everything that we call energy or force. It is the prana that is manifested as motion, the power of gravity and magnetism. The prana is manifested as the actions of the body, nerve currents, and thought. All thought and all physical motion are manifestations of prana. The sum total of all force in the universe, mental or physical, when resolved back to its original state, is called prana. The knowledge and control of this prana is what is meant by pranayama.

The control of the prana is the one goal of pranayama. This is the purpose of the training and exercises. Each man must begin where he stands, and must learn how to control the things that are nearest to him. Your body is the nearest thing to you, nearer than anything else in the universe, and your mind is the nearest of all. The power that controls this mind and body is the nearest to you of all the prana in the universe. Thus, the little wave of prana which represents your own mental and physical energies is the nearest wave of all that infinite ocean of prana. You must first learn to control that little wave of prana within you. If you analyze the many schools of thought in this country, such as faith healers, spiritualists, Christian Scientists, hypnotism, psychotherapy, etc., you may find that each attempts to control the prana. Following different paths, they stumbled on the discovery of a force whose nature they do not know, but they subconsciously use the same powers which the yogi uses and which come from prana.

The yogi believes the mind can exist on this higher plane, the superconscious. When the mind has attained to that state which is called samadhi—perfect concentration or superconsciousness—it goes beyond the limits of reason, and comes face to face with facts which instinct or reason can never know. Manipulation of the subtle forces of the body, which are different manifestations of prana, if trained, stimulates the mind, which progresses to the plane of the superconscious. This is the yoga equivalent to my superconscious mind tap.

From the explanation above, it can be seen that pranayama is not breathing, but controlling the muscular power which moves the lungs. The muscular power that travels through the nerves to the muscles and from those to the lungs, making them move in a certain manner, is the prana. Once this prana is controlled, we find that other actions of the prana in the body slowly come under control.

Every activity of mind and body demands energy. If a great deal of energy goes to one particular place, that place will be proportionately more active. The yogi aims at keeping his vital organs in a healthy state, so that they need a minimum of energy, and instead of letting the energy lie dormant he whips it into activity by the stimulating effect of breathing exercises, and consciously directs it to where he desires it to contribute a positive amount of energy. Ultimately, with the spiritual objective in view (the objective of all yoga), the energy is directed to the mind, and with its plus-quality actuates the mind to discern things spiritually and attain a form of soul healing.

23

HEALING AND THE NEW PHYSICS

David Bohm, the renowned physicist who developed the stochastic causal interpretation of quantum mechanics and advanced the notions of wholeness within the implicate order, was troubled by the term, "psychosomatic." He felt that the conceptual disjunction of mind, body, and psyche inherent in the term gave an untrustworthy picture of the underlying reality. To do justice to the intrinsic unity of the constitutional elements of our being, Bohm advocated substituting "somasignificance" for "psychosomatic." Because he firmly believed in man's essential oneness, he disdained dichotomy and trichotomy in favor of the doctrine of wholeness. Consequently, Bohm held that we all possess the ability to listen to our bodies, and to thus harness the disease process to redirect our lives.

Niels Bohr proposed that the dynamics of conscious thought occur on such a minute scale, involving such infinitesimal exchanges of energy, that only a quantum mechanical explanation could properly account for the actual phenomenon of consciousness. Walker went a step further, becoming the first researcher to formulate a provisional quantum mechanical description of human consciousness. His model postulated that the fundamental "unit" of consciousness is the quantum itself. Since *our* basic understanding of brain neurophysiology parallels these various models, we must recognize that dimensional considerations alone would compel us to seek a quantum explanation of the elemental energetic mechanisms in the brain. Simply put, an adequate understanding of the brain demands the application of quantum concepts.

The quantum conception of time differs radically from conventional, linear notions, so much so that perception of time in a quantum context can have extraordinary import. Many athletes have reported experiencing time in just such a way, their descriptions often resembling the physicists' notion of nonflowing, nonlinear spacetime. In his groundbreaking volume, *The Ultimate Athlete,* George Leonard collated a large number of such "nonordinary experiences of time."

> Thousands of such events occur every day, in sandlots and city streets and giant stadiums. For the most part, they are unreported and thus only faintly experienced. The culture goes on distracting itself with extravagant spectator events and consumer products and restless travel, all the while ignoring the vast riches that lie as close to us as our own experience. These riches are by no means limited to the field of sports, but are especially abundant there. The intensity of the experience, the intricacy of the relationships, the total involvement of body and senses, all come together in sports to create the preconditions for those extraordinary events that the culture calls "paranormal or mystical."

New models of holistic health demonstrate that matter is neither absolute nor immutable—matter can be both transformed into energy and created from energy. Energy-containing voids (black holes) can serve as both cradle and grave for matter. These various processes continue unabated, even after "death" has supposedly set in.

Pioneering quantum physicist John Wheeler wrote that:

> The world at bottom is a quantum world; and any system is ineradicably a quantum system. This suggests that eventually our concepts of how our own bodies work will have to give due regard to quantum physical events and the probabilistic, statistical subatomic world. At present, most bioscientists believe the subatomic events are too small to be of practical importance.

Some scientists have objected to this line of thinking, protesting that "electrons and human beings are not the same thing." The prejudice inherent in this rejoinder is at root quite unscientific. Adopting this principle would have led scientists to dismiss the possibility of humans ever flying—on the grounds that flight is an attribute possessed only by small animals such as bees and hummingbirds.

Although its first principles were enunciated by Max Planck as far back as 1900, quantum physics is often termed "new physics." Its conceptual framework makes demands of its disciples, requiring one to step outside the self, to transcend one's environment, and to comprehend the universe in its ineffable radiance. New physics realizes its goal only when the seeker concedes that transcending self is both impossible and unnecessary. This is also the main lesson taught in Zen Buddhism. The master guides the student to the point where conscious searching is finally abandoned. The rational mind is understood to impede acquisition of true understanding. Our greatest growth (soul healing) is achieved only through the complete integration of the spiritual and physical. In this light, perhaps the ultimate spiritual goal is not so much to transcend, but to fully acknowledge and embrace the immanent oneness of our own being.

What exactly are the capabilities of the human consciousness? Research by Ullman and Krippner at the Dream Research Laboratory of New York City's Maimonides Hospital provides the requisite background for answering this question. For example, a sleeping subject was "sent" specific images by a distant "sender" during a designated sleep phase. The subject would be awakened and asked to record the content of his dreams. An independent panel of judges searched for statistical correlations between the subject's transcribed dream and the sender's "transmissions," and were stupefied by the results. The judges soon realized that coincidence had to be ruled out as a possible explanation for the inexplicable convergence of the two data sets. Such research is relevant for our purposes because soul healing is inconceivable, apart from some form of telepathic transmission mechanism.

In the early 1980s, physicists Targ and Puthoff, working at the Stanford Research Institute (SRI), sought empirical evidence for "remote viewing" (out-of-body experiences). In hypnosis, a subject was directed to describe the environment of another individual many miles distant. Leaving their bodies enabled the subjects to locate their targets, whereupon they provided detailed descriptions of their whereabouts. Some of the subjects amazed the researchers with the stunning accuracy of their reports.

Biofeedback research provides additional grist for the mill. Laboratory subjects are essentially given an artificial "window" into otherwise hidden parts of their body—a window created by sensors and transducers that convert measured body events into a palpable form (blinking lights, moving meters, tonal variations, etc.). The subject's electronically enhanced awareness of his or her bodily processes enables them to directly affect the function being measured, relying on information gleaned from the transducers to make the desired adjustment. Subjects have learned how to regulate both heart rate and blood pressure, increase blood flow to specific regions of the body, and modulate electrical activity in various muscle groups. The subjects' ability to micromanage body processes was entirely unexpected. Many of them learned how to increase blood flow to a single finger, or to a proscribed region on the forearm. Some were even able to control the activity of muscle cells governed by a single motor nerve.

Classic learning theory falls short in accounting for the results of these kinds of biofeedback experiments. The level of minute physiological control exhibited by the subjects simply falls outside the scope of conventional dogma.

The American Association for the Advancement of Science formally addressed this issue in the 1979 symposium titled "The Role of Consciousness in the Physical World." SRI's Willis Harman proclaimed that the data then in hand could only be explained if scientists presupposed four key axioms concerning human consciousness and its attributes. Harman's axioms proposed that mind is spatially extended (the extensive aspect); that mind is temporally extended (the protensive aspect); that mind is ultimately dominant over the physical (the psychodynamic aspect); and that minds are joined (the concatenative aspect). Reject any of these axioms, and the data becomes inexplicable.

Conscious mental activity can affect the things of the physical world—including the organs, tissues, and cells that compose our bodies. Mind is an irrefutably genuine factor in the process by which health and disease unfold themselves. This axiom casts a long shadow over the results of modern medical research, pointing up a fundamental flaw in its method. At issue is a foundational assumption governing the empiricists' approach to medical experimentation: the assumption that the conscious attitudes and biases of the *experimenter* have no effect on the outcome of the experiment, and therefore can safely be ignored. The evidence controverts this assumption.

A burgeoning interest in the question of how human observers influence and affect the objects of observation has generated a growing body of apposite literature. Contemporary quantum theory has become a veritable womb for the origination of new theories designed to account for the interconnectedness of the observation process. These theories span a broad spectrum of opinion, the extremes of which are in mutual antagonism. For example, some hold that the observer's instruments so dominate the observation process that no portion of the measurements being taken are attributable to the target object itself. Conversely, others teach that events transpiring within the mind of the observer are determinative of the mensuration process, thereby hinting at the profound notion that the quantum realm may function as the vestibule through which mind and object connect—thus validating mensuration at the deepest imaginable level.

Phrases like "the physics of consciousness" have lost their utility, thanks to a regrettable escalation of their ambiguity quotient. Salvaging this important concept from the conceptual fog now obscuring its true significance will require a full, unbiased probe of the entire range of theoretical thought touched on above, including the intercalated hybrid theories situated between the radical extremes. Mainstream scientists are convinced that they have successfully systematized the position that champions the primacy of the observer's instruments on the observing process, in their minds obviating the need to consider competing ideas along the conceptual spectrum. This abridgement of vision continues to hobble those who approach the issue in so one-sided a manner.

Not surprisingly, we are left with the most well-known problems in measurement theory, those stemming from the Heisenberg Uncertainty Principle. (This physical law states that the position and velocity of an object can never be simultaneously determined.) But at the cutting edge of measurement theory, a concern with the role of the consciousness of the observer is re-emerging, gaining adherents despite the fact that the precise mechanism by which mind impacts physical reality via quantum interaction remains a fascinating mystery. Happily, the first primitive models have continued to evolve and improve as a more enlightened science gropes its way toward the truth.

Corroborating evidence for a quantum level shunt (*quantum leap*) between the realms of the mind and the body is abundant. (N.b. the term "quantum leap" is here used colloquially for didactic impact, and not in the technical sense whereby Bohr and Einstein described electrons jumping from shell to shell.) The evidence for these leaps can be clearly seen in those cases where cures have occurred quite apart from conventional medical intervention, among which faith healing, spontaneous remissions, and placebo effects deserve to be numbered. Why are these heterodox cures relevant to the present discussion? Because in each instance, the faculty of inner awareness seems to have promoted a dramatic jump—a quantum leap—within the somatic healing mechanism.

According to the new physics, all reality is interconnected at the deepest levels. Observations performed on one object can affect the data readings taken on another, regardless how one isolates the objects from one another. They may not be in physical contact at all—they may even be light years apart—but in the most profound, universal sense, they are never out of contact with each other.

Beyond spacetime we find pure consciousness. We cannot fathom its nature, but neither can we deny its imposing presence. This duality has led to a scientific impasse. Survey the panoply of inexplicable phenomena recorded in literature: psychokinesis, bending light by thought, materialization and dematerialization, astral travel, out-of-body travel, clairvoyance and precognition, reincarnation, auric fields around living things, telepathy, psychometry, teleportation, levitation, healing with the mind or hands, etc. This is quite a list! It should provoke in you the question, "Why doesn't science finally settle the legitimacy of these phenomena one way or another?" Science, however, is only as good as its methodology and starting assumptions, and in this instance, method is clearly implicated as the sticking point.

The methodology of science is erected on the twin pillars of demonstrability and repeatability. These two attributes are the chief criteria for admission of evidence into scientific discourse—whatever can't be repeated and/or demonstrated is *a priori* excluded from consideration. Scientific evidence is evidence that must be *objectively observed*, but the various phenomena listed above are paranormalities that are predominantly *subjective* in scope, depending as they do on the state of the observer. The observer must be in an altered state of consciousness (hypnosis or other alpha level) to perceive these phenomena.

How does the universe produce anything at all? A quantum wave flows between two given events in the same way that a river springs from a source and flows to a sink. The quantum wave then "turns around" in space-time and flows from the sink back to the source. The resulting self-reinforcement of the quantum wave as it undergoes retroflexion through its own space-time mirror image produces the experience we know as reality. In 1953, John Wheeler hit upon an astonishing insight, "based on dimensional considerations," that spacetime is not flat (featureless, unstructured) at the smallest scales (the so-called Planck length), but is actually a highly energetic "quantum foam." This foam is marked by the rapid creation and reabsorption of spacetime "bubbles," which meant that the so-called vacuum of empty space is actually a surging sea of quantum fluctuations. The spontaneous breakdown and regeneration of the quantum foam that forms the spatial backdrop in which reality unfolds is based on the double-flow process previously mentioned, a retroflexive process that occurs in like manner in every physical phenomenon. This is the proper birthplace of self-organization: self exists through the interaction of quantum waves with their spacetime mirrored images (retroflexive conjugates), in the same way that you interact with your own mirror image. Ponder these unsettling facts concerning human interaction with mirrors: to notice yourself in the mirror, you must forget yourself, and to forget yourself you must take note of yourself. Change is effected through self-reflection, and by observing ourselves in others we are able to change each other.

Quantum waves can move faster than light—they are "superluminal." They can go backward or forward in time. Physicists Sudarshan, Feinberg, and Recami called objects that traveled faster than light, *tachyons*. (As a technical aside, David Bohm and J. P. Vigier reasoned that superluminal transmissions arose from "wavelike, photonlike, collective motion of the quantum potential," offering a more integrated, holistic alternative to the tachyon theory popularized in the press.) Einstein and his adherents deduced that objects traveling faster than light—superluminal entities—can be observed in reversed time sequences. The mathematical underpinnings for these effects flowed directly out of Einstein's original model, were rigorously worked out, and later elevated to the status of scientific orthodoxy. Synthesizing our results, it would follow that the quantum wave is a wave of probability moving faster than light that serves as the connecting agent between our minds and the physical world.

PARALLEL UNIVERSES

Quantum physics teaches that a flipped coin lands either heads up or tails up, but never heads and tails simultaneously. For each statistical possibility, there exists a parallel universe in which that particular potentiality becomes actual reality. Thus, in one universe the coin lands heads up, but in the other it lands tails up—but you occupy both universes observing the outcome! You exist in each separate universe at once, yet there is no direct ontological bridge between the two: the complementary worlds remain hidden from one another.

Your existence spans all the parallel universes simultaneously. You may be quite ill in one, yet healthy in another. Focusing on the healthy universe (reprogramming yourself to a different frequency) initiates the restoration of health. We often have thoughts of wholeness and health when we are sick, and thoughts of illness when we are quite healthy; these may just result from our awareness of the parallel universes (frequencies). All futures and pasts exist concurrently—time is not so much a river flowing past our vantage point, of which only a fraction is discernible at any one juncture, but rather is like a huge ocean that we can take in with a single glance. If we are "hung up" on the past, the past will dominate and shape our view of the future, but changing our perception of the present will be the key to changing the future.

There is no death. There is only a shift in awareness. Because change alone rules over us, our only enemy is our own ego (our defense mechanisms). Pogo is right. We have discovered the enemy and it is us. Jesus, Buddha, and others have tried to show us how to reunite Ourselves with ourselves.

Parallel universes are born whenever an observation is made. According to quantum physicist Fred Alan Wolf in his book *Parallel Universes* (pg. 27),

> There are parallel yous and mes somehow existing in the same space and time that we live in but normally not seen or sensed by us. In these universes, choices and decisions are being made at the very instant you are choosing and deciding. Only the outcomes are different, leading to different but similar worlds.

Parallel universes are predicted by both quantum theory and Einstein's theory of relativity. General relativity theory also predicts the existence of black holes, understood by physicists Stephen Hawking and Kip Thorne to be putative bridges between parallel universes. In light of Einstein's demonstration that space, time, and matter are mutually dependent, the circle of the argument can finally be closed with the stringency of a syllogism: the parallel universes can and should be accessed, as befits beings who dream of being captains of their souls.

If quantum waves are the actual medium of thought, could they not travel outward or inward, passing through the nearest black hole into a parallel universe that may exist in our past or future? Surely, if thoughts were superluminal and were carried by quantum waves, they could travel to the edge of the universe and back almost instantaneously. (Based on the computed density of quantum foam, namely 3.6×10^{93} g/cm^3, the round trip would take only 10^{78} seconds!) Signals traveling this fast could be "reflected" backward in time.

A corollary of the parallel universe model is that certain conditions could arise as a result of a patient's inability to remain on one parallel universe. Such dimensional instability could easily account for multiple personality disorders, UFOs, schizophrenia, and other forms of psychosis. The disorienting effects of being unwillingly wrenched from world to world would obviously traumatize even the most robust psyche.

The spontaneous appearance and disappearance of UFOs also finds resolution in the parallel universe model, which accounts for their sudden arrivals and departures in terms of instantaneous shifts between worlds. Wolf (p. 310) also states:

> Our minds are thus tuned or are tunable to multiple dimensions, multiple realities. The freely associating mind is able to pass across time barriers, sensing the future and reappraising the past. Our minds are time machines, able to sense the flow of possibility waves from both the past and the future. In my view there cannot be anything like existence without this higher form of quantum reality.

In Chapter 1, I described how healing begins in the aura before it progresses into the body proper. Auras appear to be closely associated with quantum wave functions, not only those in our brain and mind but also those that traverse space-time itself. Perhaps the aura is the result of receptor cells in the human retina responding to the quantum wave movement—like a quantum fingerprint left on the retina. When the person whose aura is being observed changes his mind, it instantly changes the quantum wave between observer and the observed. Those sensitized to the subtleties of this change could discern it through one of the five somatic senses, e.g., smell something, or visualize a purple glow. The receptive observer might hear voices or perceive a foreign presence. An observer with a well-trained mind might detect quantum wave movements as pneumatic manifestations, such as thoughts or sudden feelings about the person being observed (e.g., "I know you are angry"). Finally, everyone has experienced the feeling that they knew someone they had never actually met before. On quantum principles, this phenomenon occurs naturally when you tune in to the other person's quantum wave movements.

HOLOGRAMS

Scientists have learned how to record on film the interference pattern that results when light reflected from a 3-D object interacts with a laser beam. The interaction of the reflected light and laser is referred to as a hologram. The film records the complicated diffraction pattern in the same way photographic film records light intensity and color. The usefulness of a hologram isn't evident until one reverses the process and passes a laser light back through the diffraction pattern in the film. Amazingly, the laser scatters off the ripples in the diffraction pattern and assembles a 3-D optical image of the original object that was recorded—and it hangs eerily suspended in mid-air. By looking through the flat holographic plate, you can see the original object as if it were being viewed through a window, but the actual object may no longer be present.

The hologram cannot be destroyed by cutting the plate that generates the image into smaller pieces. Each sliver and shard of the plate, when held up to the light, will still create the image of the entire original object, just as the whole plate had done. The image is weaker, but it is nonetheless complete. This amazing phenomenon not only enables 3-D viewing, but preserves complete isomorphism between the holographic image and the actual object.

Karl Pribram, neurosurgeon and hologram expert, discovered that the human brain functions holographically. Pribram conducted an elaborate mathematical analysis of interference wave functions and discovered powerful evidence of holographic object-rendering "hardware" within the brain's memory and perception centers.

According to Pribram, frequency domain is the primary reality, and is composed solely of frequencies. This frequency domain is really a "black hole" where time and space have collapsed, dissolving their natural boundaries. Within, everything occurs simultaneously. A new order of reality reigns therein, where paranormal events (telepathy, NDE, past lives or healing) are projections of a holographic reality. Causality is excluded in the absence of space and time, or in other words, when time and space collapse, so does causality.

The holographic model of memory and perception provides the only viable model that fully accounts for the brain's stupendous storage capacity—the brain would quickly fill up with visual data alone within a few years of birth, given standard models of how neurons might store information. When death approaches, one experiences the holographic reality without mediation—we become directly plugged in, as it were. That is why core experiences in NDE exude such certitude and conviction regarding their visions. The process of dying involves a gradual shift of consciousness from conventional reality to the holographic reality of pure frequencies. Once passed over into the new reality, the consciousness still functions holographically, reconstituting frequencies back into perceivable object-images.

The hologram provides a pedagogically useful analogue with which to bridge the gulf between personal and transpersonal consciousness. There are at least two kinds of consciousness: personal/individual consciousness, and transpersonal/unitive consciousness. The former is exemplified by the pattern of light seen when pressure is applied to our closed eyelids. The latter involves total absorption in pure oneness, the absence of all multiplicity, and the apprehension of the essential ultimacy of unity. This involves dissolution of the boundary between the personal self and the external world.

Unfortunately, the world has tended to see the distinction between personal and transpersonal consciousness as an "either/or" scenario, rather than a "both/and" situation. Western psychologists will not countenance the idea of a transpersonal, cosmic consciousness, interpreting it as a nonveridical, hallucinatory experience propagated by electrochemical aberrations in the brain. On the other hand, the Eastern consensus is that all personal consciousness is mere illusion. The false dichotomy carved out by these competing schools of thought continues to obstruct serious discourse well into the present day.

In conclusion, the new physics teaches us that all time is simultaneous, and unmarred by either artificial or natural demarcations or divisions. Each body is in dynamic relationship with the universe and every other body through subquantum superluminal contact. All matter, space, and time are relative. The observer is so interconnected with the thing observed that isolation and insulation are impossible, thus demoting the notion of "pure objectivity"to a polite fiction. The elemental components of the human body (molecular, atomic, subatomic) are in dynamic relationship with all the other particles throughout the universe. Lastly, the mind functions holographically. Each thought creates a discrete three-dimensional reality (parallel universe or frequency) in which anything is possible, including soul healing.

SOURCES

Bohm, D. "Quantum theory as an indication of a new order in physics. Part A. The development of new orders as shown through the history of physics." *Foundations in Physics*, 1971, 1, 4, 359–81.

Bohm, D. "Quantum Theory as an Indication of a New Order in Physics. Part B. Implicate and Explicate Order in Physical Law." *Foundations of Physics*, 1973, 3, 2, 139–68.

Pribram, K. H. *Languages of the Brain*. Englewood Cliffs, N.J.: Prentice Hall, 1971.

Pribram, K. H. "Holonomy and Structure in the Organization of Perception." In U. M. Nicholas (Ed.) *Images, Perception and Knowledge*. Dordrecht-Holland: D. Reidel, 1977.

Walker, E. H. "Consciousness and Quantum Theory" in *Psychic Exploration: A Challenge for Science*, Ed. E. D. Mitchell. New York: G. P. Putnam's Sons, 1976.

Wolf, F. A. *Parallel Universes: The Search for Other Worlds*. New York: Simon and Schuster, 1988.

24

EMPOWERMENT

When I am asked during an interview what the benefits of soul healing are, the answer is simple. First, I point out that this approach removes the fear of death (the number one fear people have–especially as they get older). Secondly, this therapy trains patients to access their higher self (superconscious mind), thus allowing them to review past lives, the future of their current life, and lifetimes yet to be lived in subsequent centuries. It is the third benefit of *empowerment* that we shall explore more fully here.

In my definition, empowerment means taking charge of one's life. It does not denote controlling others, but it *is* characterized by the prevention of any form of victimization. There are many types of victimization. For example, a mate can exhibit manipulative tendencies or make unjust demands upon you. An employer or employee may attempt to take advantage of your kind nature. Bureaucracy of all types (government, religion, and corporations) has long been guilty of exercising this principle.

A soul cannot grow as long as it is being compromised by victimization. The karmic "buck" must stop here if you are to evolve spiritually. The profile of my "typical" patient consists of a person with a low self-image, a series of "self-defeating sequences" (SDS—procrastination, overeating, etc.), and victimization. By training the patient to raise the frequency vibrational rate of their soul (subconscious rate) through the use of superconscious mind taps, the empowerment mechanism is initiated.

Further, by guiding this patient into the various future paths (frequencies) and programming to their ideal selection, this goal can be reached. The rest is merely a matter of time. My patients are actually custom-designing their own destiny, within a certain range of options predetermined by this karmic subcycle. In like manner, the theosophical theory behind choosing new lifetimes is based on the concept of empowerment.

The Plane Concept
According to the plane concept, our karmic cycle is worked out on five lower planes. On each of these lower planes an entity (soul) has a level of awareness of vibrational rate. In order to go to a higher plane, your vibrational rate must have reached a certain level. Each successive plane requires a higher vibrational rate. If it is not at this level, then the entity will seek that plane which best fits its level.

THE LOWER FIVE PLANES

1. *The earth plane or physical plane.* This is the plane that we function in now. The body is most material or physical at this level. The greatest amount of karma can be erased or added at this level. This is by far the most difficult level.
2. *The astral plane.* The body is less material here. This is where the subconscious, or soul, goes immediately following death or crossing over. Ghosts are examples of astral bodies.
3. *The causal plane.* The body is even less material at this level. The akashic records are kept here. This is where a medium projects him or herself when he or she reads your past or future.
4. *The mental plane.* This is the plane of pure intellect.
5. *The etheric plane.* The body is least material at this level. On this plane, truth and beauty are the ultimate values.

The amount of time spent on these lower planes depends entirely on the soul's achievements and remaining karmic debts. If you need to develop intellectually, you would select the mental plane. If truth is most important to your karmic cycle, the etheric plane would be the logical choice. The earth plane represents the plane of greatest elimination or addition to our karmic debts.

The Moment of Death

From the moment of death, the entity is placed in a very precarious position. This is a transition or adjustment period. We must first be made aware of the fact that we have died. This is accomplished by the very helpful guidance from highly evolved entities called Masters and Guides. These Masters and Guides have completed their karmic cycles many centuries ago. Their main purpose is to help us adjust to the fact that we have died, and to lead us to the white light that will take us to the soul plane, where we will evaluate our previous life and choose our next. At this time, we may also see and communicate by telepathy with friends or relatives who have previously died. These entities will also try to persuade us to enter the white light. If you don't enter the white light you will remain on the astral plane as a troubled spirit. Most recently departed entities will find comfort in the last surroundings they inhabited on the earth plane. Thus, they will frequent, in spirit, their house or apartment. Some of their family may be made aware of their presence and could interpret this as a ghost haunting their house. Indeed, many cases of haunted houses can be explained in this fashion.

The Soul Plane

Eventually, you will enter the white light and your destination will be the soul plane. Upon arriving at the soul plane, you will be greeted by special guides assigned specifically to you for the purpose of orientation. Your guides will spend as much time as necessary to explain the nature of reality and discuss your present purpose on this plane. You will be shown detailed events from your last life and how they fit into your karmic patterns. Also, you will be shown scenes from past and future lives and requested to study these events in detail. It is as if you were a football player studying films of the opposing team. Instead of preparing for a football game, you are preparing to choose your next life. You are given a tremendous amount of help and advice by your Masters and Guides in these all-important decisions. However, it is always *your* responsibility to make the choice concerning your next life. The soul always has free will. This is part of your empowerment. In choosing your next life, the earth place may not be to your liking. In that case you might choose any of the other lower planes (astral, causal, mental, or etheric) to work out your karmic cycle.

Life on these other planes isn't very different from that on the earth plane. People get married, have children, divorce, love, hate, etc., on all of the lower planes.

Akashic Records

These Akashic records are reportedly kept on the causal plane, but we do have access to them on the soul plane. They represent a file on the soul's growth and development throughout its many lives. They contain what the soul has learned and not learned.Thus, the soul's progression through its karmic cycle is what the Akashic records contain. By using these records, we have intimate knowledge of what we have done and what we have yet to do. This is a supremely valuable aid.

THE SEVEN HIGHER PLANES

You may choose any of the lower five planes to work out your karma, but as long as you have a karmic cycle you cannot enter the seven higher planes—your vibrational rate would be too low to permit it.

Beyond the soul plane there are seven higher planes, with the highest plane being the nameless, or God plane. On the God plane, the essence of every single one of us dwells. What this concept signifies is that God is within all of us, that we are all creators, and that we create our own realities. God is also called ALL THAT IS by devotees of this concept. Thus, this God plane is the equivalent of Heaven.

What I find particularly appealing about this concept is that there is no Hell. Hell is merely the temporary negative aspects of our lives on the lower five planes. However, there is a Heaven in this concept. Many people assume parapsychology to be an atheistic (no belief in God) or agnostic (not believing in God unless proof of its existence can be obtained) discipline, but nothing could be further from the truth. When we reach the God plane we are perfect. The subconscious—or soul—is pure.

As with the lower five planes, it is your vibrational rate that determines which of the seven higher planes you may enter. If your vibrational rate qualifies you for the eighth plane, then that is where you would properly reside. Your level of consciousness—your thoughts and actions—determines your vibrational rate.

The plane concept can best be illustrated by the diagram on the next page.

GOD OR NAMELESS PLANE (PLANE 13)			
Seven Higher Planes	Plane 12		
	Plane 11		
	Plane 10		
	Plane 9		
	Plane 8		
	Plane 7		
SOUL PLANE (PLANE 6)			
Karmic Cycle (Lower 5 Planes)	Etheric Plane	(Plane 5)	
	Mental Plane	(Plane 4)	
	Causal Plane	(Plane 3)	Akashic Records
	Astral Plane	(Plane 2)	
	Earth Plane	(Plane 1)	You are Here

Figure 3 — The Plane Concept

From this presentation I trust you can see how much control you really do wield over your past, present, and future lives. Remember, any issue can be resolved as long as the patient is sufficiently motivated to remove this SDS, and the goal is within the realm of human possibility.

Empowerment applies to all aspects of your personal and professional life. It may entail terminating a relationship, or several confrontations with a significant other to eliminate victimization. Professionally, changes of jobs, retraining, confrontations with superiors and/or subordinates, and assertiveness techniques may have to be applied to allow your soul to heal and grow. Empowerment is the opposite of codependency.

I do not mean to imply that this is either easy or can be accomplished instantaneously. Every circumstance must begin with a single step. Throughout this process, resistance will be offered by your own defense mechanisms or ego (rationalization, intellectualization, sublimation, displacement, etc.), friends, family members, professional peers, and others. It is your mission, should you decide to accept it, to maintain your position and grow.

Interestingly enough, others will also benefit by your empowerment. This will decrease the quantity but significantly increase the quality of your social and professional network. Is is only those "friends" and colleagues who are trying to manipulate you, or who are jealous of your growth (due to their own insecurities), that will object to your empowerment and attempt to dislodge you from your path.

These less than ideal souls have a perfect right to do their thing, but it is *your* responsibility to see to it that their "thing" doesn't victimize you. Can you think of any healthy reason that anyone would object to your empowerment? I can't, and I have pondered that question for twenty years.

The most important point to remember is that your empowerment will never come at the expense of another. I am not advocating that you become a more selfish, ruthless, manipulative soul. However, I do promote the concept of always being keenly aware of the dynamics of everyone around you, objectively evaluating the intent and quality of their actions or inactions.

Soul healing is more than simply overcoming illness. It is a total way of life, a path that can and must be consciously embraced. Soul healing involves growing and evolving through an illness or other hardship; it requires mastering oneself rather than conquering a symptom. Empowerment flows in the melding together of body, mind, and spirit into a functional and growth-oriented being.

The word "healing" is derived from the same root as the words "whole" and "holy." Healing, in the sense intended here, involves restoring or remembering oneness, wholeness, and holiness. Modern medicine and alternative therapies are often involved in healing. However, medical and psychological therapy concentrate solely on the elimination of the symptoms of disease. This is only one aspect of healing, so far as our broad definition is concerned.

Soul healing addresses the core of our personhood, including deep psychological processes working within every human being. It means uncovering the richness of the deep psyche and its mysterious ways. Soul healing applies not only to illness, but to the resolution of every imaginable human conflict and relationship issue. It may be expressed as the integration of body, mind, and spirit, letting go of resistance, learning to love oneself fully, correcting one's relationship with God, atonement (at-one-ment), remembering who one is, finding one's way home, seeking wholeness, or uncovering and healing the wounds we all carry. These are just a few inadequate synonyms to help describe the breadth of meaning and the full implications of the term "soul healing."

THE SOUL HEALING PROCESS

While there are stages of soul healing that we may experience in common with others, the soul healing path is primarily different for each person. Each of us has a unique story and unique experiences. Needs differ. Certain modalities and approaches are more comfortable and effective for one person than another. People seem tuned or open to different frequencies, so they often prefer one method, personality, or type of healing over another.

It is as though we are all climbing the same mountain, but are all following different paths to the summit. Some are steep and straight, while others wind around in ornate convolutions. Some are smooth, while others appear ominous, even treacherous. Some are well-marked and well-worn, while others must be forged at great personal sacrifice as one goes along. The life that one is presently living is, in fact, one's soul healing path. To respect and honor your situation, regardless of circumstance, is a crucial aspect of soul healing.

Conventional thinking judges some people to be well, while others are judged in need of healing. Conventional thinking often regards symptoms as bad, while health, wealth, and happiness are deemed to be good. Each approach to psychotherapy will be effective for some people, but not others. No one approach will work for everybody. This is partly due to the fact that each person brings a unique set of experiences, motivations, expectations, and energy into therapy.

Psychoanalysis traditionally requires a multitude of sessions, sometimes stretching over several years, to progress a client to a desired outcome. Hypnotherapy takes only weeks.

Soul healing teaches that everyone is in the process of becoming all we were created to be. Soul healing rejects the simplistic notion that some individuals are troubled and others are well, as if either state was immutable. Soul healing begins with a decision, a conscious formulation of intent. The universe then conspires (breathes together) to create conditions that guide one upon the path of healing. Symptoms, situations, and challenges are ways the psyche directs us to seek out and embrace soul healing. If we suppress a symptom or avoid a situation, the psyche will simply present it again later in a different form.

Many of us who work in soul healing believe that nothing efficacious originates outside a person. All power to change, to be healed, is created from within (superconscious mind). However, one has the capacity to drain one's own power away, usually leading to the self-deceiving protest that outside forces robbed one of one's health. If nothing else, simply taking responsibility for whatever exists or occurs in one's life is very empowering. If you created a mess, presumably you can "uncreate" it.

In the short term, taking full responsibility can cause extreme guilt, remorse, and self-recrimination. Much of this comes from old, tradition-bound attitudes about a harsh, judgmental God, or similarly harsh authority figures that have become internalized. Soul healing would contend that guilt is a primary emotion intended to be released through forgiveness of self and others.

In this sense, the soul healing process is largely about shifting one's perspective in a life-changing way. Guilt, fears, failure, low self-worth, and many other false beliefs are reinforced by the customs, laws, and institutions of society. It is no accident that the word "culture" and the word "cult" derive from the same root word. Challenging prevailing attitudes can even make one appear to be either crazy or insane. For example, how dare we forgive criminals? The entire legal system is based on the principle of projection and proving blame. Most of the medical system is built on projecting blame for disease onto entities outside of ourselves. This is a defense-mechanism mentality. An important part of changing one's perspective is to not take anything too seriously. The phrase used in the Bible is to be "in the world but not of it." Oriental philosophy speaks of the need for emotional detachment. Excessive seriousness even about soul healing can slow, or even halt, the healing process.

The multiplicity of soul healing methods reflects just how complex we human beings are. It also reflects how exotic and remarkable the universe in which we live actually is. Indeed, soul healing is about opening ourselves up to unlikely and unlimited possibilities. Some would call these possibilities "miracles." Understanding the boundless possibilities for soul healing in itself facilitates healing, because it serves to release the fear and despair that are often at the root of what must be overcome for healing to occur. Ergo, soul healing involves a systematic and comprehensive expansion of awareness.

Many assert that only love heals. All the various healing modalities and techniques serve to remind us of our intrinsic power, our wholeness, and our loveliness. When we love ourselves enough, negative energy patterns dissipate and the body heals itself. To the extent one believes wholeheartedly in any method, it will be effective for soul healing. At times, we may have to be tricked into healing by being placed in fearsome machines, by experiencing pain, or by a thousand other ways (usually based on co-dependency).

Methods are only triggers for soul healing. In fact, healing miracles occur quite commonly if one diligently searches for them. We are consciously aware of very little of all that occurs within and around us. For this reason, perhaps any and all imaginable methods or therapies may be helpful for soul healing.

The first condition necessary for successful soul healing to occur is that one must desire it. Specifically, one may desire more energy, more enjoyment, more fulfillment, or more happiness in one's life. Negative desires include the avoidance of disease, of death, fear of loss, or fear of the unknown. Fear can, however, become a useful stage of soul healing, particularly the fear that occurs when one realizes that one's life is not moving in the desired direction, or that something in one's life is missing. Fear is far more widespread than is generally acknowledged. Most of the time we succeed in ignoring fear or distracting ourselves.

A strong desire for soul healing, no matter how it is felt, is most helpful to facilitate such healing. After all, desires keep us alive and create our lives.

Stress is only a resistance created by our defense mechanisms, by our need to control, justify, or even understand an event. Learning not to judge events and situations is a great and noble part of soul healing.

At the deepest level, I believe soul healing is inevitable. For some people, the time is now. For others, it may take many years or lifetimes. We have the God-given right to suffer and be miserable for as long as we wish. We can accelerate the process if we desire it. We can ask that the veils be lifted, the clouds depart, and that all the barriers to loving oneself be overcome.

Soul healing can be impeded by an unwillingness to face oneself, or by experiencing a temporary respite from an illness or other negative situation. Illness or misfortune may actually be a way to avoid responsibility, to command the family's attention, to indulge in self-pity and feel sorry for oneself, or to avoid work.

Responsibility involves discipline. Interestingly, the word "discipline" is derived from the same root as the word "disciple." Discipline is an aspect of mastery of the challenge of life. Discipline is not so much a harsh striving to achieve a goal as it is the honing of one's skills in a given area.

Soul healing often involves the exercise of discipline, including the discipline (and courage) to follow one's own guidance. Outside forces (defense mechanisms) which control the body and emotions need to be brought under conscious control. Regimens designed to retrain the body and brain may have to be pursued. One may indeed choose illness to learn discipline. Discipline can be as simple as following a healthy diet and exercising regularly, or it may involve years of working through emotional traumas, tracing the threads of intuition to their sources deep within the psyche. At its most efficient, discipline involves accessing the superconscious mind to heal oneself.

Some people understand the power of faith and prayer. True faith helps one to stop worrying, casting out fear and causing anger about one's condition to evaporate. The exercise of faith removes stress from the body and enhances or allows soul healing to proceed more rapidly.

Openness and willingness to surrender to positive forces are important spiritual aspects of healing. The surrender is not to the illness, but to one's higher self or God's will. One must realize that God's will is more powerful than our puny egos. First, one may have to exhaust one's own solutions to eventually arrive at a place of utter despair! This is okay, if this is what it takes, for one to be finally receptive to soul healing.

The good news is that we eventually surrender not only our bad habits, but also our fears, despair, and feelings of smallness and insignificance. All such negativity is eventually placed on the altar of sacrifice and ultimately renounced. Perhaps this is the ultimate goal of healing. We renounce all that is not of God or the Higher Self, and then are truly made over in His image. To be your own soul healer is both your true purpose in the universe, the goal of life, and the aim of this book. This, by definition, will fully empower you.

Your own motivation is the key to the success of this approach. The techniques are actually quite simple and anyone can apply them. You must want, in your "heart of hearts," to accomplish these goals or else nothing will avail. How many soul healers does it take to change a light bulb? Just one, but the light bulb must want to change.

CONCLUSION

More and more, doctors and patients are looking beyond traditional medicine to alternative therapies and soul healing. The emphasis in psychoneuroimmunology on searching outside the scope of traditional therapies and concepts of the medical school classroom has made the art and science of healing more complex, more challenging, more potentially rewarding, and, for the time being, a little chaotic. However, the results are encouraging. At one time, scientific medicine had control over the art and science of healing. John Burnham, professor of history at Ohio State University, has described the status of medicine in his essay, "American Medicine's Golden Age: What Happened to It?" The prestige of the physician was interpreted by the population as "priestly functioning as they went through medical ceremonies and acted as wise and trusted personages." This mythic image of the doctor was kept alive by pop culture icons such as Marcus Welby, the wise, fatherly physician-healer able to listen and heal. But even as the media propped up doctors, their image was in decline. It was the failure of conventional medicine to successfully deal with such chronic diseases as heart disease and cancer (the major causes of death) that initiated the decay of popular esteem for medicine in the late 1950s and early 1960s. All the Ben Casey, Dr. Kildare, and Joe Gannon ("Medical Center") episodes on television could not stem the tide. Medicine's negative attitude toward psychosomatic illness, with its concomitant inability to treat such conditions, fostered a surge in soul healing modalities. The toxicity of many medications prescribed by doctors (Thalidomide was teratogenic, causing horrendous congenital deformities; the antibiotic chloramphenicol caused many deaths among children) was reported in the media. The opposition of the American Medical Association (AMA) to Medicare, and medicine's advocacy of superfluous tonsillectomies and Caesarean sections certainly did not shed favorable light on the profession. The "rich doctor" image replaced the dedicated healer image common before World War II. Finances also played a role. The cost of medical care in America quadrupled between 1950 and 1965 (from $10 billion to $40 billion). By 1970 this figure had swollen to $70 billion, representing seven per cent of the nation's GNP. By 1983, 10.5 per cent of the GNP was devoted to health care. Doctors spent less time talking to patients and more time performing lucrative hospital procedures. The 1960s ushered in new diets, exercises, and an interest in Eastern religions and rituals involving mind and body relaxation techniques. This "superhealth" desire could not be produced nor served by traditional medicine.

Burnham calls the "resurgence of romantic individualism" in the 1960s a direct result of, among other things, the media's reports on nontraditional medicine. *New York Times* reporter James Preston wrote about his experiences with acupuncture, dovetailing with the Transcendental Meditation movement that had already taken root.

Soul healing gained increasing credibility in the wake of Neal Miller's research on animal training with biofeedback conducted at Rockefeller University in New York, Dr. Benson's work with the relaxation response at Harvard, and Keith Wallace's reports on TM. A Harris Poll conducted in 1966 showed that seventy-three per cent of those who responded had a great deal of confidence in physicians; by 1982 that confident majority had shrunk to only thirty-two per cent. Traditional medicine had lost its monopoly on healing. Jan Smuts set the tone for alternative medicine in the 1926 book *Holism and Evolution* by challenging the tendency of medical science to oversimplify complex organisms and systems.

When one who seeks healing has set a spiritual ideal and has requested help from others, the sensitive centers in the body become receptive and responsive to the help that may be received. This may come from a distance, through prayer and meditation, or directly, as in the laying-on-of-hands. The channel is not the source of healing, but rather one who may aid the seeker in attuning to the Spirit within the person. It is this subconscious to superconscious (higher self) connection that lies at the foundation of soul healing.

Illness is just vibration that is out of harmony. Illness is created in the same way that anything else is created: it arises out of thought. Thus, illness is a way of learning about yourself. To be healed is to be "wholed," to be at one with the universe. Perhaps healing is a harmony of our quantum waves. By being together with each other, we enhance this harmony, just as when two pieces of a broken hologram are put together, the image generated becomes stronger.

We must choose between alternatives. Do we really want to be well? If a yes answer to this question is important to you, you are already in contact with higher consciousness. On the other hand, if these ideas seem unimportant to you, awareness of any higher consciousness reaching you is precluded. The choice is not made by "it." The choice is made by you. To hear the news, you must turn on the receiver. To turn it on, you must first want to hear the news. I believe that the process of "tuning" to higher consciousness is one of deepening self-reflection. A link is established between the patient and the harmony of the universe (*harmonics mundi*), which contains the knowledge, or "vibrations," needed to reestablish health. This, in effect, is soul healing.

Many people feel that God is responsible for any type of soul healing that occurs. There are, of course, many interpretations of just who or what God is. In metaphysics, we refer to God as a perfect, universal energy. Some use the term, *all that is*.

Quantum physicist Evan Harris Walker has defined human consciousness in mathematical terms. In *Psychic Exploration: A Challenge for Science,* Walker observed (p. 567) that "[we] are now at a point in time for which certain knowledge, factual knowledge, can provide a basis for the God concept." Walker establishes that "consciousness is a nonphysical, but real entity" (p. 547). He argues further that "the physical quantities that can serve as the connection between the consciousness and the events of the physical world are reasonably well delineated by physics."

Walker is a most interesting man. I had the pleasure of interviewing him in 1982 when I hosted a five-hour, late-night radio show called "Insights into Parapsychology." He pointed out that consciousness is not produced by the physiology of the brain; in point of fact, the reverse is true: it is consciousness that directly influences the brain.

I am marshalling these facts for three reasons. First, many people assume that those of us involved in metaphysics or parapsychology have no belief in God. Nothing could be farther from the truth. In fact, quantum physics demonstrates the existence of consciousness, which is only a step away from "proving" that God exists.

Second, quantum physics has long ago demonstrated that the presence of the observer (consciousness) affects the observations being made. This not only applies to soul healing, it even sheds light on its underlying mechanisms.

Third, the holographic theory of Pribram, in the light of quantum physics (including the proofs for the existence of parallel universes), provides a scientific explanation for both superconscious mind taps and progression hypnotherapy. This fortuitous conjunction of hard science and parapsychology gives credence to a patient's empowerment by way of soul healing.

As I pointed out earlier, our previous observations and scientific research may all be inaccurate because the role of consciousness has been systematically deemphasized by modern science. This circumstance is fortunately not the determinative one. What is significant is that soul healing is here to stay. It has always existed, and will forever remain a part of humankind's armamentarium.

We do not seek out these spiritual issues in soul healing to feel important, but because there is healing to be done. They are involved in pain, or they are needed to resolve pain. They are part of our business. Therapists who avoid such experiences are handicapped. Introducing spiritual realities like guides and higher self into a session accelerates the therapeutic process. Our work is spiritual because people are spiritual, not because we make it spiritual. Patients shouldn't come out of the experience in awe of something bigger—they should come out bigger and more empowered.

Soon, physicians may be following in the footsteps of natural healers. Barbara Ann Brennan offered this perceptive insight in her book, *Hands of Light*: "What the healer really does is to induce the patient to heal himself through natural processes. ... Your body and your energy system move naturally toward health." This is what the scientists are now discovering, as they work with the substances that are the body's own internal healing agents.

Recent studies show how common and natural soul healing is, demonstrated in problems that the stresses and strains of everyday life exhibit. Following are some examples.

- A view of nature from your hospital window can contribute more to recovery from surgery than many drugs.

- A divorce has nearly the same impact on heart disease as smoking one or more packs of cigarettes a day.
- People under negative stress are six times more likely to become infected with a cold virus and twice as likely to develop cold symptoms.
- A study at the University of Miami School of Medicine supports the therapeutic use of massage. The children receiving massage were found to have lower levels of the stress hormone cortisol in their saliva.
- Since the fall of the Berlin Wall, stress-related symptoms have been rising among West Germans and falling in the East. Stress-related symptoms appear to be related less to the absolute level of prosperity and stability than to the trajectory of social and personal change.
- In controlled tests conducted in a public hospital affiliated with the Baylor College of Medicine, C-section rates among women receiving the continuous emotional support and comfort of a female companion dropped fifty-six per cent. The length of labor was shortened by two hours, and only half as many babies required prolonged hospitalization after birth.
- A study of workers at The Boeing Company in Seattle shows the likelihood of a worker to report a back injury is more related to job satisfaction than physical factors.
- Couples with severe marital problems experienced elevated blood pressure and heart rates, and showed a significantly depressed immune response. The more negative the behavior, the more pronounced the immunological deficiency became.
- In a study of 2,700 residents in Tecumseh, Michigan, men who volunteered for community organizations were two-and-a-half times less likely to die from all causes of disease than their noninvolved peers.

In his book, *Visions and Prophecies for a New Age,* Mark Thurston stated:

> Sixty-four people were once enough to change the destiny of the United States, and this nation is approximately one-twentieth of the world's population. If we multiply 64 by 20, we have approx-

imately 1300 as a target number for the critical mass to change the destiny of humanity. Perhaps as few as just 1300 people who truly live and pray in attunement with God's plan will be the threshold amount to trigger global changes for healing.

In 1994, Americans made over 450 million visits to alternative health practitioners. During that same year they made 388 million appointments with mainstream physicians. People are looking for alternative ways to help themselves live longer and better lives. The momentum has shifted, and we are now at an auspicious crossroads for the human race, as we stand on the edge of a new era of unprecedented opportunity. By accessing our higher self, by living a life of high moral character, ethical excellence, and spiritual receptiveness, by listening to our bodies and the universe, we can all become soul healers.

APPENDIX

A

HEALING YOURSELF THROUGH HYPNOSIS

It can be frustrating to read a book such as this and not be able to identify experientially with the natural state of hypnosis. No matter how well it is explained, a naive reader often simply cannot identify with the process. I therefore include the following simple explanation and exercise that I developed in my early years of private practice.

Hypnosis is a subject of rich interest to nearly everyone. The fascination that it holds is its promise to open to a person a world of rich treasure and self-improvement, as if by magic. Nearly everyone who is human finds at some time he has a desire or need to improve himself. Hypnosis seems to provide an answer. After all, we have all seen how hypnotists have the power to make people do things, haven't we?

The hypnotist, in fact, has no power and never did—just skill. The hypnotists who come to mind were professional entertainers who deliberately tried to give the false impression that they had a "remarkable power" over their subjects and could force them to do things. The actual power behind hypnosis lies within the subject and his or her mind. Charged and unleashed, the subject is free to release all his or her mental creative power and bring it to bear with amazing results. The capacity of the human mind to solve and create is remarkable. Self-hypnosis and hypnotic techniques are a way to successfully reach and put to use more of one's own mind.

Genuine and legitimate improvements in one's self are never simple or easy. They require persistence and determination to accomplish; without these qualities, failure will follow.

SELF-HYPNOSIS

Hypnosis is pleasant. It is a state of deep concentration. Your *conscious* mind is relatively weak. It vacillates continuously and will create an endless round of excuses as to why you should not bother with what you are trying to accomplish. It lacks the kind of stabilizing force that the *subconscious* possesses.

The *subconscious* mind can best be influenced when one is in a passive or relaxed state, such as in hypnosis. This restful quieting of the mind acts to cleanse it, opening it to pure and more elevated thoughts. Hypnosis will build both mental vigor and enthusiasm because it removes all the negative fears and thoughts that act as roadblocks to energy, inspiration, and accomplishment. You must turn your wishes, ideas, or hopes into reality, or they remain meaningless to you. The subconscious is the best place to start the undertaking.

I suggest, therefore, that two ten-minute periods be put aside each day for the purpose of training your subconscious mind. The best time is very early in the morning shortly after awakening. The other period can be at your convenience during the day, except not before bedtime, unless you have difficulty in falling asleep.

Stage 1

Find a quiet room and close the door to shut out distracting sounds. Lie down on a bed or couch and relax for two to five minutes. Both the mind and body will relax as you lay inert, and this passive state will open a door to the subconscious mind. As you lie quietly, close your eyes and imagine a warm, relaxing feeling.

- Focus all your attention on the muscles in the toes of both your feet. Imagine this warm, relaxing feeling spreading and surrounding the muscles of the toes, moving to the backs of both feet and to the heels and ankles. Now imagine this warm feeling moving up the calf muscles of both legs to the kneecap and into the thigh muscles, meeting at the hip bone.
- The warm, relaxing feeling is moving up the back bone to the middle of the back, surrounding the shoulder blades and moving into the back of the neck.

- The warm, relaxing feeling is now moving into the fingers of both hands, just as it did with the toes. This feeling spreads into the back of both hands, palms, wrists, forearms, elbows, shoulders, and neck, relaxing every muscle along its path.
- The warm, relaxing feeling moves into the back of the head, scalp, and all the way to the forehead. Now, the facial muscles are relaxed; the eyes, which are closed; the chin, ear lobes, and neck. Now each and every muscle in the entire body is completely relaxed.

When you develop this generalized relaxed feeling throughout your body, with an accompanying heaviness in your arms or legs, you have finally reached a light state of hypnosis. Continue with the exercise for several days, then progress to the second stage. The instructions should become part of a mental dialogue that you will be thinking to yourself. Read it over two or three times and commit the general idea to memory, rather than trying to remember it word for word.

Stage 2

To go deeper into hypnosis is the next concern. This can be accomplished in a number of ways. One of the more common is to imagine a very pleasant and soothing scene, such as a green valley that you are looking down into from a mountain top, watching a lazy brook meander along, relaxing you more and more as you watch its slow movements. Another way is to imagine yourself descending an ancient stone stairwell very slowly, while thinking to yourself as you wind down the flight of stairs that you are going deeper and deeper with each step. The following is an example of a hypnotist deepening the hypnotic trance state:

- I want you to imagine that you are standing on the fifth floor of a large department store … and that you are just stepping into the elevator to descend to street level. As you go down, and as the elevator door opens and closes as you arrive at each floor … you will become more and more deeply relaxed … and your sleep will become deeper and deeper.
- The doors are closing now …. and you are beginning to sink slowly downwards. The elevator stops at the fourth floor … several people get out … two more people get in … the doors close again … and already you are becoming more and more deeply relaxed … more and more deeply asleep.

- And as you sink to the third floor ... and stop, while the doors open and close again ... you are relaxing more and more ... and your sleep is becoming deeper and deeper.
- You slowly sink down to the second floor ... one or two people get out and several get in ... and as they do so ... you are feeling much more deeply relaxed ... much more deeply asleep.
- Down once again to the first floor ... the doors open and close ... but nobody gets out or comes in. Already you have become still more deeply relaxed ... and you sleep still deeper and deeper. Deeper and deeper asleep ... deeper and deeper asleep.
- Down farther and farther ... until the elevator stops at last at street level. The doors open ... and everybody gets out.
- But you do not get out.
- You decide to go still deeper ... and descend to the basement.
- The elevator doors close again ... and down you go ... down and down ... deeper and deeper ... and as you arrive at the basement ... you are feeling twice as deeply and comfortably relaxed ... twice as deeply asleep.

As you develop skill with your own mind, you will be able to go in much more quickly, and even surroundings that used to be too distracting for you to handle will now become tolerable places for practicing self-hypnosis.

Since the basis of my approach to hypnotherapy is the superconscious mind tap, the following is an exercise anyone can do to achieve this state in his or her soul healing.

SUPERCONSCIOUS MIND TAP

Now listen very carefully. I want you to imagine a bright white light coming down from above and entering the top of your head, filling your entire body. See it, feel it and it becomes reality. Now imagine an aura of pure white light emanating from your heart region, again surrounding your entire body, protecting you. See it, feel it, and it becomes reality. Now only your masters and guides and highly evolved loving entities who mean you well will be able to influence you during this or any other hypnotic session. You are totally protected by this aura of pure white light.

In a few moments I am going to count from 1 to 20. As I do so you will feel yourself rising up to the superconscious mind level where you will be able to receive information from your masters and guides. You will also be able to overview all of your past, present and future lives. Number 1 rising up, 2, 3, 4, rising higher. 5, 6, 7, letting information flow; 8, 9, 10, you are half way there; 11, 12, 13, feel yourself rising even higher; 14, 15, 16, almost there; 17, 18, 19 and 20, you are there. Take a moment and orient yourself to the superconscious mind level.

Play New Age music for one minute.

You may now ask yourself any questions about any past, present or future life issue. Or, you may contact any of your guides or departed loved ones from this level. You may explore your relationship with any person. Remember, your superconscious mind level is all knowledgeable and has access to your Akashic records.

Now slowly and carefully state your desire for information or an experience and let this superconscious mind level work for you. Allow your higher self to raise the quality of your soul's energy.

Play New Age music for eight minutes.

You have done very well. Now I want you to further open up the channels of communication by removing any obstacles and allowing yourself to receive information and experiences that will directly apply to and help better your present lifetime. Allow yourself to receive more advanced and more specific information from your higher self and masters and guides to raise your frequency and improve your karmic subcycle. Do this now.

Play New Age music for eight minutes.

All right now. Sleep now and rest. You did very, very well. Listen very carefully. I am going to count forward now from 1 to 5. When I reach the count of 5, you will be back in the present, you will be able to remember everything you experienced and re-experienced, you will feel very relaxed and refreshed, and you will be able to do whatever you have planned for the rest of the day or evening. You will feel very positive about what you have just experienced and very motivated about your confidence and ability to play this tape again to experience the superconscious mind level and to continue raising the frequency vibrational rate of your soul's energy. All right now: 1, very, very deep; 2, you are getting a little bit lighter; 3, you are getting much, much lighter; 4, very, very light; 5, awaken, wide awake and refreshed.

BENEFITS OF SOUL HEALING

I would like to end this section with a list of some of the many benefits that can be attained through hypnotherapy and soul healing:

1. Elimination of insomnia.
2. Increased relaxation and the elimination of tension.
3. Increased and focused concentration.
4. Improved memory ("hypernesia").
5. Improved reflexes.
6. Increased self-confidence.
7. Pain control.
8. Improved sex life.
9. Increased organization and efficiency.
10. Increased motivation.
11. Improved interpersonal relationships.
12. Slowing down the aging process.
13. Facilitating a better career path.
14. Elimination of anxiety and depression.
15. Overcoming bereavement.
16. Elimination of headaches, including migraine headaches.
17. Elimination of allergies and skin disorders.
18. Strengthening one's immune system to resist any disease.
19. Elimination of habits, phobias, and other negative tendencies (self-defeating sequences).
20. Improving decisiveness.
21. Improving the quality of people, and circumstances in general, that you attract into your life.
22. Increasing your ability to earn and hold onto money.
23. Overcoming obsessive-compulsive behavior.
24. Improving the overall quality of your life.
25. Improved psychic awareness—ESP, meditation, astral projection (out-of-body experience), telepathy, superconscious mind taps, etc.
26. Elimination of the fear of death by viewing one's past and future lives.
27. Attracting a soul mate into your life.
28. Establishing and maintaining harmony of body, mind, and spirit.

APPENDIX B

FINDING A SOUL HEALER

As with anything else in life, there are certain therapists and therapies that one should avoid. Some of my patients have described humiliating experiences of brainwashing passing itself off as therapy. They say, "if it feels good, why not?" or, "if it makes me happy, what could possibly go wrong?"

The problem is that some pursuits of happiness may lead to destructive mind states characterized by disorientation, delusion, detachment, and withdrawal. Patients talk about, "getting it," "cosmic consciousness," "ecstasies," "breakthroughs," and so on. That by itself is fine, but when I assess their mental and emotional status and perceive major dysfunctional behavioral patterns, something is very wrong.

The purpose of this chapter is to prevent you from encountering the usual pitfalls to soul healing or any other kind of therapy. It is obvious that a "psychic counselor" who tells you that your problems are due to a "curse," and for five hundred dollars she or he will burn candles and remove this curse, is trying to scam you. Even a "metaphysical" fool and his or her money are soon parted.

AVOIDING THE PITFALLS OF SOUL HEALING

I am going to discuss the pitfalls of soul healing by dividing these obstacles into two categories. The first one deals with mass therapies and cults. The second concerns individual practitioners.

Mass Therapies

Certain mass therapies indulgently lecture their disciples for hours on the nature of reality, perception, and belief system. They initiate a series of "processes" and mental exercises intended to erase a trainee's tapes (a pejorative term for feelings and thought patterns that supposedly inhibit one from experiencing life to the fullest). They are not above incorporating verbal assaults, fear, guilt, and sensory deprivation into their "therapeutic" regimens.

These groups misrepresent their identities and intentions. They may lie about their place in their organization's hierarchy. They may ingratiate themselves with future proselytes by feigning affection for them. They may project so overwhelming an air of spiritual radiance and confidence that their influence over others becomes a foregone conclusion. They may provoke tendentious debate and escalate the rhetoric until their subjects are reeling from emotionally-charged mental conflicts urgently needing resolution. They will employ demagoguery, persuasion, propaganda, and sophisticated mass-marketing techniques to achieve their ends, and these techniques are never employed casually or informally, despite appearances to the contrary; they are premeditated to the most minute detail. Programs like these are the brainchild of Madison-Avenue experts dedicated to finding the path to maximal control.

Participants are often recruited through informal channels, such as posters, telephone and mail solicitations, and word of mouth. The individual eventually attends an emotionally intense group meeting or therapeutic session, hoping for a life-changing breakthrough. Various individual and group processes and "training" techniques are engineered to simulate the profound experiences the individual is seeking. Group leaders may lead participants in meditation or steer them into vivid fantasizing. They may lecture interminably, their speeches thick with psychological and scientific jargon. Some group leaders trace and exploit the most intense conflicts dotting each individual's lifetime, counseling their charges that conflict has hounded them from infancy, and will continue to darken their lives until they submit to the leader's wisdom.

Caught in the crossfire of verbiage and long-buried emotion, unable to break out of a physically grueling group ordeal, the individual may enter a state of explosive overstimulation or emotional collapse. These experiences may produce hallucinations or delusions, and tend to disrupt one's values and beliefs, one's marriage, and even one's family relationships. In the aftermath of such an overwhelming new experience, a state of mind may be entered that may pass for a renewal or rebirth experience.

The ability to think, to question things, to feel, is compromised. By this point, emotion, joy, and desire have departed entirely. Participants enter a phase of self-doubt, and react by mimicking the "trainers."

People flounder in alternate states of debilitating fear, confusion, and despair for months after an intense weekend marathon of "therapy." They are often prohibited from eating, drinking, taking prescription medicine, and bathroom breaks. When imposed concurrently with the emotional maelstrom buffeting the participants, such sensory deprivation techniques become indistinguishable from classic brainwashing techniques.

Noted Russian physiologist I. P. Pavlov studied these techniques at the dawn of the twentieth century. He provided the first accurate map of the sequential stages of "protective inhibition" of brain function in response to traumatic overstimulation. He concluded that dramatic conversions in such circumstances are the result of a physiological dysfunction of the brain that robs it of evaluative wisdom, making the individual uncritically susceptible to new ideas which under normal circumstances would never have been entertained.

Mass "therapies" like these, while cleverly packaged and superficially appealing, are worse than a dead end, because they can worsen one's condition. I hasten to add, lest the reader jump to the wrong conclusion, that I have nothing against meditation, yoga classes, or other group experiences, providing they do not indulge in the kind of deleterious techniques and manipulative regimens described above.

Individual Soul Healers

I have always been a great advocate of formal scientific training. Perhaps my degrees in biochemistry, dentistry, and counseling psychology favorably predispose me in this direction, but all prejudice aside, education does serve a purpose. In an ideal world, your prospective soul healer would be trained in psychology and/or medicine, but many of the techniques practiced today find no formal counterparts in the traditional curricula.

In the absence of this training, or even in its presence, certain criteria for evaluating a clinician should be employed. First, they should never, under any circumstances, require recreational drugs, especially hallucinogenic agents, as part of their therapy. The purpose of soul healing is to bring one's energy into balance and raise its quality. No drug can do that for you.

In addition, the therapeutic approach and techniques being proposed by the prospective clinician should be corroborated by background literature, preferably scientific in bearing. If the soul healer refuses to provide any such collateral information, and becomes extremely defensive in tone when you press him on this point, be very wary. If the clinician objects to your intention to secure a second opinion, or intends to treat you with a strange device, be doubly wary.

Dr. Faith Fitzgerald of the University of California–Davis Medical Center published a telling article in the *New England Journal of Medicine* that puts these issues in perspective. She reported on observations she made while traveling on the talk-show circuit, investigating a multitude of holistic apostles and the various therapies they were touting. Most of those she met were "true believers," well-meaning individuals who sincerely believed what they were teaching, who spoke with unfeigned conviction and certitude. Unfortunately, their recommendations not only differed from one another, but were sometimes even mutually exclusive. Fitzgerald, reflecting on the survey results, concluded that for many people, holistic medicine is a religion. "And as such [it] stands on a different plane of thought than does science." The practice of holistic medicine is more a matter of belief than of scientific conviction. When queried why they employ cures that appear to be, at best, inadequately tested, holistic clinicians reply that the comparative effectiveness of various therapies is a secondary issue, beyond the proper scope of their responsibility. For this reason, some holistic healers proffer treatments that are not only unconventional, but also unproven.

If such a therapist refuses to disclose the names of former patients, do not be alarmed. Confidentiality is part and parcel of professional therapy, and in fact enjoys statutory protection in all fifty states.

However, your healer should not exhibit "plaqueaphobia." By this term, I mean an explicit aversion to having anyone closely inspect the degree(s) mounted on the wall. If the clinician advertises the trappings of a formal education, what could be wrong with examining the plaques exhibited to attestat to this? Natural curiosity would impel us to study a professional's background accreditation. The problem is that if these are phony spurious degrees purchased from a diploma mill, the healer will not want you to discover this particular skeleton in their closet.

Following your treatments, you should be devoid of the extremely negative symptoms rehearsed in the preceding discussion regarding mass therapy (namely, hallucinations, delusions, complete disorientation, apathy, etc.). Your healer should be experienced in shielding techniques.

SELECTING A SOUL HEALER

Your soul healer should be knowledgeable about all aspects of Karma and be able to answer all your questions, offering appropriate guidance as needed. A review of Chapter 5, along with the books on the reading list, will provide sufficient background for posing the right kind of questions to your practitioner. If it dawns on you that you know more than the therapist does, it is time to leave immediately.

The following questions can be used as models in interviewing your prospective soul healer:

Q: Why can't people consciously recall past lives?

A: Most people's memory comes from their conscious mind proper (ego). It is the subconscious mind we have to tap to elicit past/future life memories.

Q: What methods other than hypnosis can help reveal past and future lives?

A: Meditation, spontaneous regressions and progressions, automatic writing, karmic (Vedic) astrological charts, and contacts with Masters and Guides and one's own Higher Self in dreams and daydreams.

Q: How can the present population of the world be explained by reincarnation, assuming there are no new souls?

A: The Oversoul Concept states that our soul's energy can split and occupy more than one body at a time. This concept is covered more fully in *The New Age Hypnosis Workbook* (forthcoming), and in *Past Lives — Future Lives.*

Q: Does a belief in reincarnation conflict with a belief in God?

A: Absolutely not. The God energy created the universe and our higher selves are but a component of this perfect energy source.

Q: What is the purpose of our karmic cycle?

A: Spiritual growth. We are only here to perfect our soul's energy so that we may ascend to the higher planes and finally to the God plane (heaven, nirvana, *all that is*).

Q: Do we ever change sex in our karmic cycle?

A: Yes. Although my research shows that approximately seventy-five per cent of our lives are lived as the same sex, we must change sex in order to grow spiritually.

Q: My life has been a difficult one, doctor. Could it be that I'm just not supposed to be fulfilled this time around?

A: You karmically chose all obstacles as well as assets in this and all of your lives. The new physics demonstrates that we create our own reality. Absolutely everyone has the potential to improve their lives. You are never doomed to a fate of unhappiness.

Q: What is the one true type of soul healing?

A: There is no one true type. There are dozens of methods that will work. No one therapy will work with everyone. Practitioners naturally gravitate to one or more of these types of healing approaches for their own personal reasons.

Q: Do you guarantee that your soul healing will work?

A: This is a very important question. No ethical practitioner ever makes such a guarantee. If your prospective soul healer does, do not work with him or her.

Q: Who is ultimately responsible for my soul healing—you?

A: You, the patient. A soul healer can only train you to access your own higher self and natural healing energies.

If past life therapy is part of your treatment, it is crucial that you do not allow unpleasant discoveries to result in feelings of guilt, fear, or resentment. It is almost statistically impossible *not* to have lived as a murderer, thief, or prostitute at one time, given the hundreds of past lives through which we've all passed. Remember that on balance, most of our past lives have been suffused with honesty, virtue, generosity, and kindness. The therapist should be able to help you defuse any negative revelations, guiding you to the recognition that the purpose of these lives is to allow the soul to grow. This growth requires that life be viewed from many different angles.

In his book, *The Masks of the Universe,* University of Manchester astronomer Edward Harrison maintains that we can never arrive at a single, correct picture of the universe, only a series of changing models of it. Therefore, do not be concerned if the reality you discover in alpha conflicts with the conception of the universe you have come to accept when awake and fully conscious.

When it comes to choosing a therapist, always trust your instincts. If he or she is qualified but you don't like or trust him or her, terminate the relationship. Not only will you not succeed with that particular practitioner, but you might just be susceptible to his or her negative karma.

I hope these guidelines will be helpful to you in choosing your soul healer. Ideally, they should help you avoid making a serious mistake. In the event you are already involved with a therapist who is not likely to help you, I trust you will be able to cut your losses and move on like the empowered soul you will become.

SUGGESTED READING

Reincarnation and Out-of-Body Experiences

Bruce Goldberg

Past Lives – Future Lives

The Search for Grace

"The Clinical Use of Hypnotic Regression and Progression in Hypnotherapy." *Psychology—A Journal of Human Behavior*, v. 27–1 (1990), 43–48.

"Your Problem May Come from Your Future: A Case Study." *Journal of Regression Therapy*, v. 4–2 (1990), 21–29.

"Treating Dental Phobias Through Past-Life Therapy: A Case Report." *Journal of the Maryland State Dental Association*, v. 27–3 (1984), 137–139.

Elisabeth Kubler-Ross

Death, the Final Stage of Growth

On Death and Dying

Raymond A. Moody, Jr. M.D.

Life After Life

The Light Beyond

Reunions: Visionary Encounters with Departed Loved Ones

Kenneth Ring
Heading Toward Omega: In Search of the Meaning of the Near-Death Experience
Life at Death: A Scientific Investigation of the Near Death Experience

Brad Steiger
Returning from the Light

Charles Tart
Altered States of Consciousness

Healing and Alternative Medicine

Ronald Beesley
Yoga of the Inward Path

Barbara Ann Brennan
Hands of Light

Bruce Goldberg
"Slowing Down the Aging Process Through the Use of Altered States of Consciousness: A Review of the Medical Literature." *Psychology – A Journal of Human Behavior*, v. 32–2 (1995), 19–21.
"The Treatment of Cancer through Hypnosis." *Psychology – A Journal of Human Behavior*, v. 3–4 (1985), 36–39.
"Hypnosis and the Immune Response." *International Journal of Psychosomatics*, v. 3–3 (1985), 24–26.

Louise L. Hay
You Can Heal Your Life

Dennis T. Jaffee, Ph.D.
Healing from Within

Delores Krieger.
The Therapeutic Touch: How to Use Your Hands to Help or to Heal

Kathleen McDonald
How To Meditate

Carl O. Simonton
Getting Well Again

Brad Steiger
The Healing Power of Love

Jess Stearn
Edgar Cayce: The Sleeping Prophet

Quantum Physics

Bruce Goldberg

"Quantum Physics and Its Application to Past-Life Regression and Future-Life Progression Hypnotherapy." *Journal of Regression Therapy*, v. 7–1 (1993), 89–93.

Max Jammer

The Philosophy of Quantum Mechanics

Lawrence LeShan

The Medium, the Mystic, and the Physicist

Edgar Mitchell

Psychic Exploration: A Challenge for Science

Ken Wilbur

Quantum Questions: Mystical Writings of the World's Great Physicists

Fred Alan Wolf

Parallel Universes: The Search for Other Worlds

Angels

Sophie Burnham

A Book of Angels

Angel Letters

Brad Steiger

Angels Over Their Shoulders: Children's Encounters With Heavenly Beings

INDEX

D

E

F

G

H

I

K

L

M

N

O

P

Q

R

S

T

W

Y

Stay in Touch. . .

Llewellyn publishes hundreds of books on your favorite subjects

On the following pages you will find listed some books now available on related subjects. Your local bookstore stocks most of these and will stock new Llewellyn titles as they become available. We urge your patronage.

Order by Phone

Call toll-free within the U.S. and Canada, 1–800–THE MOON.
In Minnesota call (612) 291–1970.
We accept Visa, MasterCard, and American Express.

Order by Mail

Send the full price of your order (MN residents add 7% sales tax) in U.S. funds to:

Llewellyn Worldwide
P.O. Box 64383, Dept. K317–4
St. Paul, MN 55164–0383, U.S.A.

Postage and Handling

- $4.00 for orders $15.00 and under
- $5.00 for orders over $15.00
- No charge for orders over $100.00

We ship UPS in the continental United States. We cannot ship to P.O. boxes. Orders shipped to Alaska, Hawaii, Canada, Mexico, and Puerto Rico will be sent first-class mail.

International orders: Airmail—add freight equal to price of each book to the total price of order, plus $5.00 for each non-book item (audiotapes, etc.). Surface mail—Add $1.00 per item.

Allow 4–6 weeks delivery on all orders. Postage and handling rates subject to change.

Group Discounts

We offer a 20% quantity discount to group leaders or agents. You must order a minimum of 5 copies of the same book to get our special quantity price.

Free Catalog

Get a free copy of our color catalog, *New Worlds of Mind and Spirit.* Subscribe for just $10.00 in the United States and Canada ($20.00 overseas, first class mail). Many bookstores carry *New Worlds*—ask for it!

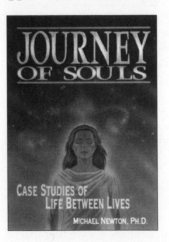

THE SECRET WAY OF WONDER
Insights from the Silence

Guy Finley
Introduction by Desi Arnaz, Jr.

Discover an inner world of wisdom and make miracles happen! Here is a simple yet deeply effective system of illuminating and eliminating the problems of inner mental and emotional life.

The Secret Way of Wonder is an interactive spiritual workbook, offering guided practice for self-study. It is about Awakening the Power of Wonder in yourself. A series of 60 "Wonders" (meditations on a variety of subjects: "The Wonder of Change," "The Wonder of Attachments," etc.) will stir you in an indescribable manner. This is a bold and bright new kind of book that gently leads us on a journey of Spiritual Alchemy where the journey itself is the destination … and the destination is our need to be spiritually whole men and women.

Most of all, you will find out through self investigation that we live in a friendly, intelligent and living universe that we can reach into and that can reach us.

0-87542–221–7, 192 pp., 5 ¼ x 8, softcover **$9.95**

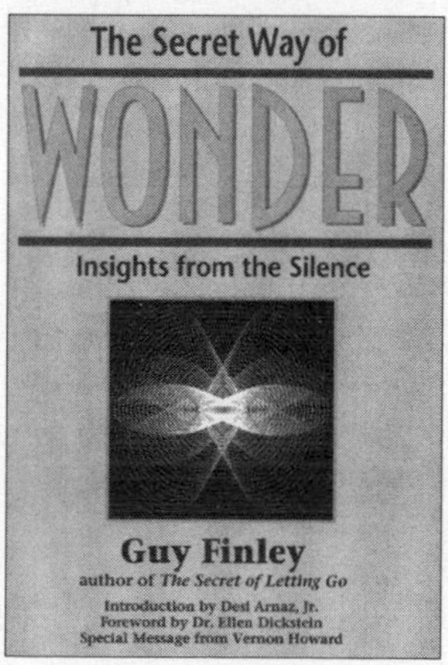